Dimensions of Thinking:
A Framework for Curriculum and Instruction

Robert J. Marzano
Ronald S. Brandt
Carolyn Sue Hughes
Beau Fly Jones
Barbara Z. Presseisen
Stuart C. Rankin
Charles Suhor

**Association for Supervision and
Curriculum Development**

125 N. West Street
Alexandria, Virginia 22314-2798
(703) 549-9110

DIMENSIONS OF THINKING
A FRAMEWORK FOR CURRICULUM AND INSTRUCTION
by
Robert J. Marzano, Ronald S. Brandt, Carolyn Sue Hughes, Beau Fly Jones,
Barbara Z. Presseisen, Stuart C. Rankin, and Charles Suhor

Published by
The Association for Supervision and Curriculum Development, 125 N. West St.,
Alexandria, VA 22314-2798

Co-published by
ERIC Clearinghouse on Reading and Communication Skills, 1111 Kenyon Rd., Urbana,
IL 61801
Mid-continent Regional Educational Laboratory, 12500 E. Iliff Ave., Suite 201, Aurora,
CO 80014
Music Educators National Conference, 1902 Association Dr., Reston, VA 22091
National Education Association, 1201 Sixteenth St., N.W., Washington, DC 20036
North Central Regional Educational Laboratory, 295 Emroy Ave., Elmhurst, IL 60126
Research for Better Schools, Inc., 444 N. Third St., Philadelphia, PA 19120

On behalf of
The Association Collaborative for Teaching Thinking

This publication is based on work sponsored in part by the Office of Educational Research and Improvement, U.S. Department of Education, under contract nos. 400-86-0002, 400-86-0045, 400-86-0004, and 400-86-0003. The publication's content does not necessarily represent the official views of OERI, the Department, or any other agency of the U.S. Government.

Printed in the United States of America

Typeset by Mid-Atlantic Photo Composition, Inc.
Printed by Semline, Inc.

Ronald S. Brandt, *ASCD Executive Editor*
Nancy Carter Modrak, *Manager of Publications*
Mary Morello Shafer and René M. Townsley, *Associate Editors*
Scott Willis, *Editorial Assistant*
Al Way, *Art Director*

ASCD Stock No. 611-87040

Library of Congress
  Catalog Card No. 87-72733
ISBN 0-87120-148-8

$10.00

Dimensions of Thinking
A Framework for Curriculum and Instruction

Contents

Acknowledgments

The Authors

Robert J. Marzano is Director of Research at the Mid-continent Regional Educational Laboratory in Aurora, Colorado. He is senior author of *Tactics for Thinking*, a teacher training program published by ASCD. He has authored articles, books, and training materials in the areas of language arts, effective schooling, and thinking skills.

Ronald S. Brandt is Executive Editor of ASCD and staff liaison for ASCD's Teaching Thinking project.

Carolyn Sue Hughes is Assistant Superintendent for Curriculum and Program Development with the Oklahoma City Public Schools. She was director of QUEST, a thinking skills program developed in the 1970s by the Parma, Ohio, Public Schools. As ASCD President in 1985-86, she organized and chaired the Association Collaborative for Teaching Thinking, a group of 28 organizations working together to promote student thinking in elementary and secondary schools. She also chaired the Wingspread II: Dimensions of Thinking Conference in 1986.

Beau Fly Jones is Program Director of the North Central Regional Educational Laboratory in Elmhurst, Illinois. Active in the development of research-based materials for inservice and preservice education, she helped produce the ASCD videotape, *Teaching Reading as Thinking*, and is senior editor of *Strategic Teaching and Learning: Cognitive Instruction in the Content Areas*, published by ASCD in 1987.

Barbara Z. Presseisen is Director of National Networking at Research for Better Schools, the Mid-Atlantic Educational Laboratory in Philadelphia. She is Chair of the Cross Laboratory Committee on Higher-Order Thinking Skills, a founder of the Jean Piaget Society, and serves on the editorial advisory boards of *Educational Horizons* and the *Teaching Thinking and Problem-Solving Newsletter.*

Stuart C. Rankin is Deputy Superintendent of the Detroit Public Schools. He has been a member of the ASCD Executive Council and Board of Directors, and he chaired the 1984 Wingspread Conference that led to preparation of this book.

Charles Suhor is Deputy Executive Director of the National Council of Teachers of English and Director of the ERIC Clearinghouse on Reading and Communication Skills. A former English teacher and K-12 Supervisor of English for the New Orleans Public Schools, his publications include over 150 articles in education journals.

Reviewers

Full responsibility for the contents of this book remains with the authors, but we are grateful to the following for their helpful comments on previous drafts of the manuscript.

Zulfi Ahmad, Cincinnati (Ohio) Public Schools
Robert Anastasi, National Association of Elementary School Principals, Reston, Virginia
Daisy Arredondo, Consultant, Lincoln, Nebraska
John Barell, Montclair State College, Upper Montclair, New Jersey
Joan Boykoff Baron, Connecticut State Department of Education, Storrs
Barry Beyer, George Mason University, Fairfax, Virginia
Sandra Black, Consultant, St. Augustine, Florida
Hilda Borko, University of Maryland, College Park
John Bransford, Vanderbilt University, Nashville, Tennessee
Evelyn Chatmon, Baltimore County (Maryland) Public Schools

Acknowledgments

Susan Chipman, Office of Naval Research, Arlington, Virginia
Arthur Costa, California State University, Sacramento
Thomas Duffy, Carnegie-Mellon University, Pittsburgh, Pennsylvania
Bessie Duncan, Detroit (Michigan) Public Schools
Sydelle Seiger-Ehrenberg (deceased)
Peter Ellsworth, University of Wyoming, Laramie
Robert Ennis, University of Illinois, Champaign
Reuven Feuerstein, Hadassah-Wizo-Canada Research Institute, Jerusalem, Israel
Lawrence Friedman, North Central Regional Educational Laboratory, Elmhurst, Illinois
Esther Fusco, Babylon Union Free School District, Babylon, New York
Meredith "Mark" Gall, University of Oregon, Eugene
J. Robert Hanson, Hanson Silver Strong and Assoc., Moorestown, New Jersey
Michael Hartoonian, Wisconsin State Department of Public Instruction, Madison
Robin Hobbs, Baltimore City (Maryland) Public Schools
M. Ellen Jay, Montgomery County (Maryland) Public Schools, Silver Spring
Dennis Kelly, Illinois State University, Normal
Mellon Kennedy, University of Illinois, Champaign
Rita King, San Diego County Office of Education, San Diego, California
Dan Kirby, University of Georgia, Athens
Herbert Klausmeier, University of Wisconsin, Madison
Susan Kline, University of Washington, Seattle
Marcia Knoll, New York City (New York) Public Schools
Alan Lesgold, University of Pittsburgh, Pittsburgh, Pennsylvania
Frances Link, Curriculum Development Associates, Washington, D.C.
Matthew Lipman, Montclair State College, Upper Montclair, New Jersey
Carolee Matsumoto, Education Development Center, Newton, Massachusetts
Jay McTighe, Maryland State Department of Education, Baltimore
John Meehan, Pennsylvania Department of Education, Scranton, Pennsylvania
Timothy Melchior, Memorial Junior High School, Valley Stream, New York
John Mellon, University of Illinois, Chicago
Eunice Boardman Meske, University of Wisconsin, Madison
Raymond Nickerson, BBN Laboratories, Cambridge, Massachusetts
Scott Paris, University of Michigan, Ann Arbor
Richard Paul, Sonoma State University, Rohnert Park, California
David Perkins, Harvard University, Cambridge, Massachusetts
Mel Preusser, Douglas County (Colorado) School District, Castle Rock
Nelson "Pete" Quinby, Barlow High School, West Redding, Connecticut
Taffy Raphael, Michigan State University, E. Lansing
Judith Segal, Office of Educational Research and Improvement, U.S. Department of
     Education, Washington, D.C.
Elliot Seif, Bucks County (Pennsylvania) Intermediate Unit, Doylestown
Irving Sigel, Educational Testing Service, Princeton, New Jersey
Edward Silver, San Diego State University, San Diego, California
B. Othanel Smith, Professor Emeritus, University of South Florida, Tampa
Robert Sternberg, Yale University, New Haven, Connecticut
Robert Swartz, University of Massachusetts, Boston
Richard Thompson, Tupelo (Mississippi) Public School District, Tupelo
Margaret Tinzmann, National College of Education, Evanston, Illinois
Ryan Tweney, Bowling Green State University, Bowling Green, Ohio
Charles Wales, West Virginia University, Morgantown
Deborah Walsh, American Federation of Teachers, Washington, D.C.
Belinda Williams, Board of Education of the City of Paterson, Paterson, New Jersey
Lee Winocur, Project IMPACT, Costa Mesa, California
M.C. Wittrock, University of California, Los Angeles

Contributors

The following wrote passages that have been included in the document: John Barell, Joan Boykoff Baron, Matthew Lipman, Margaret Tinzmann, and Belinda Williams.

Member Organizations of the Association Collaborative for Teaching Thinking

American Association of Colleges of Teacher Education
American Association of School Administrators
American Association of School Librarians
American Federation of Teachers
American Educational Research Association
Association for Supervision and Curriculum Development
Council for American Private Education
Council of Chief State School Officers
Council of Great City Schools
Home Economics Education Association
Institute for Development of Educational Activities
International Listening Association
International Reading Association
Music Educators National Conference
National Art Education Association
National Alliance of Black School Educators
National Association of Elementary School Principals
National Association of Secondary School Principals
National Association of State Universities and Land-Grant Colleges
National Congress of Parents and Teachers
National Council for the Social Studies
National Council of Teachers of English
National Council of Teachers of Mathematics
National Education Association
National Middle School Association
National Science Teachers Association
National School Boards Association
North Central Regional Educational Laboratory

Foreword

Who would not want what is taught in school to include an emphasis on student thinking? Yet we know that the activities and interaction patterns in many classrooms do not contribute to growth in thinking. Numerous attempts have been made to change the situation, with varying degrees of success and frustration. The authors of this book offer a fresh approach.

Because of the bewildering array of strategies offered by various advocates, many educators are confused about just what it means to "teach thinking" and how, other than buying a packaged program, schools can provide for it. As a partial answer, the authors of *Dimensions of Thinking* have developed a framework intended to be the basis for curriculum and staff development programs. They have organized and clarified research and theory from several sources, including philosophy and cognitive psychology, in a form intended to be useful to practitioners.

As you read *Dimensions of Thinking*, you may be challenged to rethink conventional views on such matters as student motivation and reward systems and the relationship between thinking skills and content knowledge. You will doubtless begin to wonder about the possible impact of teaching thinking on the perennial problems of student failure, disillusionment, and unmet potential. And you will probably be excited by the possibility of gains in student achievement that we usually only dream about.

Because this publication challenges traditional notions about purposes and methods of instruction, it has implications for preservice and inservice teacher education and for refocusing the efforts of supervisors, principals, superintendents, and boards of education. A powerful yet flexible model, *Dimensions of Thinking* promises to influence education far into the future.

Marcia Knoll
ASCD President, 1987-88

Preface

WHEN THE SEVEN OF US GOT TOGETHER TO BEGIN WORK ON THIS BOOK, WE KNEW it could not be done perfectly, and a few of us doubted it could be done at all. The idea of a new "taxonomy" of thinking skills was first suggested at an invitational conference hosted by the Johnson Foundation at the Wingspread Conference Center in Racine, Wisconsin, in May 1984. ASCD had called the meeting to ask interested educators how we might best contribute to the burgeoning interest in teaching thinking. The conferees suggested numerous possibilities, including preparing a resource book, producing a series of videotapes, starting a network, and cooperating with other education organizations to promote interest in teaching thinking.

In February 1985 Carolyn Hughes, then ASCD president-elect, met with representatives of other organizations to form the Association Collaborative for Teaching Thinking. The Collaborative identified five projects that member organizations thought would be useful, including one that ASCD offered to support financially: development of a framework of thinking skills.

Educators wanted a framework because they were hearing more and more about published programs designed specifically for teaching thinking. Each of these programs had its own definition of thinking and its own array of skills. If schools were to integrate the teaching of thinking with regular academic instruction, they needed to know what aspects of thinking to teach. We decided to try to answer that question as well as we could.

We began knowing that several detailed lists of thinking skills were already available, but it did not seem useful simply to rearrange them. Besides, the literature on thinking dealt not only with skills but with several other aspects of thinking, such as "dispositions" of critical thinkers, creativity, decision making, and the role of knowledge in thinking. We wanted to recognize each of these aspects of thinking in our framework if we could. We chose to call the major elements of our framework "dimensions" because, if we could draw a diagram of our model, it would have at least five dimensions.[1]

---

[1]It would, of course, be difficult to represent more than three dimensions graphically, so we have not attempted that. We acknowledge also that, as Ray Nickerson has pointed out, our use of the term is somewhat inappropriate because we are not actually referring to measurable extensions in space.

The framework presented in this book has been reviewed by numerous researchers, experts, and practitioners and revised several times in an effort to make it as accurate and helpful as possible. Some 60 people, including both researchers and practitioners, met in November 1986 for a second invitational conference at Wingspread to criticize the third draft of the manuscript, which was subsequently rewritten again in response to the conferees' recommendations. We appreciate the many helpful comments we received, and we feel the framework is stronger because of them. Additional research information on each of the dimensions may be found in a companion volume, *Dimensions of Thinking and Cognitive Instruction.*[2]

We knew when we began that our final product would not be fully satisfactory, and for good reason. Thinking is such a complex activity that it is extremely difficult to portray with accuracy and clarity. Some aspects of thinking are better understood than others, and many are the subject of considerable controversy. Some of the better published programs for teaching thinking skills are grounded in particular conceptions of thinking. They are based on a particular body of research or on a well-conceived rationale. They are coherent—but also somewhat idiosyncratic. Our aim was to assemble a cohesive framework drawn from many diverse sources. For example, we wanted to include the perspectives of both psychology and philosophy. Unfortunately, the two traditions are very different, so in a sense we were trying to reconcile the irreconcilable. Nevertheless, despite these concerns, we think practicing educators will find this framework useful.

The framework is intended for use in designing staff development programs for teachers and other educators and as the basis for curriculum planning at all levels. In the years ahead, we hope to see each of the dimensions more fully reflected in school programs and practices. Some researchers and educators are concerned about publication of a framework such as this because they oppose the teaching of skills apart from meaningful context. They see that schools frequently fall into the trap of seeming to teach skills for their own sake rather than providing for their useful application in goal-directed activities. We believe that occasional explicit instruction in core skills and processes—when related to a useful purpose—can be beneficial to students, but in general we, too, question the value of teaching skills apart from content.

We recogize that this framework can be misinterpreted and misused, but it is not intended as a scope and sequence chart for a separate thinking skills curriculum. To the contrary, we believe that whether or not schools decide to offer special thinking skills programs, thinking should pervade the entire curriculum. Accordingly, we have tried to identify aspects of thinking so fundamental that students should *use* these skills and processes repeatedly in the course of learning academic content.

---

[2]Jones, B.F., and L. Idol, *Dimensions of Thinking and Cognitive Instruction* (Hillsdale, N.J.: Erlbaum, in preparation).

1. Thinking as the Foundation of Schooling

IN RECENT YEARS, MANY AMERICANS HAVE COME TO RECOGNIZE THAT STUDENTS IN our schools do not think as skillfully and critically as we might wish. A barrage of books, articles, and reports has appeared in support of teaching thinking. For example, such prominent organizations as the Education Commission of the States (1982) and the College Board (1983) have highlighted the teaching of thinking. High-impact reports such as *A Nation at Risk* (National Commission on Excellence in Education, 1983) have pointed to deficiencies in higher-level thinking as a major weakness in American education. Widely read journals such as *Educational Leadership* have devoted entire issues to the topic.

Many of these publications cite students' inability to answer higher level questions on tests or to perform well on complex academic tasks. For example, Silver's (1986) analysis of the results of nationwide testing by the National Assessment of Educational Progress (NAEP) includes convincing examples of how students approach academic tasks in a mechanical fashion without much apparent thought about what they are doing. A classic illustration is the following NAEP problem.

Estimate the answer to 3.04 x 5.3

a. 1.6   b. 16   c. 160   d. 1,600   e. don't know

Only 20 percent of the 13-year-olds and 40 percent of the 17-year-olds got the right answer. Yet when asked to compute the answer to a similar problem, 60 percent of the 13-year-olds and 80 percent of the 17-year-olds answered correctly (Burns, 1986). Other evidence suggests that students of all ages have many misconceptions that are not being effectively addressed by existing instructional methods. Anderson and Smith (1984), for instance, have noted that elementary students can pass chapter quizzes on photosynthesis and still not understand that plants make their own food.

These and countless other examples in the reform literature suggest that America's students often lack rigorous thought and perhaps even that thinking is not valued in our schools. Indeed, the main message often communicated to students is that they should provide "the right answer."

According to Doyle's (1983) study of academic work in American schools, accountability and testing drive schooling. Students learn early in the game that all classroom activities are not equal; some things are tested, and others are not. By the time students have reached high school, they know the rule well: "Learn what will be tested." The result, despite teachers' good intentions, is devaluation of independent thought.

The Goal of Education

Such philosophers as Robert Ennis, Matthew Lipman, and Richard Paul hold that the development of rational thinkers should be the primary goal of education. Paul (1986b) envisions the end product of education as the inquiring mind:

A passionate drive for clarity, accuracy, and fair-mindedness, a fervor for getting to the bottom of things, to the deepest root issues, for listening sympathetically to opposite points of view, a compelling drive to seek out evidence, and intense aversion to contradiction, sloppy thinking, inconsistent application of standards, a devotion to truth as against self-interest—these are essential components of the rational person (p. 1).

Others would say that the goal is to develop mature thinkers who are able to acquire and use knowledge. For example, Anderson (1977) and Rumelhart (1980) stress the fundamental role of "searching for meaning" in cognition. Toward this end, model learners work actively to integrate new information with what they already know, to select what is important, to make inferences beyond the information given, and to think strategically about their own learning.

For many philosophers, psychologists, and educators, the development of rational thought and the search for meaning need no justification; their centrality to education is self-evident (Kirkpatrick, 1936). More pragmatic reasons, though, are not hard to find. Certainly the success of any democratic system depends on individuals' ability to analyze problems and make thoughtful decisions. A democracy thrives on the productivity of its diverse constituency—a productivity fostered by free, critical, and creative thought on issues of common interest.

Seiger-Ehrenberg (1985), who in her lifetime developed several thinking-skills programs, expresses the rationale for teaching thinking in terms of individual and social needs and benefits. "By the time students graduate from high school, they should be able to consistently and effectively take intelligent ethical action to accomplish the tasks society legitimately expects of all its members and to establish and pursue worthwhile goals of their own choosing" (p. 7). She defines "intelligent ethical action" as "using rational thought processes to arrive at a decision . . . taking into account . . . the well-being of those affected" (pp. 8–9). She proposes that these outcomes—which can be achieved only by teaching students to think—should be the basis for planning the entire curriculum.

The Need for a Framework for Teaching Thinking

Many programs designed specifically for teaching thinking are now available. Costa's (1985a) *Developing Minds: A Resource Book for Teaching Thinking* includes descriptions of more than 30 such programs or approaches. Although these resources are useful and show great progress in our awareness of the need to foster thinking, the different definitions of thinking and the number of available options can be confusing. In fact, it would be a mistake to assume that thinking instruction is somehow contained in this abundance of programs and that offering one or more of them is sufficient. Such an assumption is dangerous because it ignores the need to conceptualize basic skills such as reading and writing as thinking and because it ignores the need to infuse teaching thinking in all curriculum areas.

What has been missing in current theory and practice is an organizing framework for teaching thinking—a latticework to systematically examine themes common to the different approaches and relationships among them. An appropriate framework would allow practitioners in different subject areas and grade levels to develop a common knowledge base and a common language for teaching thinking. In this book we seek to develop such a framework.

Dimensions of Thinking

At the outset, it is important to acknowledge the limitations of our effort. The framework presented here is meant to be a useful tool for practitioners. It is not offered as a model of how the mind works or as an explanatory theory. Rather, we are guided by Anderson's (1983, p. 12) definition: a *framework* is a "general pool of constructs for understanding a domain, but is not tightly enough organized to constitute a predictive theory."

Such noted scholars and researchers as Perkins (1981), Sternberg (1980), Gardner (1983), Anderson (1983), and Johnson-Laird (1983) have developed highly sophisticated theories and models of cognition and intelligence. No duplication of their work is intended here. Rather, we have tried to draw from many scholarly works to identify the "dimensions" that appear to be threads running through both research and theory—perspectives that can be used to analyze various approaches to teaching thinking and to provide direction for planning curriculum and instruction. Accordingly, we have identified five dimensions of thinking:

- Metacognition
- Critical and creative thinking
- Thinking processes
- Core thinking skills
- The relationship of content–area knowledge to thinking

These dimensions do not form a taxonomy. They are neither discrete nor comparable categories. They overlap in some cases, and they relate to each other in different ways. Therefore, they do not form a hierarchy. Nor are they intended as ends in themselves. We chose them because they reflect the various domains of thinking as they are understood in terms of current research. Educators can use this framework as a resource to match the demands of the curriculum with the needs of students, knowing that this is a working document that will change as research provides new information.

The first dimension, *metacognition*, refers to our awareness and control of our own thinking. For example, students' beliefs about themselves and about such things as the value of persistence and the nature of work will heavily influence their motivation, attention, and effort for any given task.

Critical and creative thinking are dominant themes in the literature on thinking. We consider this dimension to include these two different but related ways of characterizing thinking. Regardless of the particular processes or skills involved, an individual's thinking can be described as more or less creative or critical.

We conceive of *thinking processes*, such as concept formation, comprehension, decision making, and problem solving, as another dimension of thinking. Whereas skills, such as ordering data or verifying the accuracy of statements, can be accessed randomly as the situation arises, the cognitive processes are goal oriented. To comprehend a passage, solve a problem, or engage in scientific inquiry are important academic activities in their own right. We view them as being more or less macro-level operations that take place over time in variable but somewhat predictable sequences of generic skills.

We refer to these more micro-level operations as *core thinking skills*. They are best described as basic cognitive operations used in metacognitive reflection and in the thinking processes. The skills of comparing and classifying, for example, are used frequently in decision making and problem solving.

These first four dimensions do not exist in isolation. Individuals must think *about* something, and the content of our thinking greatly influences how we think. For example, our ability to classify and order data probably depends more on our knowledge of the topic than on our knowledge of the skills of classifying and ordering. Knowledge is related to the other dimensions in complex and subtle ways.

A key characteristic of the dimensions is that they occur simultaneously. An individual may be thinking metacognitively ("Do I understand this word? Is it important to what follows?") while using skills and processes ("How can I represent this problem? What would I need to do to produce a *good* essay?") in critical and creative ways. When writing a paper, for example, a student might be monitoring attitudes, such as the desire to go out and play ball rather than study, while using a specific thinking skill such as summarizing.

Our framework does not distinguish as separate dimensions several aspects of thinking that need to be addressed in any organized effort to foster student thinking and therefore might have been included as additional dimensions. One of these is cognitive development: the growth in students' capacities for thinking as they mature and gain experience. Another is cognitive style. Research and everyday experience confirm that individuals think differently, so schools must not expect a single style of thinking to fit all students equally well. We also considered having a separate chapter on attitudes and dispositions but decided to discuss this important aspect of thinking in the context of the other dimensions.

The Razor's Edge

Before discussing the dimensions in depth, we want to warn against teaching them as ends in themselves. We do not recommend that a district or school use this or any other framework as the basis for a scope and sequence chart calling for isolated instruction in thinking. Rather, students should *use* the skills, processes, and metacognitive strategies in connection with learning regular classroom content. They should view the skills as means to comprehending a theory, solving a problem, or drafting an essay.

We do not mean to suggest, however, that students do not need practice in a given skill or that they should never be taught specific skills in adjunct courses. Clearly, some students need more practice than others, and trying to learn skills and content at the same time may overwhelm some of them. Nevertheless, even when cognitive and metacognitive skills are taught directly, the goal should be to learn valuable information. To be effective, drill and practice must have functional meaning (Sticht & Hickey, in press). Meaningless drill and practice will not produce thinking students.

Teachers in every subject area, then, have a dual agenda. They need to develop in all students a rich knowledge base, and they need to provide students with a repertoire of cognitive and metacognitive skills and strategies that will enable them to use the knowledge efficiently in meaningful contexts.

Thinking in Historical Context

Any conception of thinking is always from the perspective of a particular time frame. Thinking was perceived differently in the 10th century than it was during the Enlightenment. Different times have their own unique thought processes, and current thought patterns reflect the present era.

Our effort is but one of a long list of similar attempts to map what is known about thinking onto curriculum and instruction. More than 70 years ago, Dewey (1916) wrote, "The sole direct path to enduring improvement in the methods of instruction and learning consists in centering upon the conditions which exact, promote, and test thinking." Similarly, in 1961 the National Education Association identified the improvement of thinking as central to American education:

Thus in the general area of the development of the ability to think, there is a field for new research of the greatest importance. It is essential that those who have responsibility for management and policy determination in education commit themselves to expansion of such research and to the application of the fruits of this research. This is the context in which the significant answers to such issues as educational technology, length of the school year and content of teacher education must be sought and given (Educational Policies Commission, 1961, pp. 14-15).

Just as educators' interest in thinking can be traced back several decades, interest in thinking and its relationship to human behavior is as old as civilization itself. The study of thinking has at least two strong traditions—the philosophical and the psychological.

A Great Tradition: Philosophy

The roots to the philosophical interest in thinking reach back to the classical past. Greene (1984) notes that in the Western world, philosophy preceded by at least 2,000 years the growth of what we now call science.

Indeed, philosophy was seen as the queen of sciences. To think or reason, according to early philosophers, was to take the stance of the objective and contemplative spectator and, in doing so, to discover truth. Plato described the philosopher-king as one who could discern through introspection the forms or ideas behind appearances. Aristotle described this process of discerning truth through rational thought as grasping the design or *telos* of reality. In *The Nichomachean Ethics*, Aristotle also saw reason as a guide to correct behavior: "To know what excellence is is not enough; we must endeavor to acquire it and to act accordingly."

Inquiry is one of the philosopher's primary tools. According to Socrates, the philosopher continually uses discussion and argument to try to "attain to each thing itself that is; he doesn't give up before he grasps by intellection itself that which is good itself" (in Goldman, 1984).

The spirit of inquiry runs through the entire history of philosophy. It shaped many of the modern notions of science. For example, in the 17th century, Descartes wrote that the philosopher's primary responsibility was to develop an accurate method of investigation. As a mathematician, Descartes gravitated toward developing a system closely related to analytic geometry. Dewey observed that, because inquiry leads to change, a democratic society should nurture the spirit of inquiry, lest society stagnate and the energies of its citizens turn inward, destructively.

Philosophy, then, has been inexorably tied to the study of thinking. Such great scholars as Hegel, James, Spinoza, and Bacon, along with those mentioned above and many others, have greatly influenced how we think today and how we view thinking. The current interest in teaching thinking, then, is fundamentally a philosophical issue—but it is also a psychological issue.

The Second Great Tradition: Psychology

Not until about the mid–19th century did scholars view the human mind as a "working mechanism" with underlying operations that could be scientifically studied (Rowe, 1985). The biologists Darwin (1809-1882) and Spencer (1820-1903) observed correlations between the evolutionary increase in the flexibility of animal behavior and the increasing size of animals' brains. In short order, the attention to identifying the operations that constitute thinking increased. The first psychological laboratory was founded in Leipzig by Wundt and his students to investigate the basic building blocks of all cognition, which they thought to be sensations and perceptions. Since those early days of psychology, the study of thinking has taken many forms, among them Gestalt psychology, behaviorism, psychometrics, and information-processing theory.

Primarily concerned with perception, Gestalt psychology assumes that all organisms have an innate tendency to organize information taken from the environment. But the organization cannot be explained as a simple matter of small, independent parts combined in some cumulative fashion. Instead, human beings organize information in a *gestalt* (a structure, form, or configuration) different from the sum of its parts. Such scholars as Wertheimer, Necker, Koehler, Luchins, Dunker, and Taylor used the notion of a gestalt to explain many aspects of thinking.

Although Gestalt psychology focuses strongly on perception, behavioral psychology is primarily concerned with learning. In behavioral or stimulus-response psychology, the probability of a given response in an organism is directly related to how the response is associated with the stimulus; more frequently practiced responses will be more likely to endure. Much of the current emphasis on skill practice in the classroom stems from this principle. Theorists commonly associated with behaviorism include Thorndike, Hull, Osgood, and Skinner.

Another strong trend in the psychological tradition is the psychometric approach. Psychometrists tend to focus on the products of behavior rather than on performance itself; thus, test scores are analyzed with sophisticated statistical techniques. In this approach, the tasks presented to students in aptitude and intelligence tests are considered valid indicators of intelligence. Early analysis of such tests indicated that a general factor or aptitude appeared central to all forms of intelligence. Recently, other factors have been identified, such as crystallized intelligence (information we learn from our culture) and fluid intelligence (genetically determined abilities such as the capacity of one's short-term memory). Psychologists commonly associated with the psychometric approach include Guilford, Thurstone, Cattell, Carroll, and Horn.

The psychometric approach to psychology has included a focus on children's developing intelligence. Binet and Simon's early research sought to identify schoolchildren unlikely to succeed in normal classrooms. Piaget and Inhelder's studies of child logic and reasoning paralleled Montessori's examination of children's learning and pedagogy, while Gesell sought to understand the social psychological and parenting influences on youthful development. Bruner, Berlyne, and Kagan have conducted many studies that seek to understand the developing mind of the child as part of a larger explanation of human development and psychology.

The most recent psychological approach to the study of thinking is information processing. This approach focuses on how we acquire, transmit, store, and transform information. Many successful analyses of thinking—for example, most of what we know about the limitations of human memory—have been made using this approach. Information-processing theory has made possible the development of powerful computer models (commonly called *artificial intelligence*) that simulate human thought. Among many others, Newell, Simon, Greeno, Schank, Abelson, Rumelhart, Minsky, and Papert are pioneers of this approach.

Dual Perspectives

Philosophy and psychology, the two traditions contributing most to the study of thinking, each provide a perspective essential to fostering thinking in the classroom. The philosophical tradition deals broadly with the nature and quality of thinking and its role in human behavior. The psychological tradition explains the workings of specific cognitive operations. Both perspectives must be considered in the development of a framework for teaching thinking.

In the following chapters, we draw from both traditions to discuss the five dimensions of thinking and their implications for educational practice. We see the potential impact of this framework as both powerful and broad—powerful because it could drastically restructure the conceptualization and implementation of schooling; broad because it could affect, among other elements, curriculum design, assessment techniques, and pedagogy. At the same time, we recognize that educators will need to continually modify the framework to account for new insights into the nature of thinking.

We recognize as well that because, like most educators, we are more deeply steeped in the traditions of cognitive and educational psychology than in philosophy, our resulting framework is necessarily "biased" in that direction. We hope in time to see the insights of philosophy incorporated more fully into the practice of education, further illuminating the dimensions of thinking.

2.
Metacognition

ALTHOUGH *METACOGNITION* IS A MAJOR FOCUS IN THE THEORY, RESEARCH, AND practice of teaching thinking, the term is not easily described or defined. Flavell (1976, 1977, 1978), one of the pioneers in the study of metacognition, describes it this way:

> Metacognition refers to one's knowledge concerning one's own cognitive processes and products or anything related to them. . . . For example, I am engaging in metacognition . . . if I notice that I am having more trouble learning A than B; if it strikes me that I should double check C before accepting it as a fact. . . . Metacognition refers, among other things, to the active monitoring and consequent regulation and orchestration of these processes . . . usually in the service of some concrete goal or objective (1976, p. 232).

In simpler terms, metacognition is being aware of our thinking as we perform specific tasks and then using this awareness to control what we are doing. Paris and his colleagues (Paris, Lipson, & Wixson, 1983; Paris & Lindauer, 1982) clarify metacognition in their discussion of "strategic thinking." Citing research on experts and novices, Paris notes that a major distinction between the two is that experts engage in self-regulated, purpose-driven behavior more often than novices. For example, math and science experts constantly compare their results with estimations or expected outcomes; novices often fail to define goals and subgoals clearly, or they may neglect to check their answers against a mental representation (e.g., Schoenfeld, 1985).

The components of metacognition are described in many ways. Flavell (1978) stresses knowledge about person, task, and strategy. Brown (1978) emphasizes planning, monitoring, and revising. Our description will be in accord with the view of Paris and Winograd (in press) that metacognition involves two primary aspects: knowledge and control of self and knowledge and control of process.

Knowledge and Control of Self

Commitment

Intuitively, most teachers recognize that students' commitment to academic tasks is a major determinant of their success. Students do not do well if they do not try, regardless of the quality of the lessons or the materials. Commitment is not a matter of chance; people have the power to generate commitment at any time. In fact, Perkins (1985) has found that highly creative people generate commitment in situations where others do not.

Blasi and Oresick (1986) note that commitment is fundamentally a decision—a decision to put energies into a task. Paris and Cross (1983) refer to this aspect of metacognition as aligning "skill with will."

In the classroom, discussion and example can clarify the nature and importance of commitment. Students can easily find examples of people who have accomplished great feats because of strong commitment, but they are often surprised that they themselves have the power to generate commitment to any task. Commitment is not something out of their control; they *choose* to be committed to their work, or they choose not to be committed.

Many students and some adults mistakenly associate commitment with their feelings about their work. ("If I'm excited about what I'm doing, if it's fun, then I must be committed to it. If I'm not excited or it's not fun, then I'm not committed.") In fact, the situation is more complicated. Mandler (1983) explains that our energy level or excitement is generated from the limbic system of the brain. This system is sometimes controlled by the information from the outside world, but more commonly, the system simply reacts to internal bodily functions. If our internal systems are not functioning well because we have not eaten properly or had enough sleep, then we will have difficulty generating energy and excitement. Still, it can be done. So students should not view how they feel as the primary determiner of whether they are going to work hard or not. Rather, they should consider whether they have *chosen* to be committed.

Attitudes

Closely related to the level of commitment are our attitudes as we engage in tasks. The tripartite model of human behavior (Weiner 1972, 1983) postulates that behavior can be explained as the interaction of three main components—attitudes, emotions, and actions. Sometimes, emotions cause attitudes that then affect behavior. But attitudes can also cause emotions that, in turn, affect behavior.

Such theorists as Weiner (1983), Covington (1983), and Harter (1980) have discussed the power of attitudes as simple and straightforward as "Effort pays off."

Effort pays off. More specifically, the area of study in cognitive psychology called attribution theory has shown that thoughts or "ideations" about a task greatly affect how we approach the task. Weiner (1983) has found that people commonly attribute success to one of four causes: ability, effort, other people, or luck. Certainly "luck" and "other people" are not useful attributions. What happens when your luck runs out or you are alone? At first, ability seems most useful—if you think you have the "right stuff," you can do anything. Unfortunately, ability attribution frequently backfires. Regardless of how much ability you think you have, there will inevitably be tasks for which you are not skilled. Students who attribute success solely to ability will probably not even attempt many new tasks, or will do them half-heartedly, because they will assume that they do not possess the necessary talent. The most useful attribution, therefore, is effort—the belief that intense, extended effort will generally lead to success.

I can perform the task. Research on locus of control and self-determination or self-efficacy suggests that a sense of personal control over the outcome of a task determines how efficiently a student approaches it (Weinstein, 1982). Motivating for and performing a task are a function of students' belief that they can perform the task. If students believe that success depends on some outside source, they will have little motivation and probably will not perform well. However, students need not necessarily believe they can *easily* perform the task—only that they can *possibly* perform it. Or, in negative terms, students cannot believe that the task is impossible.

Chapter 3, "Critical and Creative Thinking," describes several dispositions characteristic of good thinkers. Teachers can also cultivate other attitudes in students:

- Be persistent.
- Strive to work beyond what you think you can do.
- Be aware of and use the resources around you.
- Learn from failure.

Before students can become aware of their attitudes and control them as a part of a general metacognitive strategy, teachers can guide them toward two understandings: that attitudes affect behavior and that people have some control over their attitudes. By discussing real-life examples of how positive attitudes allowed people to overcome hardships or accomplish great feats, students can learn how attitudes affect behavior. Teachers can also point to examples of successful student learning, especially when a student has overcome a problem.

Since students may not believe they have control over their attitudes, developing this understanding may take time. One approach is to identify instances either within the content (in a reading text or a history lesson, for example) or within the classroom when a change of attitude was pivotal to a given outcome, and then to discuss how that change came about.

Another approach is to identify and discuss negative attitudes toward a particular class; then, as an experiment, students can work from the positive counterpart of that attitude. For example, a student might identify the negative attitude, "This class is boring for me." The student would then try to behave as though the class were interesting. The teacher might say, "For today, try to pretend this class is interesting to you. Do those things you would do if it were interesting. Try to have the thoughts you would have, the feelings you would have, if the class were interesting to you."

Changing our attitudes, even when only pretending, may dramatically affect our experience at a particular moment. Psychologist Robert Hartley (in Chance, 1987) found that asking children ages 6 to 10 to pretend they were good at solving problems by modeling the behavior of someone they knew who was good actually increased their problem-solving ability. "When youngsters pretended to be someone clever, they did as well as their more reflective classmates, making the same number of mistakes and taking the same amount of time as students who had been their betters" (p. 10).

Attention

The final area of self-regulation in metacognition is being aware of and controlling our attention level. Psychologists note that, at any given time, we are bombarded with stimuli. We cannot possibly attend to all of them, so we focus on some and ignore others (Norman, 1969). As with commitment and attitudes, many people mistakenly believe that attention is beyond their control. There are, however, two basic types of attention: automatic and voluntary.

Automatic attention is reflexive—a reaction. For example, young infants exhibit automatic attention when they turn their heads in the direction of a loud noise. When operating under automatic attention, we attend to the most unusual stimulus or the one with the greatest intensity (Luria, 1973).

Voluntary attention is under conscious control and is active rather than passive. For example, we operate under voluntary attention when we decide to notice the detail in a picture we are looking at. We operate under voluntary attention when we refocus on a task, realizing we have been daydreaming for the last five minutes. Voluntary attention causes students to sit up straight and concentrate on what is happening in class after realizing their attention has been drifting.

Students should realize that different tasks require different attention levels. When reading for pleasure or for the general idea, for example, they need not focus on details. For these tasks, they should attend to text aids such as headings and graphics. In looking for facts, the opposite is true: they should attend to dates or key words relative to the facts. Also, students need to understand that studying usually does not require giving equal attention to all the materials available; rather, they need to select what is important and focus their attention on those things. To learn this flexibility, students need opportunities during class to practice using different attention levels and selecting what is important, with feedback about the appropriateness of their decisions.

Thus, three aspects of self-regulation relate to metacognition:

- Monitoring and controlling commitment
- Monitoring and controlling attitudes
- Monitoring and controlling attention

Incorporating these aspects of metacognition into students' repertoire of knowledge involves much effort and practice in meaningful, content-relevant situations. One approach is to address metacognitive issues explicitly. Once students have discussed these aspects, they can practice during regular classroom activities. Before students engage in an activity, the teacher can remind them of the three components and ask them to note their level of commitment, the attitudes they have about the upcoming activity, and their level of attention. This reminder might take only a few moments, or the teacher might spend 10 to 15 minutes having students discuss the three components of self-regulation. Students could also write in their journals about their commitment, attitudes, and attention, telling how their new self-awareness affects their behavior. In short, students can approach self-knowledge and self-control as a field experiment or group inquiry about the nature of self-regulation and its effects on performance.

Although this approach may be appealing in its directness, some researchers contend that it takes valuable time away from learning the content. Proponents of this view advise teachers to focus on developing strategic thinking: Teachers should model the thoughts, commitments, beliefs, and attitudes of successful learners as they approach particular problems or decisions, identifying positive and negative attributions as they arise in day-to-day activities, and providing opportunities for students to reflect on the consequences of specific actions and thoughts in the learning process.

Knowledge and Control of Process

In their discussion of knowledge and control of process, Paris, Lipson, and Wixson (1983) stress two important elements: the types of knowledge important in metacognition and the executive control of behavior.

Types of Knowledge Important in Metacognition

Three types of knowledge are important to metacognition: declarative, procedural, and conditional (or contextual). *Declarative knowledge* is factual. When you know declarative information, you know *that*. For example, a student might know *that* most newspaper stories introduce "who, what, when, and where" in the opening paragraphs and *that* his comprehension goals differ when he reads a newspaper and when he reads a poem.

Procedural knowledge includes information about the various actions that must be performed in a task. It is knowing *how*. For example, a student's procedural knowledge might include knowing *how* to skim, *how* to scan, *how* to summarize, and *how* to infer unstated information. "Procedures describe a large range of actions involved in any task such as reading. They are the repertoire of behavior available to an agent who selects among them to attain different goals" (Paris, Lipson, & Wixson, 1983, p. 303).

Conditional knowledge refers to knowing why a given strategy works or when to use one skill or strategy as opposed to another. Knowing *when* to skim, *why* attitude is important, and *why* one approach to solving a problem is better or more efficient are examples of conditional knowledge. Researchers such as Schoenfeld (1985) emphasize the importance of conditional knowledge. In fact, Collins and Brown (in press) have identified this type of knowledge as a critical ingredient in successful training programs (see also Winograd and Hare, in press).

To exert metacognitive control over a process, then, students must know *what* facts and concepts are necessary for the task; *which* strategies, heuristics, or procedures are appropriate (conditional knowledge); and *how* to apply the selected strategy, procedure, or heuristic. For example, if students were to think metacognitively about writing a report, they would consider the relevant concepts and data to include, but they would also think about such things as how specific versus how general to be, how to organize the data, how well each argument or generalization is supported, and whether or not a given bar graph supports a particular point.

These three types of knowledge—declarative, procedural, and conditional—are essential aspects of metacognition. Ideally, teachers should be able to identify these components for the tasks presented to students and to systematically teach and reinforce them.

Executive Control of Behavior

Maintaining executive control, the second aspect of metacognition related to process, involves evaluation, planning, and regulation. In Paris, Lipson, and Wixson's (1983) model, *evaluation* includes assessing our current knowledge state—taking our mental temperature: "Do I understand the symbolism in this novel? Did I understand what I just read? Have I ever seen a problem like this one before? Do I understand the legend on this map? Is there more information I should gather before I try writing this essay?" Evaluation occurs throughout an entire process and is both the beginning and the end point for a task. It also includes assessing whether we have the resources needed for the task. Working hard will get us only so far; for many tasks, we must apply specific resources. Finally, evaluation includes assessing task goals and subgoals. ("Where do I want to end up when I am done? What other goals do I want to accomplish along the way? If I can't achieve the final goal, what subgoals can I achieve?")

Planning involves deliberately selecting strategies to fulfill specific goals. Here declarative and conditional knowledge comes into play. Students must know an array of specific procedures related to a task to select the most appropriate procedure at any given point. Piaget (1963) has observed that trial-and-error reasoning characterizes goal-related thinking before the concrete operational stage; planfulness appears in later childhood.

Regulation involves checking your progress toward the goals and subgoals identified. Failing to regulate is "blind-rule following" (Brown, 1978). From this perspective, regulation is the process of continually assessing how close to our goal or subgoal we are. ("Let's see, am I closer to my goal now than the last time I checked? Am I making progress toward my goal or am I digressing?") Then, carrying out appropriate revisions is critical.

Teachers need to model the process of planning, monitoring, evaluating, and revising and then gradually give students responsibility for these tasks. In fact, students should recognize that experts (e.g., teachers) devote substantial energy to planning, monitoring, evaluating, and revising; that experts often have problems carrying out a plan or revision; and that they sometimes fail, but that they learn from their failures (Collins, Brown, & Newman, 1986).

Occasionally it may be useful to ask students to consciously focus on the metacognitive components of a task. Costa (1984) suggests that students think of tasks as having *before*, *during*, and *after* components. Although the model should not be applied mechanically, students can come to see that evaluating, planning, regulating, and revising take place at each stage.

For example, assume that students in a science class are building a model of an atom. *Before* they actually start, they might evaluate their current state of knowledge about atoms. ("Do we know everything we need to know about atoms before we start this project?") Then they would plan a course of action based on their evaluation of their current state of knowledge, setting explicit goals and subgoals with time lines.

During construction of the model, the students would continue to evaluate their state of knowledge. They might find they were missing important pieces of declarative, procedural, or conditional knowledge. They would then temporarily stop construction and gather that information. They would engage in planning during the construction of the model. ("Given our resources and our time line, what should we do next? What's the best strategy for depicting that third layer of electrons?") Also, students would continually regulate their progress toward their goal. ("How close are we to our finished product? Are we losing ground, or are we making steady progress here?")

After completing the project, students would again evaluate their knowledge about atoms, considering declarative, procedural, and conditional knowledge. ("What new facts have we learned about atoms from constructing the model? What new procedures have we learned about model construction? What have we learned about how the condition in which an atom exists changes some of the characteristics?") Students would even engage in planning after completing the project; however, the planning would be future-oriented. ("What else do we want to learn about atoms? How are we going to obtain that information?") Students would then engage in regulation by assessing how well they accomplished their initial goals. ("Did it turn out the way we wanted it to? How successful were we?")

Although we have for purposes of analysis separated self-knowledge and self-control from knowledge and control of process, they are not in practice separate. When students are exerting metacognitive control over process, they are also exerting self-control. While they evaluate, plan, and regulate (before, during, and after a task), they may also be monitoring and controlling commitment, attitudes, and attention.

Implications

What does an emphasis on metacognition mean for the classroom teacher and for students? First, emphasis on students' self-control and responsibility for that control in the classroom can be overt and direct. Students can learn that self-monitoring is a valued, high-level skill. They can systematically develop commitment, a positive and personal attitude toward learning, and attention through introspection and practice.

The notion of the teacher as a disciplinarian is, therefore, greatly diminished. In situations where students have little self-control, they need to learn to develop and foster that control as a means to attaining better academic progress. Student self-control is considered as important and deserving of direct attention as any academic goal; indeed, the achievement of academic goals is directly dependent on self-control. This view echos the message of the work world to education: that one of the important skills for students entering the work force is knowledge and control of themselves so that they can work autonomously and effectively with others in sometimes difficult situations.

3. Critical and Creative Thinking

A PERSISTENT CONCERN IN SCHOOLS IS THE QUALITY OF STUDENTS' THINKING: HOW it measures up to standards of good thinking. Although desirable thinking has been characterized in many ways (productive, rational, logical, and so on), the term most commonly used for the type of thinking that schools try to encourage is critical thinking. Creative or inventive thinking is a second type of thinking encouraged in schools. We believe that critical and creative thinking should not be considered cognitive processes comparable to problem solving and decision making. Instead, these terms imply judgments about the quality of the thinking involved—a judgment about the relation of thinking to some ideal model. As we solve a problem or make a decision, we do it more or less creatively, more or less critically.

People tend to view critical thinking as primarily evaluative and creative thinking as primarily generative. But the two types of thinking are not opposites; they complement each other and even share many attributes. Paul and Bailin (undated) contend that distinguishing clearly between them is impossible because all good thinking involves both quality assessment and the production of novelty. Critical thinkers generate ways to test assertions; creative thinkers examine newly generated thoughts to assess their validity and utility. The difference is not of kind but of degree and emphasis.

The moral for educators is to avoid implying that critical thinking and creative thinking are opposite ends of a single continuum. Instead, school programs and practices should reflect the understanding that highly creative thinking is often highly critical and vice versa. For example, a student working on a project might think imaginatively in choosing a way to represent a situation. ("Rather than make the report a regular essay, I think I'll write it as a conversation between the two opposing political leaders.") At the same time, the student might think objectively about the information presented in the report ("Let me see, is what I am saying really accurate? What is my source on this issue? Should I cite my reference here, or can I assume that this is common knowledge?") Furthermore, even a standard essay will be good only to the extent that the student imaginatively ties it into experience (i.e., thinks creatively) and assesses that experience critically.

Critical Thinking

Critical thinking is sometimes defined narrowly ("assessing the accuracy of statements") and sometimes more globally. Ennis (1985), who at one time preferred the narrower meaning, now defines critical thinking as "reasonable, reflective thinking that is focused on deciding what to believe or do" (p. 54). This broader interpretation, he explains, is more in keeping with general usage and is consonant with a view of good thinking as including a generative element. As shown in Ennis's analysis (Figure 3.1), thinking is "reasonable" when the thinker strives to analyze arguments carefully, looks for valid evidence, and reaches sound conclusions. The goal of teaching critical thinking is to develop people who are fair-minded, objective, and committed to clarity and accuracy.

The concept of critical thinking dates back to Socrates. A basic thread running through philosophy from its earliest conception has been the cultivation of rational thinking for the purpose of guiding behavior. In his analysis of the goals of education, Goodlad (1984) found that this aim is reflected in the adopted goals of most states and school systems, mostly because critical thinking is considered essential for democratic citizenship. For example, many of the abilities listed in *A Handbook of Basic Citizenship Competencies* (Remy, 1980), such as "identify and, if necessary, develop appropriate criteria for making a judgment," are similar to those appearing on lists of critical thinking skills.

The skills associated with critical thinking (Figure 3.1) are labeled somewhat differently from the way we have defined the core thinking skills discussed in Chapter 5 (see also Walsh & Paul, undated, pp. 13-15). The critical thinking skills defined by philosophers are sometimes relatively specific refinements of these more generic skills. For example, as one of his "elementary clarification" abilities, Ennis lists "asking and answering [clarification] questions." In purpose and circumstance, Ennis's example is a sharper, more specific version of the core skill described in Chapter 5 as "formulating questions." Similarly, Ennis lists several abilities related to making and judging inferences; we lump them into the single core skill of "inferring."

Examples of using critical thinking skills (from Figure 3.1) in ordinary school content include:

Figure 3.1

Goals for a Critical Thinking Curriculum

Working definition: Critical thinking is reasonable, reflective thinking that is focused on deciding what to believe or do. Critical thinking so defined involves both dispositions and abilities:

A. Dispositions
1. Seek a clear statement of the thesis or question
2. Seek reasons
3. Try to be well informed
4. Use credible sources and mention them
5. Take into account the total situation
6. Try to remain relevant to the main point
7. Keep in mind the original or basic concern
8. Look for alternatives
9. Be open-minded
   a. Consider seriously other points of view than one's own ("dialogical thinking")
   b. Reason from premises with which one disagrees—without letting the disagreement interfere with one's own reasoning ("suppositional thinking")
   c. Withhold judgment when the evidence and reasons are insufficient
10. Take a position (and change a position) when the evidence and reasons are sufficient to do so
11. Seek as much precision as the subject permits
12. Deal in an orderly manner with the parts of a complex whole
13. Be sensitive to the feelings, levels of knowledge, and degree of sophistication of others
14. Use one's critical thinking abilities

B. Abilities
   Elementary clarification:
   1. Focusing on a question
      a. Identifying or formulating a question
      b. Identifying or formulating criteria for judging possible answers
      c. Keeping the situation in mind

   2. Analyzing arguments
      a. Identifying conclusions
      b. Identifying stated reasons
      c. Identifying unstated reasons
      d. Seeing similarities and differences
      e. Identifying and handling irrelevance
      f. Seeing the structure of an argument
      g. Summarizing

   3. Asking and answering questions of clarification and challenge, for example:
      a. Why?
      b. What is your main point?
      c. What do you mean by . . .?
      d. What would be an example?
      e. What would not be an example (though close to being one)?
      f. How does that apply to this case (describe case, which might well appear to be a counter-example)?
      g. What difference does it make?
      h. What are the facts?
      i. Is this what you are saying: _____?
      j. Would you say some more about that?

   Basic support:
   4. Judging the credibility of a source; criteria (that are often not necessary conditions):
      a. Expertise
      b. Lack of conflict of interest
      c. Agreement among sources
      d. Reputation
      e. Use of established procedures
      f. Known risk to reputation
      g. Ability to give reasons
      h. Careful habits

Figure 3.1, continued

5. Observing and judging observation reports; criteria (that are often not necessary conditions):
   a. Minimal referring involved
   b. Short time interval between observation and report
   c. Report by observer, rather than someone else (that is, the report is not hearsay)
   d. Records are generally desirable. If report is based on a record, it is generally best that:
      (1) The record was close in time to the observation
      (2) The record was made by the observer
      (3) The record was made by the reporter
      (4) The statement was believed by the reporter, either because of a prior belief in its correctness or because of a belief that the observer was habitually correct
   e. Corroboration
   f. Possibility of corroboration
   g. Conditions of good access
   h. Competent employment of technology, if technology is useful
   i. Satisfaction by observer (and reporter, if a different person) of credibility criteria

Inference:
6. Deducing and judging deductions
   a. Class logic—Euler circles
   b. Conditional logic
   c. Interpretations of statements
      (1) Negation and double negation
      (2) Necessary and sufficient conditions
      (3) Other logical words: "only," "if and only if," "or," "some," "unless," "not both," and so on

7. Inducing and judging inductions
   a. Generalizing
      (1) Typicality of data: limitations of coverage
      (2) Sampling
      (3) Tables and graphs
   b. Inferring explanatory conclusions and hypotheses
      (1) Types of explanatory conclusions and hypotheses
         (a) Causal claims
         (b) Claims about the beliefs and attitudes of people
         (c) Interpretations of authors' intended meanings
         (d) Historical claims that certain things happened
         (e) Reported definitions
         (f) Claims that something is an unstated reason or unstated conclusion
      (2) Investigating
         (a) Designing experiments, including planning to control variables
         (b) Seeking evidence and counterevidence
         (c) Seeking other possible explanations
      (3) Criteria—given reasonable assumptions:
         (a) The proposed conclusion would explain the evidence (essential)
         (b) The proposed conclusion is consistent with known facts (essential)
         (c) Competitive alternative conclusions are inconsistent with known facts (essential)
         (d) The proposed conclusion seems plausible (desirable)

8. Making and judging value judgments
   a. Background facts
   b. Consequences
   c. Prima facie application of acceptable principles
   d. Considering alternatives
   e. Balancing, weighing, and deciding

Advanced clarification:
9. Defining terms and judging definitions; three dimensions:
   a. Form
      (1) Synonym
      (2) Classification
      (3) Range
      (4) Equivalent expression
      (5) Operational
      (6) Example and nonexample

Figure 3.1, continued

    b. Definitional strategy
       (1) Acts
          (a) Report a meaning
          (b) Stipulate a meaning
          (c) Express a position on an issue (including "programmatic" and "persuasive" definition)
       (2) Identifying and handling equivocation
          (a) Attention to the context
          (b) Possible types of response:
             (i) "The definition is just wrong" (the simplest response)
             (ii) Reduction to absurdity: "According to that definition, there is an outlandish result"
             (iii) Considering alternative interpretations: "On this interpretation, there is this problem; on that interpretation, there is that problem"
             (iv) Establishing that there are two meanings of a key term, and a shift in meaning from one to the other
             (v) Swallowing the idiosyncratic definition
    c. Content

10. Identifying assumptions
    a. Unstated reasons
    b. Needed assumptions: argument reconstruction

Strategy and tactics:

11. Deciding on an action
    a. Define the problem
    b. Select criteria to judge possible solutions
    c. Formulate alternative solutions
    d. Tentatively decide what to do
    e. Review, taking into account the total situation, and decide
    f. Monitor the implementation

12. Interacting with others
    a. Employing and reacting to "fallacy" labels, including:
       (1) Circularity
       (2) Appeal to authority
       (3) Bandwagon
       (4) Glittering term
       (5) Name-calling
       (6) Slippery slope
       (7) Post hoc
       (8) Non sequitur
       (9) Ad hominem
       (10) Affirming the consequent
       (11) Denying the antecedent
       (12) Conversion
       (13) Begging the question
       (14) Either-or
       (15) Vagueness
       (16) Equivocation
       (17) Straw person
       (18) Appeal to tradition
       (19) Argument from analogy
       (20) Hypothetical question
       (21) Oversimplification
       (22) Irrelevance
    b. Logical strategies
    c. Rhetorical strategies
    d. Presenting a position, oral or written (argumentation)
       (1) Aiming at a particular audience and keeping it in mind
       (2) Organizing (common type: main point, clarification, reasons, alternatives, attempt to rebut prospective challenges, summary—including repeat of main point)

• Students recall or are told about an incident (real or imagined) in which a student was accused of breaking a school rule (such as smoking in the building or stealing another student's property). They work in pairs or trios to develop criteria for judging observation reports and determining the credibility of sources. After comparing their lists with Ennis's (items 4 and 5), they read several conflicting accounts of the Boston massacre and apply the criteria to that incident.

• During an election campaign, students watch examples of television political announcements and review campaign literature (from candidates on both sides). Students look for examples of "fallacies" (item 12a).

• As they read each other's compositions on the desirability of requiring all young people to enroll for a year of voluntary service, students analyze the writers' arguments by identifying stated and unstated reasons and summarizing main points (Figure 3.1, item 2).

These examples illustrate that critical thinking is far more than a set of skills. Paul (1984) argues that it is a major aspect of one's character. Students must recognize, he says, the natural human tendency to consider our own values and views superior to those of others, and we must continually strive to overcome this tendency. Paul (1987) distinguishes between "weak sense" and "strong sense" critical thinking. People who use their skills of analysis and argumentation primarily to attack and discredit those who disagree with them are practicing critical thinking in the weak sense. "A strong sense critical thinker is not routinely blinded by his own point of view. . . . He realizes the necessity of putting his own assumptions and ideas to the test of the strongest objections that can be leveled against them" (pp. 3-4).

As an example of fostering critical thinking in the weak sense, Paul (1987) cites a set of writing prompts from a state test. On an exercise requiring students to state their views on the Cuban missile crisis, the information provided assumes that the U.S. position in the dispute was entirely right and that the Soviet position was entirely wrong. This is not an isolated example, according to Paul. "I know of no textbook presently in use in a large public school system that . . . highlights the importance of strong sense critical thinking skills. Monological thinking that presupposes an American world view is clearly dominant" (p. 20).

Paul (undated) believes that to counteract this egocentric, ethnocentric tendency, schools must engage students in dialectical and dialogical thinking. Dialogical thinking involves a dialogue or extended exchange between different points of view or frames of reference. Dialectical thinking is dialogical thinking conducted to test the strengths and weaknesses of opposing points of view.

Dialogical thinking in an 8th-grade social studies class could be elicited through a discussion of whether it was right for American pioneers to take permanent possession of land that had been American Indians' hunting grounds. The exchange would be more dialectical if some students spoke, after appropriate preparation, from the Indians' point of view, while another group represented the settlers. A third group could decide which arguments were more persuasive, and then all students would be given an opportunity to express their own views.

Over time and with regular practice, students should begin to internalize the dispositions of critical thinking. Like attitudes, dispositions are highly general operating principles that govern behavior. Also, like attitudes, they are probably stored as linguistic propositions in the mind and are observable as inner speech. Ennis (1987) lists the important dispositions of critical thinking:

- Seek a clear statement of the thesis or question.
- Seek reasons.
- Try to be well informed.
- Use and mention credible sources.
- Consider the total situation.
- Try to remain relevant to the main point.
- Keep in mind the original or basic concern.
- Look for alternatives.
- Be open-minded.
- Take a position (and change a position) when the evidence and reasons are sufficient to do so.
- Seek as much precision as the subject permits.
- Deal in an orderly manner with the parts of a complex whole.
- Use critical thinking abilities (skills).
- Be sensitive to others' feelings, level of knowledge, and degree of sophistication.
- Use one's critical thinking abilities.

For example, when thinking about a topic or interacting with others about it, a person with these dispositions would probably engage in self-talk like the following:

Let's see, am I clear about what we're discussing here? Why would he be trying to persuade me to take that position? I don't have all of the facts; I'd better clarify the issue. Am I being open-minded about what he is saying to me, or have I already concluded that he can't be right? I'm starting to be convinced; I'd better modify my original opinion.

Developing such an inner dialogue fosters self-awareness and a better understanding of others. Ideally, through the reinforcement of critical thinking skills and dispositions, children

can be taught comprehensive principles of rational thought. They can learn to consider it natural that people differ in their beliefs and points of view and they can learn to grasp this not as a quaint peculiarity of people but as a tool for learning. They can learn how to learn from others, even from their objections, contrary perceptions, and differing ways of thinking (Paul, 1984, p. 12).

Creative Thinking

Creative thinking, like critical thinking, is defined in various ways. Halpern (1984) states that "creativity can be thought of as the ability to form new combinations of ideas to fulfill a need" (p. 324). Incorporating the critical thinking notion of dialectical thinking, Barron (1969) notes that "the creative

23

process embodies an incessant dialectic between integration and effusion, convergence and divergence, thesis and antithesis" (p. 112).

Perkins (1984) highlights an important characteristic of creative thinking:

Creative thinking is thinking patterned in a way that tends to lead to creative results. This definition reminds us that the ultimate criterion for creativity is output. We call a person creative when that person consistently gets creative results, meaning, roughly speaking, original and otherwise appropriate results by the criteria of the domain in question (pp. 18-19).

Perkins implies that to teach for creativity, students' output must be the ultimate criteria. However diverse students' different thoughts might be, they bear little fruit unless translated into some form of action. That action may be internal (e.g., making a decision, reaching a conclusion, formulating a hypothesis) or external (e.g., painting a picture, making a pun or an analogy, suggesting a new way to conduct an experiment). But creative thinking must have some outcome.

It is probably no accident that Perkins's emphasis on action or output in creative thinking is similar to Ennis's emphasis in his definition of critical thinking (reasonable, reflective thinking focused on deciding what to believe or do). Indeed, because of this similarity of purpose and direction, we discuss critical and creative thinking as a single dimension of thinking—both important to effective output in any endeavor. Although the definitions for creativity are diverse, the components or aspects of creative thinking are increasingly well defined. Below are five aspects of creative thinking drawn from various theoretical bases.

1. *Creativity takes place in conjunction with intense desire and preparation.* A common fallacy about creativity is that it does not require hard work and forethought. Harman and Rheingold (1984) note that the usual preconditions for creativity are precise, intense, and prolonged grappling with an issue. They quote the great composer Strauss as saying:

"I can tell you from my own experience that an ardent desire and fixed purpose combined with intense resolve brings results. Determined, concentrated thought is a tremendous force. I am convinced that this is a law and it holds good in any line of endeavor" (p. 75).

Similarly, in his profile of the creative individual, Raudsepp (1983) writes:

The popular notion that the creative individual relies mainly on effortless inspiration and enforced spontaneity is a widespread misconception. . . . Creative achievement requires a hard core of self-discipline and arduous, unceasing dedication (p. 178).

Perkins (1985) says simply: "Creative individuals almost invariably are hard workers; they must invest in their pursuits the kind of time and effort many individuals would consider unreasonable" (p. 9).

2. *Creativity involves working at the edge rather than the center of one's capacity.* This idea is central to the creative process (Perkins, 1981, 1984). Time

and effort aside, creative individuals stand ready to take risks in pursuit of their endeavors and keep rejecting obvious alternatives because they are striving to push the limits of their knowledge and abilities. A classic example is the wide range of substances Edison explored in his attempts to develop a durable replacement for the carbon filament in the electric light bulb:

Southern moss, palmetto monkery grass, Mexican hemp, jute, bamboo, coconut palm, and manila fiber were dipped in rock-candy syrup and carbonized strands were plucked from Kruesi's and Mackenzie's beards, and bets were placed whether Kruesi's black hair or Mackenzie's red hair would prove the longer lasting. . . . A thread snipped from a spiderweb turned beautiful light pink and produced green phosphorescence (Conot, 1979).

Creative thinkers are not satisfied simply with "what will get by." Rather, they have an ever-present urge to "find something that will work a little better, be more efficient, save a little time."

3. *Creativity requires an internal rather than external locus of evaluation.* Underlying creative people's ability to take risks is trust in their own standards of evaluation (Perkins, 1984, 1985). Creative individuals look inwardly to themselves rather than outwardly to their peers to judge the validity of their work. Therefore, Raudsepp (1983) asserts that the creative person tolerates and often consciously fosters working in isolation, creating a buffer zone that keeps the individual somewhat insulated from standard norms and practices. Not surprisingly, many creative people are not initially well received by their contemporaries.

Closely related to the locus of evaluation is the question of motivation. Perkins (1985) asserts that creativity involves intrinsic more than extrinsic motivation. Intrinsic motivation is manifested in many ways: avowed dedication, long hours, concern with craft, involvement with ideas, and most straightforwardly, resistance to distraction by extrinsic rewards such as higher income for a less creative kind of work (p. 10). In fact, considerable evidence indicates that strong extrinsic motivation undermines intrinsic motivation (Amabile, 1983). Of course, this evidence is consistent with the discussion of attitudes about self in Chapter 2. Encouraging students to emphasize their success at tasks can eventually undermine self-esteem. Rather, we should help students to work more from their own internal locus of evaluation and encourage them to engage in tasks because of what they might learn or discover.

4. *Creativity involves reframing ideas.* This aspect of creativity is the most commonly stressed, although different theorists describe it in different ways. The concept of flexibility as described by Perkins (1984) and Raudsepp (1983) falls under this category; divergent thinking as described by Guilford (1956) and lateral thinking as described by de Bono (1970) also fit here.

To understand how an idea is reframed, we should first consider how an idea is framed. Information-processing theorists (e.g., Rumelhart & Ortony, 1977) assert that we interpret the world through structures called schemata: knowledge structures in which related information is clustered. (For a more detailed discussion of schemata, see Chapter 5.) People use schemata to make sense of the world. Smith (1982) speaks broadly of schemata as theories about what the world is like—"theories of the world in our heads." He writes that schemata are "the basis of all our perceptions, and understanding of the world, the root of all learning, the source of all hopes and fears, motives and expectancies" (p. 57).

These structures have been used to describe virtually every type of cognitive function, from visual perception (Lindsay & Norman, 1977) to understanding language (Rumelhart, 1980). These human "theories of the world" are essential to our learning and making sense of the world. However, there is a curious paradox about schemata. Just as they are the basis of human perception and understanding, so too are they "blinders" to interpretations that fall outside their scope. To illustrate, stop reading for a moment and try to connect the nine dots in Figure 3.2 using four connected straight lines. If you have never seen this problem before, you probably had difficulty solving it, maybe because you approached the problem with a specific set of expectations—a specific schema—you assumed that the four lines had to remain within the perimeter of the nine dots. To solve the problem, you must go beyond the perimeter of the dots, as shown in Figure 3.3.

Figure 3.2

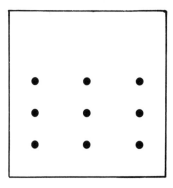

Figure 3.3

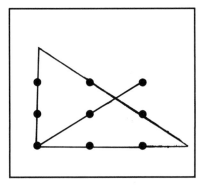

Creativity involves the ability to go beyond the schema normally used to approach a problem—to "go beyond the lines"—and reframe the problem so it might appear in a different light. Characteristically, the creative person has the ability to look at a problem from one frame of reference or schema and then consciously shift to another frame of reference, giving a completely new perspective. This process continues until the person has viewed the problem from many different perspectives.

Reframing oftens involves the use of models, metaphors, or analogies. When straightforward analytic or inferential tactics fail to produce a creative solution, the creative person can often forge links with different structures. As these structures are elaborated, new, powerful solutions may result (Rankin, 1964).

Black (1962) and Samples (1976) have provided examples of creativity in both the sciences and the arts. Scientists working on the theory of electricity made a major advance when they saw similarities in structure between electricity and fluids. The creative imagery of poetry often involves the use of metaphor and analogy. Representation and symbolism are trademarks of inventiveness in art and music. These methods of reframing mean that creative thinking requires breadth and depth. Teaching for creative thinking requires the use of activities that encourage students to see similarities in events and entities not commonly linked.

5. *Creativity can sometimes be facilitated by getting away from intensive engagement for awhile to permit free-flowing thought.* Some theorists have pointed to various ways in which creative people block out distractions, permitting insights to come to the forefront of consciousness. Stein (1974) notes that Zola pulled the shades during the day to avoid light; Proust liked to work in a cork-lined room; Ben Jonson wrote best while drinking tea and enjoying the odor of orange peel; Schiller had rotten apples on hand; both Milton and Descartes liked to lie down and stretch out. The working principle underlying all these efforts was to create an atmosphere in which unconscious thought could surface.

Harman and Rheingold (1984) point to major scientific breakthroughs that occurred during periods of "unconscious thought":

Mendelev reported seeing the periodic table in a dream "where all the elements fell into place as required. Awakening, I immediately wrote it down on a piece of paper. Only in one place did a correction later seem necessary" (p. 71).

Kekule's daytime dream of molecular structure has been called "the most brilliant piece of prediction in the whole history of science" (p. 40).

After much preparation, considerable intensity, and many attempts to grasp insight in various ways, at some point creative people seem to "let go" of their rational, critical approach to problems of composition and invention and allow the ideas to flow freely, with little conscious control.

The explanations for this phenomenon are diverse. Harman and Rheingold (1984) assert that the unconscious mind processes much more information than we are aware of; it can access information impossible to gain through rational analysis. By implication, then, the unconscious mind engages in a much more comprehensive, diverse form of processing than the conscious mind. Therefore, we should actively try to develop techniques (such as meditation) for accessing the unconscious, for it is a rich source of otherwise inaccessible information.

Others argue strongly against the assertion that the mind can work on problems at an unconscious level. For example, Perkins (in Brandt, 1986) refers to the fallacy of "extended unconsciousness":

Suppose you are trying to solve a math problem. You might imagine that you could come up with the answer having worked unconsciously on it for hours, much as you would work on it consciously. That's what I mean by extended unconscious thinking. And that's what I claim doesn't occur. When it seems to happen, short conscious chains of thought that happen quite rapidly really account for the sudden emergence of a solution.

Perkins's comments are consistent with Sternberg and Davidson's (1986) discussion of insight. For them, insight is a predictable, explainable process that includes selectively encoding, combining, and comparing information. Therefore, an understanding of the process will enable us to cultivate insight.

Regardless of whether the unconscious mind actually processes information or the conscious mind does it so quickly that we do not notice, many creative people find that when they stop working on a problem for a while, they sometimes gain useful, new perspectives. Take, for example, Bertrand Russell's description of how he used "unconscious thinking":

I have found, for example, that if I have to write upon some rather difficult topic, the best plan is to think about it with great intensity—the greatest intensity of which I am capable—for a few hours or days, and at the end of that time give orders, so to speak, that the work is to proceed underground. After some months I return consciously to the topic and find that the work has been done. Before I had discovered this technique I used to spend the intervening months worrying because I was making no progress; I arrived at the solution none the sooner for this worry, and the intervening months were wasted, whereas now I can devote them to other pursuits (Russell, 1971, p. 154).

Whether Russell's processing of the information actually occurred "underground" is probably irrelevant in terms of developing techniques for classroom use. Creativity sometimes involves stepping away from a task, especially when the task is particularly galling and intractable. During these breaks in the action, the mind (consciously or unconsciously) often generates insights that can help to complete the task.

Application

We have discussed critical and creative thinking in the classroom together rather than separately to stress that they are complementary and that both are necessary to attain any worthy goal. Both can and should be taught in the context of regular academic instruction. Whenever students are formulating a question, analyzing a text, or defining a term with clarity, accuracy, and fair-mindedness, they are developing the skills of critical thinking. Whenever they solve an unstructured problem (as in an electricity shop or a home-economics laboratory) or plan a project, they are developing their creative abilities. Whenever they consider diverse points of view and imaginatively, empathically, and accurately reconstruct them, they are thinking both creatively and critically.

However, the kind of teaching found in many classrooms will not necessarily produce a high level of critical and creative thinking. Goodlad's (1984) study of representative American schools established that students in typical classrooms are seldom asked to express an original idea, let alone offer opinion or evidence of any sort. If schools are to develop more skillful thinkers, far more thoughtful interaction must occur in classrooms, ranging from large-group discussion of controversial issues to small-group and paired problem solving (see the section on oral discourse in Chapter 4).

One way to foster good thinking in the classroom is to make students aware of its characteristics, either by informing them directly or by helping them discover for themselves. A teacher using the latter approach might have students study the lives of highly critical and creative thinkers or interview local people known for the quality of their thinking. Students could also identify times in their own lives when they were functioning critically and creatively and try to describe their thinking to others. When students have developed criteria for evaluating thinking, the teacher might encourage a metacognitive approach by saying:

For the project we are going to work on this week, try to be aware of how much you are practicing critical and creative thinking. Ask yourself: Am I clear about what I am trying to accomplish? Am I trying to be well informed about the topic? What sources have I consulted? Have I considered a variety of points of view, or only those I favor? Am I doing this as well as I possibly can?

Teachers can foster critical and creative thinking in other ways:

- Prepare curriculum materials to supplement regular textbooks. The Center for Critical Thinking and Moral Critique at Sonoma State University, California, has produced a handbook with specific examples of remodeled lessons in K-3 language arts, social studies, and science textbooks. For example, for a lesson on body language from a language-arts text, the authors (Paul, Binker, & Charbonneau, 1986) suggest that rather than using the language in the text, the teacher use the vocabulary of critical thinking: "What can you *infer* this person wants to say? What can you *conclude* about this picture? Why?" (p. 75, italics added).
- Conduct discussions and debates on controversial subjects. Johnson and Johnson (in press) have helped teachers organize for "structured controversy" in which pairs of students argue an issue with other pairs of students, then change sides and defend the opposite point of view against other pairs.
- Have students role-play historical incidents in which protagonists held conflicting views.
- Have students attend community meetings or watch television programs that express different viewpoints.
- Have students write letters to the editor expressing their opinions on a current local issue.
- Have older students analyze newspaper articles and other material to find examples of apparent bias.

- Have students confront questions with multiple answers. Instead of saying, "Do these 10 division problems," ask, "The number 4 is the answer to what questions?" Instead of saying, "Find all the yellow blocks and put them on the table," say, "Identify the characteristics that a single block might have, such as yellowness, cubeness, smallness, or smoothness."

- Have students read and discuss literature that reflects values and traditions different from theirs.

- Invite people with controversial views to speak to classes. (To maintain community support, and in the spirit of critical thinking, also invite someone with a different point of view.)

Some of these suggestions may not appeal to some parents, and perhaps not to some administrators and board of education members. Schools do not always have a clear mandate to teach critical and creative thinking, and in some communities teachers do not have a free hand in how to teach such things. We believe, however, that critical and creative thinking are essential in a democratic society and that their development may require that students be exposed to ideas and values different from those of their parents. As long as a spirit of inquiry and respect for family values and traditions is maintained, we believe most parents and communities will support activities like those we have suggested.

Critical and creative thinking can also be taught with the aid of methods and materials especially designed for that purpose. Several excellent programs are described in the ASCD publication *Developing Minds* (Costa, 1985a). For example, the Philosophy for Children program uses stories about children and their thinking to stimulate classroom discussion of classic philosophical issues (Lipman, Sharp, & Oscanyan, 1980). Conducting such discussions would be difficult for most teachers without the special materials and training programs developed by the Institute for the Advancement of Philosophy for Children.

A less demanding approach such as de Bono's (1983) CoRT "tools" can be used to reinforce elements of both critical and creative thinking. For example, de Bono's PMI (in which students are asked to systematically list the plus, minus, and interesting points about a seemingly trivial idea) and his OPV (in which students are asked to assume other people's viewpoints) are methods readily implemented in the classroom.

A potentially powerful technique for encouraging creative thinking is Perkins's (1986) "knowledge as design." Students are helped to see the artifacts in their environment as designs created by people in response to a need. From this standpoint, a screwdriver, Boyle's law, and the Bill of Rights are all structures devised to accomplish a particular purpose. Perkins (1984) proposes that to make sense of the world and to produce designs of their own, students can ask four questions about any piece of knowledge:

- What is its purpose?
- What is its structure?
- What are model cases of it?
- What are arguments that explain and evaluate it?

Implications

Specific teaching strategies and techniques can help, but an equally important influence on the quality of students' thinking is the school's intellectual climate and the example set by teachers. Teachers who want their students to think critically and creatively need to model that same kind of behavior themselves:

- Provide opportunities for students to explore diverse points of view in a supportive environment;
- Seek and provide reasons for what they are doing;
- Try to remain relevant to the main point of a discussion;
- Be open-minded, encouraging students to follow their own thinking and not simply repeat what the teacher has said;
- Change their positions when the evidence warrants, being willing to admit a mistake;
- Be sensitive to others' feelings, level of knowledge, and degree of sophistication;
- Exhibit intense desire and preparation to achieve a goal; and
- Seek imaginative and appropriate solutions.

Closely related to teachers' behavior is the development of a classroom climate conducive to good thinking. In *On Becoming a Person*, Rogers (1961) mentions psychological safety and psychological freedom as necessary ingredients of such a climate. (Rogers was referring to creative thinking, but we believe his remarks also apply to critical thinking.) We foster psychological safety when we accept people as being of unconditional worth, when we create an atmosphere of empathy and understanding rather than external evaluation. We foster psychological freedom when we permit the individual freedom of symbolic expression. According to Rogers, students cannot think well in a harsh, threatening situation or even in a subtly intimidating environment where group pressure makes independent thinking unlikely. Although formal institutional requirements for compulsory attendance, discipline, testing, and grading make it nearly impossible for schools to meet these conditions fully, teachers can make their classrooms more thoughtful places by being businesslike but warm and friendly and by demonstrating in their actions that they welcome originality and differences of opinion.

Critical and creative thinking are at the heart of the current emphasis on thinking skills. Most schools will have to make many changes to cultivate these ways of thinking more fully, but the rewards are worth the effort.

4. Thinking Processes

ANOTHER MAJOR DIMENSION OF THINKING IS THE SET OF MENTAL OPERATIONS WE call processes. Thinking processes such as concept formation, decision making, research, and composing, are often rich, multifaceted, and complex, involving the use of several thinking skills. As explained in the next chapter, what we call thinking skills are simpler cognitive operations such as observing, comparing, or inferring. Thinking processes are broader in scope, more "macro," and take a longer time to complete.

Some authorities treat critical and creative thinking as processes, since both involve the use of numerous skills that may be employed in the development of a product, such as a decision or a composition. As explained in Chapter 3, we prefer to use these terms to characterize the quality or nature of thinking. A person conducting research or engaging in discussion does so more or less critically or creatively. Critical and creative thinking are not separate processes; they are descriptions of the way processes are carried out.

In this chapter, we consider eight thinking processes:

- Concept formation
- Principle formation
- Comprehension
- Problem solving
- Decision making
- Research

- Composition
- Oral discourse

We selected these processes because they are commonly mentioned in theoretical and research literature, they are conceptually clear and therefore teachable, they are recognized as fundamental to instruction in many content areas, and they are essential tools for achieving most goals in the real world.

These processes are not distinct from one another; they overlap. For example, research may lead to the discovery of a new principle that later generations of students will learn through principle formation aided by oral discourse in the classroom. We accept this "messiness," since people do not typically think in neat packages. The processes do, however, relate in many ways to curriculum goals, and an understanding of the processes can transform our pedagogy.

The first three processes—concept formation, principle formation, and comprehension—appear to be more directed toward knowledge acquisition than the other five. Concept formation is a foundation for the other processes. For example, when students encounter new content, they must establish the essential concepts before they can comprehend more densely organized information. Similarly, principle formation and comprehension may be the basis for the other processes—for example, when a student invokes previously learned principles to solve a problem.

The next four processes—problem solving, decision making, research, and composition—often build on the first three because they involve the production or application of knowledge. Finally, oral discourse is a process for both acquiring and producing knowledge. Figure 4.1 depicts the interrelationships among the processes.

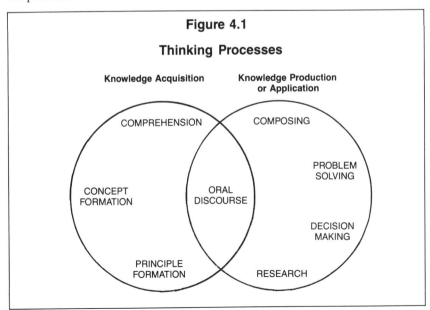

Figure 4.1

Thinking Processes

Knowledge Acquisition

Knowledge Production or Application

COMPREHENSION

COMPOSING

PROBLEM SOLVING

CONCEPT FORMATION

ORAL DISCOURSE

DECISION MAKING

PRINCIPLE FORMATION

RESEARCH

Figure 4.1 is intended as a rough schematic introduction to relationships that are not easily explained by narratives or charts. Although we will describe thinking processes as sequences of skills, we are not implying that the processes should be taught as prescribed procedures. Steps and stages should be considered repertoires or arrays of alternatives rather than blueprints for instruction. The processes might best be called "semi-ordered" (van Dijk & Kintsch, 1983). They are working hypotheses about the best way to accomplish a goal, general procedures developed through years of human experience to be used flexibly by teachers and adapted by students.

For example, 1st- or 2nd-graders beginning a unit on community helpers need to form concepts related to the postal service. They need to be able to recognize concept labels such as *mail, post, mailbox, post office, address, postage, delivery,* and *sorting;* they also need to know distinguishing attributes of the concepts represented by each label. As they form concepts, students gain increasing ability to comprehend further information about the concepts. The American child who reads British children's books about the postal service will come to comprehend that the English child who "posts" a letter is doing what Americans call "mailing" a letter.

Over time, the child begins to form principles, which describe relationships between two or more concepts. A student who understands the concepts of address, sorting, and delivery, and who comprehends information about what happens to a letter from the time it is placed in a mailbox until it reaches its destination, is ready to relate these concepts by forming such principles as "A clear, accurate address is needed for a letter to be delivered to the right person," or "Mail is usually not delivered if it does not have enough postage."

If students are to go beyond minimum understanding to apply their knowledge or to produce new knowledge, they need opportunities to engage in several thinking processes. For example, 2nd-graders may receive instruction in composing letters as part of a unit on the postal service. They may engage in oral discourse as they learn more about the postal service. Opportunities to use problem solving may emerge as they try to figure out why some of them do not receive responses to their letters. They may visit their neighborhood post office, using written sources and personal interviews to learn when it was built, what factors determined its location, or how it relates to a larger postal facility. They may engage in decision making as they consider which of several possible locations would be best for a new post office.

Concept Formation

Concept formation is one of the most misunderstood thinking processes. Some educators use the term *concept* to describe statements of general information, such as "Water seeks its own level."

The definition offered by Klausmeier (1985) is most useful for instructional purposes. He sees a concept as a mental construct commonly symbolized by a word in a society. He writes that a "concept consists of a person's organized information about one or more entities—objects, events, ideas, or processes—that enable the individual to discriminate the particular entity or class of entities and also to relate it to other entities and classes of entities" (p. 276).

A key component of this definition is the label or word representing the concept. Concept knowledge and word knowledge seem inexorably linked in the thought and language of a given culture. As Carroll (1964) points out, "A meaning of a word is, therefore, a societally-standardized concept, and when we say that a word stands for or names a concept, it is understood that we are speaking of concepts that are shared among members of a speech community" (p. 187).

This relationship between a word and a concept implies that information that cannot be stated as a single word or as a word plus a few modifiers is not a concept. "Water seeks its own level," then, is not a concept. Such a statement is more properly called a principle and should be approached instructionally from a somewhat different perspective.

Another implication is that vocabulary knowledge is one of the cornerstones of learning. Indeed, if a label (or word) is a necessary component of a concept, then we do not fully possess a concept until we have a label for it. Linguists such as Whorf (1956), who assert that language shapes perception, support this position. Condon (1968) observes that when we impose a label on phenomena, we create a reality that previously did not exist: "For better or for worse, when names are learned we see what we had not seen" (p. 31). Therefore, vocabulary knowledge is the outward indication of an individual's store of concepts, and so vocabulary knowledge is a strong predictor of general aptitude (Anderson & Freebody, 1981), for it demonstrates an individual's knowledge of the concepts considered important in a society.

Finally, the relationship between words and concepts suggests that we must link teaching concepts to teaching vocabulary. Indeed, students often need to learn clusters of vocabulary words related to the material under study. Of course, many theorists and researchers argue against direct vocabulary instruction (e.g., Nagy, 1985; Nagy & Herman, 1984; Nagy, Herman, & Anderson, 1985), and many direct approaches to vocabulary instruction (e.g., memorization of definitions in word lists) are unproductive. Still, we favor the view held by Stahl and Fairbanks (1986) and many others (e.g., Tennyson & Cocchiarella, 1986) that direct instruction in vocabulary, using techniques consistent with concept-formation research, can be a powerful, lasting educational intervention.

Several models for instruction in concepts are available (e.g., Bruner, Goodnow, & Austin, 1977; Taba, 1967). We have adapted here a model by Klausmeier (1985; Klausmeier & Sipple, 1980) that, while not necessarily superior to the others, incorporates many components of other models along with current information-processing theory.

Levels of Concept Formation

Klausmeier (1985) states that concept formation progresses through four levels: the concrete level, the identity level, the classificatory level, and the formal level. Attaining a concept at the *concrete* level occurs when we attend to something one or more times; discriminate it from other things; remember it; and then later attend to, discriminate, and recognize it as the same thing. For example, a young child attends to a clock on a wall, discriminates it from other objects, represents the clock internally, retrieves the earlier representation of the clock, and recognizes it as the same thing attended to earlier. Thus, the child knows the concept of that particular clock at the concrete level.

Attaining a concept at the *identity* level occurs when we recognize an item as the same one previously encountered when observed in a different context. For example, the child who recognizes a clock, even when it is removed from the wall of one room and placed in another, has attained the concept of that particular clock at the identity level.

To learn a concept at the *classificatory* level, we must have learned at least two examples of the concept at the identity level. Attaining the lowest classificatory level of a concept occurs when we consider at least two different examples of a concept equivalent. For example, the child who treats the clock on the wall and another one on the desk as equivalent has attained the concept of the clock at a beginning classificatory level.

Finally, attaining a concept at the *formal* level occurs when we can correctly identify examples of the concept, name the concept and its distinguishing attributes, give a societally accepted definition of the concept, and indicate how examples of the concept differ from nonexamples. (We use "distinguishing attributes" here as a kind of shorthand, noting that few if any concepts are subject to absolute definition in the Aristotelian sense.)

For instructional purposes, Klausmeier breaks concept formation into three phases instead of four. The first instructional phase fosters knowledge of a concept at the concrete and identity levels; the second instructional phase, at the beginning classificatory level; the third, at the mature classificatory and formal levels (see Figure 4.2).

Concept formation can be a long, detailed process—one that teachers cannot expect to occur incidentally. Klausmeier (1985) believes that most students cannot attain academic concepts at the formal level unless they receive explicit instruction. Some highly abstract concepts resist even direct instruction.

Unfortunately, many textbooks do not promote understanding concepts at the formal level. Peters (1975) noted that textbooks commonly introduce a concept with a general definition and one example without comparing it to either related concepts or nonexamples. Peters found that students given explicit instruction following procedures similar to those in Figure 4.2 performed significantly better on measures of concept understanding than students taught using a standard textbook approach.

Figure 4.2

Klausmeier Concept Formation Model

Phase 1: Concrete level and identity level

1. Make available an actual item or a pictorial or other representation of it.
2. Give the name of the item and aid the learner to associate the name with the item.
3. Immediately provide students with situations in which they must recognize the item (concept) and provide immediate feedback as they do so.
4. Make the item (concept) available later and determine whether students recognize it.
5. Repeat the preceding sequence (1-4) as necessary.

Phase 2: Beginning Classificatory Level

1. Make available at least two different examples and one or two quite obvious non-examples of the concept.
2. Aid the learner to associate the name of the concept with examples (this differs from step 2 of Phase 1 in that the student is required to provide the name for the concept in this later phase).
3. Aid the learner to identify and name the salient attributes of the concept.
4. Aid the learner to define the concept.
5. Arrange for students to recognize the concept in newly encountered examples and non-examples of the concept.
6. Provide for information feedback.

Phase 3: Mature Classificatory and Formal Levels

1. Prepare students to learn the concept by establishing an intention for them to become aware of related concepts, enabling them to become aware of related concepts and providing them with information about the relationships among the target concepts and other concepts.
2. Provide examples and non-examples.
3. Help the learner acquire a strategy for identifying examples and non-examples by identifying those attributes most commonly associated with the concept.
4. Have students articulate the name of the concept and its salient attributes.
5. Provide for complete understanding of the concept by having students define it.
6. Provide for use of the concept in oral and written language.
7. Provide for feedback as to the accuracy of students' knowledge and use of the concept.

Just as teachers should plan instruction in ways that help students to develop concepts, curriculum planners should identify concepts essential to each content area at each grade level. For example, mathematics students need to learn such concepts as number, equality, and pattern. Students learning social studies need such concepts as democracy, government, freedom, and justice. A well-planned curriculum will ensure that students recall key concepts over the years, learning them in greater depth as their maturity and understanding increase.

Principle Formation

Principles are generalizations that describe relationships between or among concepts in a discipline. A principle is formed when the learner recognizes a relationship that applies to multiple examples.

A principle may be communicated as a *proposition* that expresses the relationship. Some theorists (Kintsch, 1974, 1979; van Dijk, 1980) believe that linguistic information is stored as propositions or statements that can be true or false. Van Dijk sees propositions as "conceptual structures that are the minimal bearers of truth or satisfaction" (p. 207). Therefore, *Doris* and *water* are concepts, not information that can be examined for truth or falsity. But "Doris is ill" and "Water runs downhill" are propositions because we can ask whether they are true or false.

Propositions that apply to multiple examples are principles. We can imagine concepts as nodes of information stored in the mind. If these nodes were not connected, they would be stored independently as isolated concepts. For example, suppose the concepts *letter, stamp, mailman, delivered, address,* and *postage* were stored independently. We might picture them in the mind as shown in Figure 4.3.

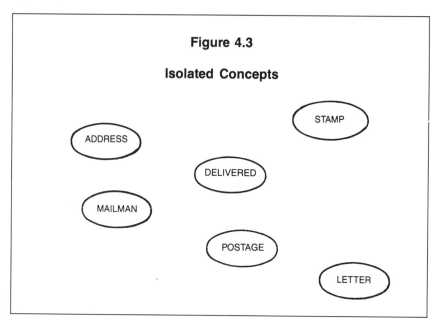

Figure 4.3

Isolated Concepts

Now imagine that these concepts are connected in the following ways: A *letter* needs a *stamp* to show *postage* has been paid. A letter is *delivered* by a *mailman* to an *address*. A *letter* without a *stamp* will not be *delivered*. The six independent concepts have been organized into three principles, as depicted in Figure 4.4.

We can infer from Figure 4.4 that the mind connects concepts into various principles. We might also infer that, before we can form principles in a given area of study, we must know the pertinent concepts in that area. Therefore, teaching vocabulary (concepts and the words that stand for them) is an integral part of content-area instruction.

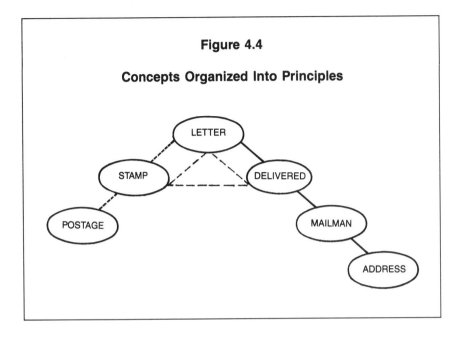

Figure 4.4

Concepts Organized Into Principles

Kinds of Principles

Because principles describe relationships, they help to organize information in a discipline. But what *kinds* of relationships are the basis of principles? Katz (1976) and Klausmeier (1985) classify principles as cause and effect, correlational, probability, and axiomatic.

Cause-and-effect principles articulate relationships that have an underlying "if-then" meaning—for example, the propositions "Tuberculosis is caused by the organism *mycobacterium tuberculosis*"; "One effect of morphine is to produce sleep" (Katz, 1976, p. 14). In every content area, several important if-then principles help organize information.

Correlational principles express a relationship in which an increase in one state or event is predictably related to an increase or decrease in another state or event—for example, "Tall people tend to weigh more." In correlational principles, no cause-effect relationship has been established, though causality is not ruled out. Rather, a relationship seems to exist by virtue of apparent systematic increases or decreases in states or events.

Probability principles indicate the likelihood that a state or event will occur. The underlying relationship is between the number of actual events and the number of possible events—for example, "The probability of getting heads on only one toss of a coin is .50"; "The probability of giving birth to a boy during any one pregnancy is .52" (Katz, 1976, p. 15).

Finally, *axiomatic principles* are universally accepted truths; or, at least, they are treated as though they are universally accepted truths. In a sense, they are probability principles for which the probability is considered 1.0. According to Katz (1976), axiomatic principles represent the largest category of principles. Some examples of axiomatic principles are fundamentals, laws, and rules.

A *fundamental* is a principle essential to a science, religion, philosophy, or art. A fundamental of democracy is that "all men are created equal." A *law* is a code of conduct formally recognized as essential in a society. For example, most societies have a written or unwritten law against stealing. A law can also be a scientific observation about an event that will always occur. A *rule* is a principle that states expected behavior. It is "softer" than a law; the consequences are usually not as great if a rule is broken. For example, many rules exist on how to use the English language in various social situations.

In presenting this classification of principles, we do not mean to imply that students should classify the principles in a content area. Rather, a teacher should guide students during instruction to discover or invent principles that organize blocks of information in the discipline.

Although principles are recognized as an important part of learning a discipline, Roth (1985) and Anderson and Smith (in press) found that in the area of science, even secondary students commonly do not grasp the principles underlying scientific phenomena studied in class. They might be able to answer factual questions, but only mechanically. When facing questions that require deeper understanding, their reactions show that they have failed to integrate the new information.

As students begin a new unit, the teacher will probably direct principle formation by targeting certain principles. The teacher may teach a principle deductively by stating it, explaining it, and having students generate many examples (Katz, 1976). Indeed, the teacher can guide students to discover principles by presenting several examples and nonexamples and having students articulate the principle that can be generalized from what they have observed.

Gagne and Briggs (1979) outline a series of instructional events a teacher might use to guide students to form principles or rules (p. 142):

1. Tell the learners about the form of the performance expected when learning is completed.

2. Question them in a way that requires the restatement of the previously learned concepts related to the rule.

3. Use verbal statements to induce learners to demonstrate concrete instances of the rule; provide feedback about the correctness in each case.

4. Ask the learners to demonstrate concrete instances of the rule; provide feedback about correctness.

5. Through questions, require them to make a verbal statement of the rule.

6. Provide for "spaced review" a day or more after instruction to aid students' retention of the new rule; present new instances for recall and demonstration.

As students gain understanding in a content area, they can direct more of the principle formation. Armed with an understanding of the content and the different types of principles, students can generate and articulate organizational principles on their own.

For example, a 7th-grade science teacher taught the principle, "All living things need oxygen." She began by asking the students to review what they had already learned about characteristics of all living things. The students recalled that living things have cells, require food, reproduce, grow, and adapt to their environment. The teacher observed that the students had not mentioned oxygen and asked, "What kinds of living things need oxygen?" The students responded that animals need oxygen.

Leading the students to the central issues, the teacher asked, "What leads you to believe that plants don't need oxygen?" Using their prior knowledge, the students recalled that plants give off oxygen but take in carbon dioxide. The teacher reminded the students that they had said plants need food, and oxygen is used to help living things burn food. She asked, "How do plants burn food if they don't use oxygen?" The students' difficulty in responding made them recognize that they needed to find out for sure whether plants use oxygen.

The teacher then introduced an experiment. Into various test tubes, the students placed samples of living plants (seeds), living animals (snails), dead seeds (boiled beans), and glass marbles. Into each of these tubes and an empty one, they poured a 1 percent solution of methylene blue, a liquid that reveals, by its color, the presence or absence of oxygen. They corked each tube and set it aside until the next day. Before concluding the lesson, the teacher asked the students how they expected to tell which of the test tubes contained something that had consumed oxygen. They agreed that when they looked at the test tubes the next day, they would conclude that no oxygen had been consumed if the solutions were still blue, but that oxygen had been consumed if the solutions were clear.

The next day, the teacher asked the students to observe the color of the liquid in each test tube. They recognized that the solution in the test tubes with nonliving items was still blue, while the solution in the tubes with the snails and the living seeds had turned clear. The students could assert that the seeds must have used up oxygen. The teacher then asked them to generate a statement summarizing why all the test tubes with living things had turned clear. Their responses led to statement of the principle, "All living things need oxygen." Next, the teacher elicited further applications of the principle by asking such questions as "What are some living things, besides seeds and snails, that need oxygen?" As students responded, the teacher asked them to support and even demonstrate their assertions.

Although principle-formation sequences take time to develop and carry out, students are likely to retain the principles they have learned through the process. Instructional strategies of this sort are needed because principles are important to learning any discipline.

A student may, however, be able to state the words that represent a principle without being able to apply it. We cannot assume that students have learned a principle just because they can state it. For example, students will have learned

41

the distributive principle of mathematics only when they can apply it to problems such as $4 \times \$3.20 = ?$ or $(97 \times 39) + (3 \times 39) = ?$. Students who can state the formula for the perimeter of a rectangle, $P = 2(l + w)$, have not learned it unless they can also identify the length and width and show how to use the relationships in finding the perimeter. Empty verbalism is not enough. The goal in teaching principles is for students to *recognize* and *apply* the relationships as well as to communicate the relationships by stating the principle.

Comprehension

Comprehension is the process of generating meaning from varied sources—directly observing phenomena; reading, looking at a sign, cartoon, painting; listening to a lecture or discussion; viewing a film. Regardless of the source, the process of comprehending involves extracting new information and integrating it with what we already know to generate new meaning.

Much research has focused on comprehension in reading (e.g., Commission on Reading, 1985). The debates about the precise nature of reading comprehension have been heated. But even though we are not sure exactly how reading comprehension works, we are fairly confident about some strategies for teaching students to improve their comprehension.

Most models of reading comprehension view the process in terms of generating meaning. Readers (listeners, observers) must create meaning from the signs or symbols presented to them. The meaning (especially meaning contained in written or oral information) is not an objective, rigid entity for the readers to somehow absorb. Rather, comprehending is a subjective process that involves interpreting information and relating it to what we already know.

As subtle as this characteristic seems, it has profound implications for teaching comprehension. It implies that learners are likely to find some meaning in what they read or hear because they bring to bear what they already know about the topic. A useful metaphor for the comprehension process is that of weaving a tapestry—taking what we already know about the topic and integrating it with new information presented in the text to create a new "picture" of the topic. The weaving metaphor puts the emphasis on the reader or listener (where it should be), not on the absorption of pre-set content.

Many strategies designed specifically for reading can be adapted to the broad process of comprehending as defined in this framework. Reciprocal teaching, developed by Palincsar and Brown (1984, 1985), is such a strategy. In this strategy, students take turns "playing teacher." They summarize, generate questions, clarify, and predict. *Summarizing* involves identifying and integrating important information in the text. It provides a basis for *generating questions*, which involves identifying information significant enough to be the substance for questions. When *predicting*, students hypothesize what will come next in the text; they must retrieve and activate their prior knowledge of the topic.

Reciprocal teaching relies heavily on oral discourse. The teacher and students share responsibility for summarizing, generating questions, clarifying, and predicting—and the responsibility for advancing the discourse is consciously shifted to the students. Figure 4.5 contains an excerpt from a transcript of a reciprocal teaching lesson.

Figure 4.5

Sample Episode of Reciprocal Teaching

Student 1:	My question is, what does the aquanaut need when he goes under water?
Student 2:	A watch.
Student 3:	Flippers.
Student 4:	A belt.
Student 1:	Those are all good answers.
Teacher:	Nice job? I have a question too. Why does the aquanaut wear a belt? What is so special about it?
Student 3:	It's a heavy belt and keeps him from floating up to the top again.
Teacher:	Good for you.
Student 1:	For my summary now . . . This paragraph was about what the aquanauts need to take when they go under the water.
Student 5:	And also about why they need those things.
Student 3:	I think we need to clarify "gear."
Student 6:	That's the special things they need.
Teacher:	Another word for gear in this story might be equipment, the equipment that makes it easier for the aquanauts to do their job.
Student 1:	I don't think I have a prediction to make.
Teacher:	Well, in the story they tell us that there are "many strange and wonderful creatures" that the aquanauts see as they do their work. My prediction is that they will describe some of these creatures. What are some of the strange creatures that you already know about that live in the ocean?
Student 6:	Octopuses.
Student 3:	Whales!
Student 5:	Sharks!
Teacher:	Let's listen and find out. Who will be our teacher?

K-W-L is another general reading strategy useful for teaching comprehension. Developed by Ogle (1986) and based on the research of Anderson (1977) and Anderson and Smith (1984), K-W-L stands for (K) What I know, (W) What I want to find out, and (L) What I learned. Before reading, students identify what they know about the topic and what they want to find out. They then read a selection and identify what they have learned.

Reciprocal teaching and K-W-L can be easily adapted to many content areas. Summarizing, generating questions, clarifying, and predicting can be applied to information presented in any medium. So, too, can students use the tactics of identifying what they know, what they would like to know, and what they have learned with any source of information.

Other reading strategies can also be applied as generalized comprehension strategies. For example, strategies developed by Jones and her colleagues (Jones, 1985; Jones, Amiran, & Katims, 1985; Jones, Friedman, Tinzmann, & Cox, 1984; Palinscar, Ogle, Jones, & Carr, 1986) are cast as activities that occur before, during, and after reading and listening. Figure 4.6 is an adaptation of this model.

Figure 4.6

Comprehension Strategies

Before Reading/Listening

1. Preview the Information
   a. Survey the text features (title, subtitles, and graphics) or the preliminary information.
   b. Survey the organizational patterns.
   c. Survey the content focus.

2. Activate/Access Prior Knowledge
   a. Recall content and vocabulary.
   b. Recall relevant categories of information and organizational patterns.

3. Focus Interest/Set purposes
   a. Ask questions.
   b. Predict content and organizational patterns.

During Reading/Listing

1. Confirm/Reject Predictions
   a. Assimilate new ideas.
   b. Withhold judgment.

2. Clarify Ideas
   a. Attend to key vocabulary.
   b. Generate new questions.
   c. Evaluate ideas.

3. Construct Meaning for Each Segment of Information
   a. Select important ideas.
   b. Connect and organize ideas.

After Reading/Listening

1. Construct Meaning for the Information as a Whole
   a. Categorize/integrate information.
   b. Summarize key ideas and their connection.

2. Assess Achievement of Purpose
   a. Confirm predictions.
   b. Identify gaps in learning.
   c. Extend learning to answer new questions/fill in gaps.

3. Consolidate/Apply Learning
   a. Transfer to new situations.
   b. Rehearse and study.

For example, in a social studies tutorial, Steve reported that he had trouble understanding his history textbook. When asked to describe his approach to reading the text, he described sitting with his book in front of him, starting at the beginning of the chapter, and reading each page—seemingly, a reasonable way to proceed. But when he had finished reading, Steve did not really know what the chapter said, though he had taken a long time. Steve's response indicated his belief that meaning was found in the book and that his job was to somehow transfer the book's meaning into his head. He expressed surprise at the idea that he needed to bring meaning to the page and combine what he knew with what the author said to create new meaning.

Steve's next assignment was a chapter entitled "The Depression and the New Deal." When asked to do so, he glanced through the chapter and noticed subtitles and political cartoons. He noted that the chapter began with a brief summary and concluded with questions about the content. When asked what he already knew about the Depression, Steve recalled hearing his grandparents describe hardships during that period. He thought he had a general idea of the Depression, but he said, "I've never even heard of the New Deal! I don't know anything about that." When the teacher asked if he could think of any situation when someone might ask for a new deal, Steve referred to a new deal in a card game. "People call for a new deal," Steve said, "when everyone has a bad hand and wants a chance to start over."

Steve verbalized the implications of this metaphor. "Maybe the Depression was like a card game when everyone had a bad hand. Things were so bad, maybe people wanted a chance to start over—maybe they thought they needed a new deal!" The teacher affirmed that Steve's idea was reasonable and identified it as a prediction for him to verify as he read. Looking through the chapter, Steve identified unfamiliar sets of letters—TVA, WPA, NRA, CCC, and AAA. He built questions around these; other questions emerged from the political cartoons.

So Steve approached the reading task with positive anticipation. He had some hunches he wanted to check out. Besides, he wanted to look for clues to make information easier to remember. Confirming his hypothesis about the New Deal, he noted that three key words about the period all started with R—relief, recovery, and reform. He used these three R-words to classify information he was learning about the TVA, WPA, and CCC. He created further questions when he realized that he wasn't sure how building dams might improve the Tennessee Valley.

Steve communicated a new sense of power in the reading situation. He made a B + on his chapter quiz and continued to use the new strategies in future reading assignments.

Problem Solving

The ability to solve problems is a prerequisite for human survival (Rowe, 1985). Moreover, many situations we encounter in our daily lives are essentially problem-solving situations. In cognitive psychology, *problem solving* has been used extensively, describing almost all forms of cognition. For example, Anderson (1983) classifies any goal-directed behavior (conscious or unconscious) as problem solving. Wickelgren (1974) describes problem solving as an attempt to reach a specific "goal state." Van Dijk and Kintsch (1983) state that problem solving occurs when a particular goal requires certain mental operations and steps.

Educators view problem solving more narrowly, using the term most commonly to refer to fairly specific types of tasks presented to students in mathematics, science, and some social science courses. Frederiksen (1984) observes that instruction in problem solving generally emphasizes well-structured problems— "the kind of problem which is clearly presented with all the information needed at hand and with an appropriate algorithm available that generates a correct answer, such as long-division, areas of triangles, Ohm's law and linear equations" (p. 303).

This is a severe limitation because many problems that students face in real life and the important social, political, economic, and scientific problems in the world are "fuzzy" and "ill-structured" (Simon, 1973). Some theorists classify problems into two broad categories, well-defined and ill-defined, holding that students should receive systematic practice in both types.

An enduring controversy in the problem-solving literature concerns whether we should teach students specific strategies for solving various types of problems or whether we should teach one or more general strategies that will apply to many problem types. The "specific" approach sacrifices generalizability for power; the "general" approach, power for generalizability.

We hope the few general strategies presented below will help teachers identify and create more specific strategies for the problems inherent in their content areas. We recommend that teachers become familiar with the different types of problems by studying sources such as *How to Solve Problems* (Wickelgren, 1974), *Problem Solving and Comprehension: A Short Course in Analytical Reasoning* (Whimbey & Lochhead, 1985), *Understanding and Increasing Intelligence* (Sternberg, 1985b), and *Thinking Skills: Making a Choice* (Wales, Nardi, & Stager, 1987).

Some general problem-solving processes are lists of unordered strategies. For example, Cyert (1980) presents 10 heuristics, paraphrased by Frederiksen (1984):

1. Get the total picture; don't get lost in detail.
2. Withhold judgment; don't commit yourself too early.
3. Create models to simplify the problem, using words, pictorial representations, symbols, or equations.
4. Try changing the representation of the problem.
5. State questions verbally, varying the form of the question.
6. Be flexible; question the flexibility of your premises.
7. Try working backwards.
8. Proceed in a way that permits you to return to your partial solutions.
9. Use analogies and metaphors.
10. Talk about the problem.

A teacher might present these heuristics to students and then model them, using different problem types. A chart of the heuristics might be prominently displayed in the classroom. As students work through practice problems, they can select the heuristics that seem most applicable to the problems presented. Sometimes, students can use most or even all of the heuristics to deal with a particular problem. Presumably, these heuristics can become integrated over time into the students' general approach to solving many types of problems.

Other general problem-solving strategies are more linear and more strongly imply a sequence for applying the heuristics. A widely used model of this type is the IDEAL problem-solving process, developed by Bransford and Stein (1984; Bransford, Stein, Delclos, & Littlefield, 1986). IDEAL stands for (I) Identifying the problem, (D) Defining the problem, (E) Exploring strategies, (A) Acting on ideas, and (L) Looking for the effects.

During the I stage, the student identifies problems as a far more subtle process than the title indicates. This stage involves recognizing problems sometimes hidden in commonplace situations or seemingly innocuous data. "If people do not realize the existence of a problem, one cannot expect them to look for a solution" (Bransford, Sherwood, Rieser, & Vye, 1986, p. 22). The authors report studies on "expert versus novice" problem solvers indicating that experts are more likely to notice problems in the domain of their expertise.

During the D stage, the problem is defined. People often agree that a problem exists but disagree on how it should be defined (Bransford & Stein, 1984). Problem definition is especially important because it influences the types of solutions considered (Sternberg, 1977, 1981a, 1981b; Newell & Simon, 1972). Central to problem definition is problem representation—the translation of the problem as stated into some other form. Representation is a kind of planning in which the original problem is replaced with an abstract version that retains the central features and is used as a guide in solving the original problem (Larkin, 1980). Many, if not most, scientists use imagery and graphic representation as an important part of the problem-solving process. Tweney, Doherty, and Mynatt (1981), in *On Scientific Thinking*, devote an entire section to the use of imagery in science. They cite original works of Einstein, Kuhn, and Planck, indicating that their ability to represent a problem as a mental image or a diagram was central to defining a problem.

E in the IDEAL model stands for exploring strategies. At this stage, the problem solver entertains various strategies for reaching a solution. Expert problem solvers also commonly look for analogies and metaphors when exploring a problem. For example, Clement (1983) notes that experts in mathematics and science commonly look for analogies and metaphors between the problem at hand and other situations.

Bransford and Stein (1984) recommend that students consider three major strategies during the exploration phase: breaking the problem into manageable parts, using special cases, and working backwards. People who fail to break complex problems into smaller problems (subproblems) frequently conclude that complex problems are impossible to solve. For example, regardless of the language used (e.g., LOGO, BASIC, Pascal), computer specialists commonly build a complex program by a series of interconnecting subprograms or subroutines. The same strategy can be used when trying to solve a mathematics problem or generate a geometric proof. Using special cases refers to simplifying a problem by considering a "trimmed" version of it. For example, students might explore strategies for resolving interracial conflict by considering what helps when two friends resolve a misunderstanding. Working backwards involves beginning with the goal and then gradually tracing the steps backwards. A student can plan a term paper by beginning with the major sections of the paper and planning around that outline—realizing that the conclusion cannot be written until after the library research is done.

The last two stages of IDEAL, acting on ideas and looking for the effects, are closely related. Newell and Simon (1972) refer to these stages as "means-end analysis"—the activities in which the problem solver repeatedly compares the present state of things with the desired goal and asks, "What is the difference between where I am now and where I want to be? What can I do to reduce the difference?" In general, the A and L stages have a strong evaluation component. The individual periodically monitors progress by determining how close or far away the goal is, changing strategies if there is little or no progress in the desired direction.

We should present students many different problem types, along with strategies for solving them. Also, students must believe that problems have solutions and that they as individuals can develop strategies for finding solutions. Similarly, in our instruction, we should demonstrate the power of oral discourse—large- and small-group discussion—in the problem-solving process.

Decision Making

Decision making is closely related to problem solving; in fact, the distinction between the two is sometimes hard to discern. Halpern (1984) states that a decision always involves two or more competing alternatives that may or may not be obvious to the decision maker. The decision maker has to choose or invent an alternative that is best, relative to some criteria—a process that involves a decision.

Decision making can be stressful. For example, Sorensen (1965) describes the harmful effects John F. Kennedy felt from the decision-making process used during the Berlin blockade. However, decision making is an activity that we all engage in many times each day. We make decisions about what to include in the day and how to order the things we will do. For these everyday decisions, we do not usually engage in a complex process, nor should we. But when complex situations arise that require analysis or deal with weighty matters, it is useful to proceed in a systematic way so that we can select the best alternative.

Many educators believe that decision making should be the focal point of education, along with the thinking skills that serve it and the knowledge base that supports it. Wales, Nardi, and Stager (1986) have developed a model for the decision-making process that involves four operations: state the goal, generate ideas, prepare a plan, and take action. Each of the operations requires a decision, and in each the decision maker identifies problems (analysis), creates options (synthesis), and makes a decision based on evaluation. This scheme is depicted in Figure 4.7.

The four operations, each with three steps, make up a 12-step decision-making process. To illustrate this model, consider a situation that occurred in a middle-grade classroom. The students had been studying the solar system and the visit of Halley's Comet. They had worked in small groups to prepare reports on each of the planets and on the comet. The following student comments on the steps in the process demonstrate the model.

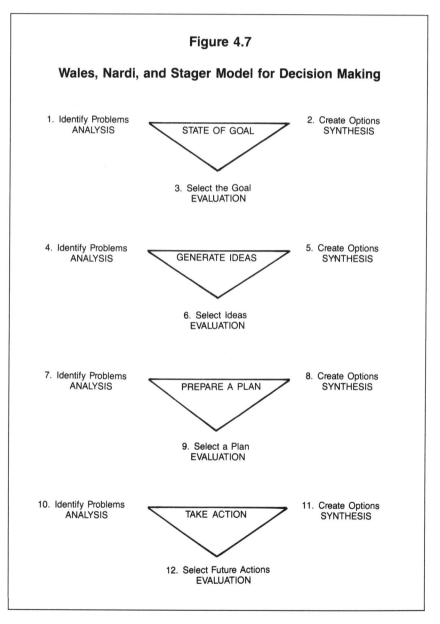

Figure 4.7

Wales, Nardi, and Stager Model for Decision Making

1. Identify Problems
   ANALYSIS

   STATE OF GOAL

2. Create Options
   SYNTHESIS

3. Select the Goal
   EVALUATION

4. Identify Problems
   ANALYSIS

   GENERATE IDEAS

5. Create Options
   SYNTHESIS

6. Select Ideas
   EVALUATION

7. Identify Problems
   ANALYSIS

   PREPARE A PLAN

8. Create Options
   SYNTHESIS

9. Select a Plan
   EVALUATION

10. Identify Problems
    ANALYSIS

    TAKE ACTION

11. Create Options
    SYNTHESIS

12. Select Future Actions
    EVALUATION

State the Goal

1. *Identify problems in the situation.* We want to create a model of the solar system to show other classes what we've learned. We'd like it to be a scale model, but the solar system is very large, and the comet is small in comparison.

2. *Create goal options.* We could use the athletic field to provide space. We might use the cafeteria. We might use our classroom.

3. *Select the goal.* The athletic field has enough space, but we can't control the weather. Our models could be ruined by rain. In the cafeteria, our model would be in the way, so we couldn't leave it in place long. We'd better try to fit it into our classroom so it will be in a protected area where we can work on it over a period of time. We'll need to find a way to adjust the scale to the size of our classroom.

Generate Ideas

4. *Identify goal problems.* We discovered that the sun is so much bigger than the planets and the comet that it could fill the whole room. The space between the planets is a problem, too.

5. *Create idea options.* We could ignore the space between the planets. We might use a smaller scale for the sun than for the planets.

6. *Select ideas.* Let's try using two different scales. Each group will do some calculations on their own planet or the comet to come up with possible scales.

Prepare a Plan

7. *Identify the new problem situation.* Some of us are still wondering if a scale model is really a scale model if two different scales are used. If Mercury is only one-half inch in diameter, how can we show anything we've learned about it in our model? Halley's Comet is even more of a problem. We might not even be able to see it, even using the larger of two scales.

8. *Create plan options.* We can try some more possibilities. Let's figure out how small a model might be while still having enough details to recognize. Then we might see how that compares to the relative size for Neptune and Jupiter.

9. *Select a plan.* We've found a way: We'll need three scales—one for the sun, another for the big planets, and a third for the little planets.

Take Action

10. *Identify plan problems.* We'll need to have our materials for making the models on Monday. How can we be sure we have what we need?

11. *Create action options.* Some of us will bring balls. Others will bring balloons to mold papier-mâché. We'll need wire. The solar system will need to be hung high enough so that we don't bump our heads.

12. *Select the next actions.* We finally finished. The other classes will visit tomorrow. Each group will explain the part we studied and built.

Wales, Nardi, and Stager's (1986) model has broad applications. In the example above, the students made a series of decisions that enabled them to reach their goal. They gradually decided to adjust their concept of a scale model when they discovered problems created by the size of the solar system. Through the process of oral discourse, the students shared information and ideas leading to the compromises necessary to reach a decision. The model is particularly useful when decisions involve a series of options.

A decision-making model designed by Lyle and Sydelle Ehrenberg is particularly effective when we need "to decide which one of a number of alternatives is the best choice to satisfy the requirements of a given situation" (Ehrenberg, Ehrenberg, & Durfee, 1979, p. MC-1). The Ehrenbergs outline a three-phase process for making choices (Figure 4.8).

Figure 4.8

Ehrenberg Model for Making Choices (Decision Making)

1. Clarify, verify the requirements of the given situation. Anticipate the characteristics of <u>any</u> item that would meet <u>all</u> of the requirements of the situation—the "ideal."

2. Identify, clarify, verify the characteristics of <u>each</u> alternative. Compare the characteristics of each alternative with the "ideal" (the characteristics identified in #1). Select the alternative that best matches the "ideal."

3. Verify the choice by identifying the characteristics of the selected alternative that make it <u>more likely</u> to satisfy the requirements of the situation <u>than any of the others</u>.

To illustrate, consider the process a middle-grade class followed to create small businesses as part of an economics unit. Before the companies could be established, the class needed to decide what products to manufacture. The students defined the problem as identifying products that could be produced in class and marketed for a profit. They listed the characteristics that would meet those requirements:

- Products desired by students
- Cost of materials less than sale price
- Products priced low enough for students to buy
- Products that can be made in a short time
- Products that can be made in a classroom or school kitchen

Alternative products were suggested as various students displayed samples they had made of the possible product. The class narrowed the alternatives by discussing the characteristics of the items using the identified criteria. A dozen samples were made of each item on the narrowed list, and test marketing was conducted within the school to determine comparative sales appeal. The students kept records of the cost of materials, production time, and responses during the test marketing. Finally, the class decided on four products and established a company to manufacture and market them. Sales were conducted during recess. A final verification activity took place when students calculated expenses and income to determine net profits for the various products.

Some decision-making models are geared specifically to create quantitative comparisons for guiding a selection among alternatives. The *Odyssey* program (Chance, 1986) describes decision making as primarily quantitative; it encourages students to identify the considerations they desire relative to their solutions and then asks students to weight each consideration relative to its importance, selecting or rejecting an alternative based on its considerations. Halpern (1984) calls *Odyssey* the "worksheet" approach. If the middle-grade class doing the economics unit had used this approach, their decision might have been guided by a chart like the one in Figure 4.9

The ratings for sales appeal were weighted 2; other considerations, 1. The ratings for sales appeal were multiplied by 2 before the ratings were totaled. In this case, the class decided to manufacture products E, F, G, and J, based on the worksheet results.

We think schools should explicitly teach at least one decision-making process and should provide students with academic and real-world situations for practicing decision making. We suggest, however, that teachers should caution students that they may neglect to include some elements that should actually have been considered, including unanticipated side effects of what may appear to be the best alternative.

Research (Scientific Inquiry)

Research, the sixth major thinking process, is defined here as scientific inquiry. It differs from problem solving in that its purposes are explaining and predicting (Halpern, 1984) rather than simply finding a correct answer. Although scientific inquiry uses both problem solving and decision making (indeed, all the other processes are involved in one form or another), it is primarily directed toward understanding how something works and how to use this understanding to predict phenomena. Many different conceptualizations of science have been offered over the centuries (see the selections by Bacon, Newton, Descartes, Einstein, Popper, and Kuhn in Tweney, Doherty, & Mynatt, 1981), but all share several characteristics: describing phenomena, formulating hypotheses, and testing hypotheses.

Describing phenomena involves such skills as observing, identifying components and attributes, classifying, and comparing. The overall intent of describing phenomena is to integrate what is perceived with what is known. The researcher attempts to identify the characteristics of what is being observed then, through comparison with other known entities, to determine where the phenomena under investigation fit into the existing knowledge base. This skill forms the basis for suggesting hypotheses.

Figure 4.9

Sample Decision Making Worksheet

ALTERNATIVE PRODUCTS		A Shaggy Pencils	B Chocolate Covered Bananas	C School Pennant	D Pizza	E Chocolate Marshmallows	F School Buttons	G Rice Krispie Munchies	H Pencil Case	I Caramel Apples	J Wristband Wallet
CONSIDERATIONS	Weight										
Time to make # per hour	1	3	3	1	2	3	2	4	2	3	2
Sales Price − Cost of Materials Profit Margin	1	2	2	1	2	4	3	4	2	3	2
Can be made in class or school kitchen: not too messy— equipment available	1	4	2	3	1	2	3	3	4	1	4
Shelf Life: Will keep if not sold same day.	1	4	0	4	1	3	4	3	4	3	4
Sales Appeal: How fast did samples sell? How did students react in interview?	2	1 $\times 2$ 2	4 $\times 2$ 8	1 $\times 2$ 2	3 $\times 2$ 6	3 $\times 2$ 6	3 $\times 2$ 6	4 $\times 2$ 8	2 $\times 2$ 4	3 $\times 2$ 6	3 $\times 2$ 6
Affordable— Can most students afford? Will they buy more than one?	1	2	3	1	4	3	2	4	1	2	2
Weighted Total		17	18	12	16	21	20	26	17	18	20

Ratings
4 - Excellent
3 - Good
2 - OK
1 - Not so good
0 - Poor

Traditionally, we have expressed *formulating hypotheses* in terms of induction and deduction. Induction is the act of observing events and then making inferences to generate hypotheses based on those observations. Deduction is generating hypotheses based on a principle believed to be true. Scientists, philosophers, and psychologists, however, have challenged simplistic views of induction and deduction (Medawar, 1967; Eco, 1976; Johnson-Laird, 1983). It seems reasonable, for example, that hypotheses can be generated both inductively and deductively, and some argue that pure induction is not possible. As Popper comments in *Conjectures and Refutations* (1962/1978):

The belief that we can start with pure observation alone, without anything in the nature of a theory, is absurd; as may be illustrated by the story of the man who dedicated his life to natural science, wrote down everything he could observe, and bequeathed his priceless collection of observations to the Royal Society to be used as inductive evidence. This story should show us that though beetles may be collected, observations may not (p. 46).

Popper's point is that observation is always selective; it always stems from some preconceived notion of the way things are or should be. Therefore, some theorists have concluded that generating hypotheses is far less structured than originally assumed and that it is primarily a process of creating "models" of reality. Rankin (1964) notes that the relationships between things observed and things already known are at first diverse and ill-defined. Over time, they begin to crystallize into a model. Only after we have developed mental models can we generate hypotheses.

Similarly, Johnson-Laird (1983) asserts that all hypotheses come from mental models. Tweney (1986) suggests that scientists construct these mental models in many different ways. More specifically, scientific thinking is a function of imagery, analogy, and metaphor, as well as logical reasoning, any of which can be used to generate and evaluate mental models.

The implication for teachers is that, after observing the phenomena under investigation, students should be asked to create some type of mental model of the phenomenon before they generate hypotheses. For some students, these mental models may be images, for others a graphic representation, for others an analogy, and for others a metaphor. In any event, students should ground their observations in some model that they can relate back to when constructing hypotheses. In actual science, the models are generally concrete—it is a common myth that science is abstract; even the most complex mathematical equation is, for the expert using it, something tangible, vivid, and real (Tweney, 1987). Students, too, must base their scientific thinking on concrete knowledge.

Testing hypotheses includes some type of data analysis. Based on the nature and purpose of the study, several approaches to data analysis and hypothesis testing can be used. Experimental studies seek to control extraneous variables while determining the effects of selected independent variables (those that can be manipulated) on selected dependent variables (those that are observed to see whether they are affected by the manipulation). Correlation studies attempt to determine the amount and nature of commonality among phenomena. Case studies and ethnographic studies seek to explain phenomena through in-depth analysis of single cases. Hypothesis testing always involves either *confirmation* (consistency between the hypothesis and the observation) or *disconfirmation* (inconsistency between the hypothesis and the observation). Students must learn that both are important; there is a pervasive tendency to ignore disconfirmation in some highly inappropriate ways (Tweney, Doherty, & Mynatt, 1981).

We are not suggesting that students should be taught the different modes of data analysis and hypothesis testing. But they can practice general scientific inquiry using the following process:

1. Identify the problem; describe the subject or phenomenon under study.
2. Identify relevant information; identify what you already know about it.
3. Generate hypotheses.
   a. Try to create linkages or relationships with things you already know. Don't limit your thinking at this stage.
   b. Develop a principle, theory, or model about what you are studying.
   c. From your model, generate hypotheses, predictions, or questions to be answered.
4. Test hypotheses.
   a. Design a scientific procedure (e.g., an experiment) that will guide your investigation of your hypothesis, prediction, or question. Be aware of the assumptions you are making.
   b. Conduct the investigation and gather information.
5. State conclusions.
   a. Organize and analyze the information, relating it back to your hypothesis, prediction, or question. Check to see how consistent your findings are with what you know about the phenomenon.
   b. Determine the extent to which your findings can be used to predict other phenomena by designing new scientific procedures (e.g., new experiments).
   c. Determine what observations might disconfirm your hypothesis, and design new procedures as a further test.

The teacher can first present this strategy to students and then model it, using a classroom experiment. Once students understand the general strategy, they can use it as they engage in classroom tasks that require scientific inquiry.

Classroom applications of research occur most frequently in science and social studies courses. One 7th grade science teacher used a "paper towel lab" to help students apply their thinking skills in the research process. She began by asking students to place themselves in the role of consumer researchers. Their problem was defined as determining which of six brands of paper towels was the best value. She selected brands representing a range in price, quality, and design.

Using recall, students identified relevant information. They listed on the chalkboard the uses of paper towels and qualities related to those uses (strength when wet, absorbency, lint, cost). For each quality, students suggested possible ways of comparing the towels.

55

Working in pairs, students generated specific hypotheses beginning with words such as "_____ is the best paper towel for the money because. . . . " The student pairs then wrote out specific, step-by-step instructions for testing their hypothesis, trying to control as many variables as possible. For example, to test for absorbency, two students wrote: (1) Place one paper towel in a bowl with 50 milliliters of water for 15 seconds; (2) lift the paper towel from the bowl; (3) measure the water remaining in the bowl; (4) compare the amount of water remaining in the bowl for the different brands of towels.

After testing, the students analyzed their information and stated their conclusions. Sometimes they decided that the hypothesis used to test a characteristic was too different from normal use to be relevant for prediction. For example, not many people will ever be concerned about how many pennies a wet paper towel can support.

In a 4th grade social studies class, the students used the research process to learn about the history of their highly integrated community. Their goal was to prepare a slide-tape for the 25th-anniversary celebration of the local community association that had worked to keep the community integrated. They defined the problem as finding out what factors had helped the community become and remain integrated.

The students collected information from original documents, such as news articles, programs, and photographs on loan from the community association, and they sorted the items into trays labeled with dates for five-year periods. Groups of students were responsible for oral and written summaries of the various periods. Individuals who had lived in the community for a long time were invited to speak to the class and respond to questions.

Students generated hypotheses on why people chose to move into and to remain in the community: questions about the quality and price of housing, the quality of the schools, and social interactions with neighbors. They designed a simple survey to check these hypotheses and went door to door asking questions. They recorded such data as when people had moved to the community, the number and ages of their children, their occupations, and their race. The students reported what they had learned about the history and sociology of the community in a slide-tape that they took pride in showing.

Although research activities should not be limited to science and social studies, those disciplines present many opportunities for students to develop the thinking skills needed for scientific inquiry. If social studies and science teachers provide frequent practice in applying thinking skills to conduct research or scientific inquiry, students will be able to apply the process in future life situations.

Composition

Composition is the process of conceiving and developing a product. Although in education we often identify this process as writing, composing is also needed to create a dance, a song, a painting, or a sculpture. Because of its importance to education and because it has been most frequently studied as a thinking process, composition in written form is the primary focus of this section. Nickerson (1984) sees writing as one of the most crucial cognitive operations: "Writing is viewed not only as a medium of thought but also as a vehicle for developing it" (p. 33).

Flower and Hayes (1980a, 1980b, 1981) have developed a "cognitive process theory" of composition. Although it has been criticized (Cooper & Holzman, 1983), the theory is still extremely useful. As Applebee (1984) notes, it is "the most thoroughly formalized model for the writing process" (p. 582).

Flower and Hayes (1980a, 1980b, 1981) criticize simplistic models which assert that the writing process occurs in a series of linear stages—prewriting, writing, and revising. They believe the writing process is far from linear; rather, it is interactive and recursive. Although they present their model in a diagram (Figure 4.10), they caution against interpreting it as a series of steps. The various aspects of composition—like the other thinking processes—may occur in varying sequences.

According to Flower and Hayes (1980a, 1980b, 1981), the writing process includes planning, translating, and reviewing—all under the control of the writer as monitor. These components interact with the writer's long-term memory and the elements of the task environment. A central premise of their theory is that writers are constantly, instant by instant, orchestrating a battery of cognitive operations as they plan, translate, and review.

During *planning*, writers form an internal representation of the knowledge they will use in writing. They organize information and set goals. Building an internal representation involves several operations; the most obvious is generating ideas, which includes selecting and retrieving relevant information from long-term memory. Sometimes, this information is already so simple or so well-developed that the writer can immediately produce clearly organized ideas. At other times, the writer may generate only fragmentary, unconnected, even contradictory thoughts.

Another part of planning is organizing information, which can take the form of simply chunking information into relevant categories, generating new ideas as a result of seeing relationships, or even envisioning how information will be represented in discourse. Goal setting is a rarely studied aspect of planning. The goals that writers give themselves are procedural and substantive, often both at the same time. For example, "I have to relate this engineering project to the economics of energy to show why I'm improving it and why steam turbines need to be more efficient." Generating and organizing new ideas are important aspects of setting goals for writing that occur throughout the process. "Just as goals lead a writer to generate ideas, those ideas lead to new, more complex goals" (Flower & Hayes, 1981, p. 373).

Translating, the second major component of the writing process, is the operation that puts ideas into visible language. Translating requires the writer to juggle all the special demands of written language, which include such abstract elements as audience, tone, and syntax, as well as the motor task of forming

Figure 4.10

Flower and Hayes Composing Model

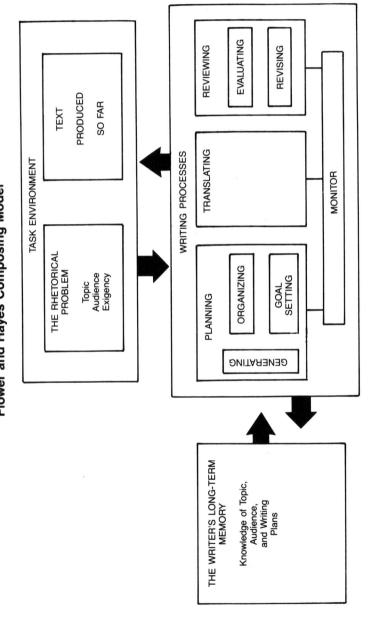

letters (or keyboarding). If the writer cannot meet these demands quickly and even automatically, the demands may impede the writing process by requiring the writer's attention. Some children who are articulate in oral language are, therefore, poor writers; their weak sense of audience, lack of fluency in motor skills, or other deficiencies in translation "short-circuit" the writing process.

Reviewing, the third component, consists of evaluating and revising. Reviewing might be a planned action in which the writer chooses to read critically what has been written. In some cases, the writer may produce a series of drafts and receive systematic feedback from peers or from the teacher. Reviewing may also be an unplanned action, triggered by a sense of "something wrong" in the text—grammatically, syntactically, or rhetorically—when the writer pauses to evaluate and revise.

As Figure 4.10 indicates, the components of the writing process are all under the control of a monitor—the writer functioning as strategist in a metacognitive sense, determining when to move from one operation to another. For example, the monitoring operation determines how long to continue generating ideas before attempting to write, or whether to try to write polished, exact prose as quickly as possible or to organize the manuscript mentally or in a rough outline before starting to write. This monitoring is what we describe as "control" in the discussion of metacognition. Scardamalia, Bereiter, and Steinbach (1984) have shown that much of children's lack of fluency lies in their lack of "executive routines," which promote strategic switching among the various components of the writing process.

While acknowledging Flower and Hayes's (1980a, 1980b, 1981) criticism of linear models as too simplistic, we recognize the value of instructional models laid out as sequenced classroom activities. Most such models caution against rigidly applying sequences. They emphasize that teachers should recognize the "looped" recursive nature of the writing process when implementing process instruction.

A wealth of professional materials exists on process approaches to teaching writing (e.g., Koch & Brazil, 1978; Chew & Schlawin, 1983; Proett & Gill, 1986). Most follow a model that includes prewriting, drafting, revising, and proofreading (with some variations in terminology). Oral discourse is an essential part of both the prewriting and revising activities. Process-based instructional models stress the importance of writing for real audiences rather than for the teacher only. Consequently, the products of the writing process are somehow published, displayed, enacted, or otherwise transmitted to the intended audiences. In short, students are encouraged to see writing as a purposeful communication activity rather than as a "dummy run" produced for the teacher and for testing situations (Britton et al., 1975).

A class of primary students used the composing process to write plays. Having heard, read, and dramatized several fairy tales, they decided to create a fairy tale of their own to act out for other classes.

The teacher asked the class to recall the usual components of fairy tales. She listed responses on the board as children identified such ingredients as a dear, kind person; a wicked person; some kind of trouble; and magic. The teacher stimulated dialogue by asking: "What are some of the things a dear, kind person in a fairy tale might say? How might other characters respond? What are some things an evil person might say?" She recorded ideas on chart paper, and the children orally improvised sample conversations between characters.

In columns on the chalkboard, the teacher wrote "good, kind person," "evil character" and "trouble." For each column, the children suggested possible attributes of characters and kinds of trouble. They talked through possible ways, magical and natural, of resolving trouble. They set their goals as they chose the kinds of characters to include in individual plays.

The children were able to move from their oral discourse into brief, individual, fairy-tale plays because they had prior experience writing group plays and were familiar with the format for scripting. After writing the first drafts, the children read them aloud. The class discussed new ideas and suggestions for improvements. After reading the revised plays, the class discussed criteria for deciding which plays to act out for other classes. The students selected four plays using their criteria. In one case, they combined elements from two plays into a single drama. Small groups further revised the plays and practiced acting them out. Parent volunteers typed and reproduced the four plays so each child could have a script. The plays were presented to parent and student audiences.

The process approach to writing carries strong implications for classroom instruction. The approach contrasts dramatically with rule-based writing instruction, which demands knowledge of formal grammar despite overwhelming evidence of its ineffectiveness (Mellon, 1969; Sherwin, 1969; Hillocks, 1986). The role of long-term memory and background knowledge in the writing process suggests that we cannot expect students to write well on unfamiliar topics. Teachers must either encourage students to choose topics for which they have a strong experiential base or provide opportunities to develop an experiential base before writing. Also, students should have the benefit of using a wide range of skills in the writing process. All students should recognize the roles of planning, organizing, and monitoring, yet each individual should be permitted to apply elements and sequences in the writing process in ways that are individually useful. Students also need frequent opportunities for practice, with peer and teacher feedback, to develop fluency and skill in written language.

Finally, what we know about written composition has implications for other forms of composition. Composition is the process of developing a product. In education, that product is commonly written discourse, but the products can take many other forms. Painting a picture, designing a dance routine, building a machine, and writing a song are all forms of composing.

We believe that the composition model presented here can be adapted to any product. The composer in nonverbal sign systems still must generate ideas from long-term memory, using content knowledge and past experience with similar products. That information is organized either in concrete terms (a plan of action for developing the product) or in abstract ways (vague images of what the completed product will be like). During translation, the composer begins representing the product in the chosen medium of expression. For example, a composer painting a picture might make a rough sketch during the initial stages of translation and then a rough, full-sized version of the picture, leading to a wholly realized product. A composer building a machine might make a scale model during the first stages of translation and then a prototype for use in field testing. During review, composers of nonwritten products evaluate and revise the product, making minor or major changes in form and substance.

We do not want to overemphasize similarities in the details of composing in different forms, nor do we want to suggest that written composition is normative. Nevertheless, we see in the Flower and Hayes (1980a, 1980b, 1981) model considerable adaptability to many acts of composing that are part of the disciplines taught in our schools.

Oral Discourse

Oral discourse—sometimes called dialogue—is the process of verbal interaction between two or more people. Oral discourse is inherently inventive and inherently social. In its inventive aspects, oral discourse is among the most fundamental of human abilities. Through this process, vague impressions, undefined feelings, and unexamined experiences are given shape with the act of speaking. Through oral discourse, people impose order on the randomness of perception and help each other make sense of themselves and the world.

The theory and research of Piaget (1967, 1972, 1976), Vygotsky (1962), and others point to the centrality of oral discourse in the process of making meaning. Children artlessly "soliloquize before others," in Piaget's phrase, before learning; Vygotsky notes that children use language as the basic means for testing their perceptions and continually reshaping their view of the world.

Other sign systems such as drawing and music are available for expressing and communicating a sense of the world. But the core process in formulating and sharing human experience is oral expression. As Eco (1976) points out, language is "the most powerful semiotic device that man has invented." Similarly, Piaget (1971) notes that "language is but one among . . . many aspects of the semiotic function, even though it is, in most instances, the most important." Even those who most commonly and intensively work with nonlinguistic sign systems— painters, musicians, architects, and mathematicians—articulate their intentions and describe their methods through oral discourse. Carroll (1974), discussing graphic arts, states that "the various forms of pictorial expression are almost always accompanied by language and often require language to make them intelligible."

Before discussing oral discourse in the classroom, we should distinguish between the spontaneous invention of oral discourse and the product orientation of written composition. Admittedly, informal letter writing, free writing, and journal writing simulate to some extent the immediate invention and expressiveness of oral discourse. But as the writing-process model discussed in the previous section suggests, written composition (and composition in other arts) involves awareness and skills, such as planning and revising, that go beyond those of oral discourse. In oral discourse, speakers do not set out with the intention of creating a work in a recognized artistic mode. Rather, they improvise, embarking on an exchange of utterances that, though rule-based, might take a potentially infinite number of syntactic, discursive, and semantic forms (Miller, 1973). With the possible exception of jazz improvisation and certain forms of "automatic art," the rapid initial shaping of ideas from human consciousness is unique to oral discourse (Suhor, 1986).

An essential quality of oral discourse, then, is its immediate, creative nature. Unlike the other processes, the skills involved in producing oral discourse follow no general sequence. Putting nonlinguistic thought into words is an act of rapid invention bringing into existence for the individual new distinctions that did not clearly exist before their verbalization. Thus, oral discourse may lead to the acquisition of knowledge as well as the application or production of knowledge. Students need to develop an awareness of their inner and outer dialogues as creative processes. Speaking to oneself or to others actually shapes knowledge and beliefs.

Classroom instruction in oral discourse has frequent applications both in and out of school. Among Tough's (1974) list of basic discourse abilities are awareness

- of how to take turns in conversation,
- of how to listen,
- of ways of asking for different kinds of information,
- of how to speak to others and appreciate their needs
- that others have a point of view, and
- that others' points of view may be different from our own.

At a more generative level, students can learn the role that intentions play in shaping language. Van Dijk (1980) states that all discourse comes from specific "intentions"; they represent the message behind the message. Schlesinger (1971) states that the intentions behind utterances are the kernels of creation. Even when the speakers are unaware, speech reflects their intentions. Halliday (1975) and Tough (1976) have identified some basic intentions behind oral discourse— informing, persuading, regulating, generating or expressing emotion, acquiring information, and stimulating divergence.

An essential quality of oral discourse as used in classroom instruction is goal-directedness. In the classroom, oral language is used consciously as a tool for learning (Moffett, 1968). The teacher's main role is to facilitate the develop- ment of oral language that leads to discovering and exploring ideas in a particular discipline. Stanton (1984) calls this type of classroom dialogue "thinking to- gether" and sees its goal as achieving "cognitive focus and mutual construction of knowledge" (p. 156). The teacher acts as orchestrator of ideas and "cognitive referee," ensuring that relationships are formed in the flow of discussion. As Thaiss (1986) states:

The teacher, in supervising conversation, can perform the analytic function of pointing out new ideas that the conversation has led to, and can ask salient questions that push children to consider apparent contradictions or new information. The teacher can also help children learn how to bring a conversation back from free brainstorming for focus on an original question, and thus how to use the insights the brainstorming has given them. In this way, teachers help their students achieve versatility as learners, speakers, and listeners, while keeping discussion within the context of the curricular program (p. 5).

Viewing classroom discourse as "supervised conversation" has wide applicability. Hillocks's (1986) meta-analysis of composition research reveals that in the most effective approach to teaching composition, the teacher leads the discussion to prepare for writing. Virtually all teaching models of process instruction in written composition include oral discourse as part of prewriting. Before the first written draft, ideas are shaped in the give-and-take of discussion.

A number of tools are available to the teacher as the supervisor of conversation. Reciprocal teaching has already been mentioned. Another powerful tool is *scaffolding*. A metaphor created by Bruner (1978) in his discussion of parent-child interactions, scaffolding refers to the supportive oral language prompts that encourage pertinent language in the classroom. These prompts are gradually withdrawn, like the scaffolds of a building, as students gain independence in using language.

Inquiry teaching is another tool for oral discourse. Long respected as an interactive method in science and social studies instruction, inquiry teaching has been refined in terms of oral discourse strategies. Collins (1986), for example, analyzed transcripts of an inquiry-based science class. He found that the teacher's agenda of goals was updated during the discussion as gaps and misconceptions in the students' knowledge became apparent. Within the framework of joint inquiry, then, the teacher uses oral discourse to highlight what is known and not known and to set future directions for the class's activities.

Cooperative learning embraces much more than oral discourse, but guided classroom interaction is an essential component. In *Circles of Learning*, Johnson and others (1984) speak directly of both the inventive, meaning-making values of oral discourse and its social, value-shaping benefits. They refer to the power of classroom dialogue in "formulating"—that is, using "vocalization to make overt the implicit reasoning processes" (p. 47). Social skills are taught directly because face-to-face interaction results in "positive interdependence." Conflicts are wholesomely aired and negotiated, with perspective taking and peer regulation flowing from the focused discussion (pp. 15-33).

Philosophers have long stressed the social and ethical benefits of oral discourse in education. Paul (1986a) points out that such traits as intellectual empathy, fair-mindedness, faith in reason, and movement toward reciprocal rather than egocentric attitudes can emerge from purposive dialogue about significant issues. Student oral discourse also supports democratic values by involving students in examining stereotypes, forming and testing consensus, and dealing with reasoned dissent. Paul's view of Socratic teaching goes well beyond the traditional Socratic questions, sequenced by the teacher, to guide students' reasoning toward predetermined conclusions. Like scaffolding, Paul's dialogical instruction (described in Chapter 3) aims at producing the autonomous learner who can generate as well as respond to thoughtful questions.

A final observation about social aspects of oral discourse relates to the one-way messages transmitted by mass media—especially television—in our society. Many educators consider oral discourse in the classroom a primary means for ensuring an ongoing critical analysis of media. The Commission on Media (1984), for example, states that "students must learn to understand the power of the media in order to avoid being controlled by them" and calls for verbal exchange in the classroom to critique the "values and stereotypes" that appear on television.

Oral discourse, then, can and should be used in developing all the other thinking processes and the core thinking skills. We believe that the currently popular writing-across-the-curriculum movement should mean *language* across the curriculum, with oral discourse at the center. Oral discourse is a key psychological event in which the "blooming, buzzing universe" described by William James is rendered sensible through the act of shaping and sharing unformed ideas. It is a key pedagogical method because students who make meaning by stating academic knowledge in their own words demonstrate a depth of understanding well beyond what is reflected in recitation or in the recognition-testing of many paper-and-pencil tests. To become conversant with a subject is to have used oral discourse in significant and personal ways.

Implications

The thinking processes for knowledge acquisition—concept formation, principle formation, and comprehension—help students build a foundation for learning any discipline. An approach to curriculum planning that incorporates thinking processes can begin by listing answers to these questions:

- What *concepts* might we want students to develop in this course? What are the concepts that students might need to understand?
- What *principles* might students need to understand the relationships in this course?
- What information might students need to *comprehend* in American literature or vocational agriculture?

Since we cannot teach every conceivable concept or principle in any one course, we must make choices. From our lists, we need to select the most important information, concepts, and principles around which to build curricular units.

Although students and teachers use knowledge-acquisition processes to build a foundation for learning any content area, the knowledge is useful only to the degree that students can apply the knowledge or produce new knowledge. Therefore, as we write each unit of curriculum, we need to design opportunities for students to use their knowledge to compose, to solve problems, to make decisions, or to conduct research for discovering new knowledge. Each unit in the curriculum should provide structured opportunities to use at least one of these processes, and in planning the overall curriculum we should provide a balanced menu of opportunities to apply the various knowledge-production or knowledge-application processes.

Students and teachers use oral discourse to learn all the other thinking processes. For example, using oral discourse students verbalize the similarities among examples of a concept, brainstorm ideas for a written composition, and debate the merits of alternative solutions to a problem. Because the thinking processes are complex and require significant classroom time, we need to develop curriculums that incorporate opportunities for students to use thinking processes to learn more effectively.

Relationships Between Processes and Skills

We have presented classroom examples of thinking processes, simply mentioning the thinking skills as integral components of the processes. We may have created an impression that the thinking skills develop automatically, without instruction, and that only complete thinking processes should be intentionally taught. Although thinking is a normal activity that certainly occurs without instruction, we can improve students' ability to perform the various processes by increasing their awareness of the component skills and by increasing their skill proficiency through conscious practice.

In a tennis game, a player uses several component skills. A player's ability to execute a backhand or forehand return can be improved by practicing the two returns in isolation. The beginning tennis player may know enough about serving to put the ball in play, but proficiency develops not only in game situations but through awareness and independent practice of component skills. A good tennis teacher provides isolated practice in serving and in backhand and forehand returns, although she also provides ample opportunity for the student to actually play tennis. When the student is playing, the coach offers feedback on how the player is applying the skills.

Similarly, a classroom teacher can enable students to improve their ability to compose, to solve problems, or to make decisions by helping them develop proficiency in thinking skills, such as observing, comparing, or inferring. While teaching a lesson using a thinking process, the teacher may observe that students are not careful observers or do not logically support inferences. Just as a tennis instructor may coach a player to "keep your eye on the ball" or "get your racket back," the teacher may need to coach students to "look again to see what else you can observe" or "explain how the instance you cited supports your position." Based on observations of the students' thinking processes, the teacher may need to provide some isolated skill practice. Both on the tennis court and in the classroom, the teacher's coaching during a thinking process—like an athletic coach's reminder during a game—helps students recall and apply what they learned during practice.

Thinking Processes

In the next chapter, core thinking skills are presented roughly in the order in which they frequently appear in analyses of the various thinking processes (Rankin & Hughes, 1986, 1987a, 1987b; Hughes, 1986). Figure 4.11 shows this relationship.

Figure 4.11

Core Thinking Skills As They Frequently Occur in Thinking Processes

---

FOCUSING SKILLS

Defining Problems　　　　　　　　　　　　　　Setting Goals

INFORMATION GATHERING SKILLS

Observing　　　　Formulating Questions

REMEMBERING SKILLS

Encoding　　　　Recalling

ORGANIZING SKILLS

Comparing　　Classifying　　Ordering　　Representing

ANALYZING SKILLS

Identifying Attributes　　　　　　Identifying Relationships
and Components　　　　　　　　　and Patterns

Identifying Main Ideas　　　　　　Identifying Errors

GENERATING SKILLS

Inferring　　Predicting　　Elaborating

INTEGRATING SKILLS

Summarizing　　　　Restructuring

EVALUATING SKILLS

Establishing Criteria　　Verifying

Thinking processes often begin with an unresolved problem, a need, or an indeterminate situation. We focus to define the problem or situation and to set goals. We gather information by observing and formulating questions or activate prior knowledge by remembering. We may deliberately encode newly acquired information to ensure that it is accessible when needed.

At certain points in the thinking process, we may need to organize information by comparing, classifying, or ordering, or by representing the information in a different form. We analyze the data, checking for accuracy and identifying the main idea, attributes and components, and relationships and patterns. We may also generate additional ideas by inferring, predicting, and elaborating. Occasionally we connect and combine information, summarizing and restructuring what has been generated. Eventually we arrive at a solution, construct new meaning, or create a product. To evaluate, we establish criteria and verify aspects of the proposed solution or product.

Because this general pattern of skills is characteristic of descriptions of most thinking processes, it can be helpful for designing units of instruction. Students can be guided through the entire process to help them gain experience with each phase. Teachers should recognize, though, that the various skills are used at many different points in any thinking process. For example, we may verify the accuracy of information during analysis but use the skill of verifying again during evaluation. Making a prediction may reveal the need to gather additional information. And we will probably compare information at several points in the process.

The teacher's challenge is to see opportunities for using thinking processes to enhance student learning in any content area, teaching the component thinking skills as necessary. The next chapter identifies some of these core thinking skills and suggests strategies for teaching them.

5. Core Thinking Skills

As noted in Chapter 4, we describe cognitive processes as complex opera-tions that usually require substantial amounts of time and effort as well as the orchestration of numerous skills. Unfortunately, the distinction between a process and a skill is necessarily fuzzy. The difficulty arises partly because the way people use skills depends on the process and content area in which the skill is used. For example, summarizing may simply require finding a main idea that is stated explicitly. At other times, summarizing may involve a highly complex combina-tion of skills for selecting and sequencing information from a dense verbal and graphic text. Moreover, summarizing may involve different knowledge and proce-dures depending on whether one is summarizing a chapter in a science text or the plot of a novel.

Problems of definition are compounded by the fact that an individual skill may build on other skills. For instance, making an inference requires recalling, comparing, and identifying relationships. In effect, a thinking skill can be viewed as a microprocess. Although such ambiguities abound, we felt obligated to make choices and elaborate on them, giving the appearance of certainty where explora-tion and tentativeness would perhaps be more appropriate.

Our sense is that core thinking skills are those essential to the functioning of the other dimensions. They may be used in the service of metacognition, the cognitive processes, or critical and creative thinking; they are means to particular tasks, such as critically analyzing an argument. A good example is the skill of setting goals. When used in the service of metacognition, goal setting is directed largely toward personal, introspective goals—goals related to the use of particular cognitive abilities. In critical thinking, the goal being set may be more external to oneself, such as solving a pollution problem or responding to a television editorial. Further, highly able thinkers often use core thinking skills in clusters, so while our presentation of them in a list may suggest that they are discrete, in actual use the opposite is true.

We believe it may be useful to differentiate between processes and skills largely in terms of whether they are *goals* or *means to achieve a goal.* The processes commonly used in classroom activities are relatively goal-oriented. Students engage various skills in order to conceptualize, to comprehend, to compose something, to solve problems, and so on. They do not summarize for the sake of summarizing, nor do they set goals as ends in themselves. Our view, then, is that processes involve using a sequence of skills intended to achieve a particular outcome.

We used several criteria to select the skills discussed in this chapter. Each is documented in various strands of psychological research or in philosophy as important to learning or thinking. Each appears to be teachable, as established through research studies, field testing, or widespread use in the classroom. Each is valued by educators as important for students to learn. Using these criteria, we have identified 21 thinking skills grouped into 8 categories, as noted in Figure 5.1.

We emphasize that these skills may be used at any point in a thinking process and that the same thinking skill may be used repeatedly. We caution that listing the skills as we have should not be interpreted to support teaching each skill separately. Sometimes that may be appropriate, especially for students having

---

Figure 5.1

Core Thinking Skills

Focusing Skills

1. Defining problems
2. Setting goals

Information Gathering Skills

3. Observing
4. Formulating questions

Remembering Skills

5. Encoding
6. Recalling

Organizing Skills

7. Comparing
8. Classifying
9. Ordering
10. Representing

Analyzing Skills

11. Identifying attributes and components
12. Identifying relationships and patterns
13. Identifying main ideas
14. Identifying errors

Generating Skills

15. Inferring
16. Predicting
17. Elaborating

Integrating Skills

18. Summarizing
19. Restructuring

Evaluating Skills

20. Establishing criteria
21. Verifying

---

difficulties with a particular skill. However, we generally support the current movement among many researchers away from isolated skills instruction, that is, skills instruction in which learning the skill is an end in itself.

This list should not be considered inviolate. It is a working document, a preliminary effort to define skills that appear to be in the repertoire of the model learner, as defined in the light of current research. As such it addresses a practical question that we hear so often: What criteria and principles can schools use to define and integrate the skills we teach?

We believe it is also important to distinguish between *skills* and *strategies*. A skill is a mental activity such as predicting, summarizing, or comparing. A strategy is a particular way of executing a given skill. Using a specific set of summarizing rules or employing a particular procedure for predicting are examples of strategies.

Proficient thinkers have a repertoire of strategies and skills far beyond those given here. Much of the research on thinking derives from efforts to document differences in thinking strategies used by highly proficient and less proficient students, as well as from efforts to teach students to use more effective strategies. A key characteristic of proficient students is their knowledge of procedures and conditions for applying specific strategies for the skills they use. A major thrust of this literature argues that skills instruction in schools and in many thinking skills programs does not provide opportunities for most students to acquire this knowledge. Where it is available, therefore, we will provide information about strategic procedures and conditions, hoping it will be useful to teachers and supervisors.

Focusing Skills

Focusing skills come into play when an individual senses a problem, an issue, or a lack of meaning. Focusing skills enable him or her to attend to selected pieces of information and ignore others. The two focusing skills we chose to include in this framework, defining problems and setting goals, are often used early in a thinking process, but they may also be used at any time during a task to clarify or verify something or to redefine or refocus one's efforts. Focusing skills may also be used at the end of problem solving, comprehending, or other processes as a way of establishing "next steps."

Defining Problems

Definition—Defining problems refers primarily to clarifying situations that are puzzling in some way. This may include asking and answering such questions as:

- What is a statement of the problem?
- Who has the problem?
- What are some examples of it?
- By when must it be solved?
- What makes it a problem? Or, why must it be solved?

These questions help the learner identify the "problem space" or boundaries of the problem as well as clarify its nature (Newell & Simon, 1972).

Giving some attention to defining problems is crucial when the problem is ill-defined or unstructured, such as finding ways to conserve eroding soil or determining the reasons for behaviors of the characters in *Lord of the Flies*; however, the same questions are important even with well-structured problems such as how to finance a car (Frederiksen, 1984). Defining problems is important not only in problem solving but also in many of the other processes, such as scientific inquiry.

Key Concepts and Issues—Once a problem has been "found," most research on problem solving emphasizes the importance of clarifying the situation early in the process, but students tend to ignore this step, perhaps because of the way problem solving is taught (Bransford, Sherwood, Rieser, & Vye, 1986). For example, students are often given problems for practice that are not of real significance to them. A page of story problems that are nothing but computational exercises in sentence form can be solved simply by changing the sentences into computational algorithms. To ask the question "Whose problem is it?" would seem strange and pointless in this situation. Such exercises are appropriate for practicing computation, but they do very little to help students apply mathematics to solve real-world problems.

Indeed, many situations call for "problem finding"—recognizing a problem when there appears to be none. For example, students do not always recognize that their writing cannot be understood by their intended audience. They produce writing that only they can understand (writer-based prose) and express surprise when a reader is confused. As part of writing instruction, teachers need to help students discover that taking the reader's point of view is indeed a real problem and that solving it requires definition and clarification.

Strategies—A general principle for teaching students to define problems is to begin with problems that are clearly structured and then move to more unstructured problems. The problem-defining questions listed above can be used to guide the discussion. A discussion of the national debt—a complex, familiar, unstructured problem—might be preceded by discussion of something simpler and more familiar, such as a personal debt, as noted in Figure 5.2. Such questions can lead students to define a problem more carefully, to change or reshape a problem, or even to reassess whether a situation is a problem in the first place. Equally important, applying these questions to familiar problems helps students link the new information to prior knowledge.

Comments on Classroom Applications—A key issue for most skills in this chapter is whether or not students benefit from isolated skills instruction. Is it useful to teach defining problems as an end in itself? While many thinking skills programs attempt to do that, there is considerable debate among researchers about whether generic skills instruction helps students to solve problems in the content areas.

It is clear that all content areas provide opportunities for students to define and clarify problems. Nevertheless, most students will need to be explicitly taught

---

Figure 5.2

Instruction Using a Familiar Problem to Help Define an Unfamiliar Problem

Teacher	Possible Student Answers
What is the problem?	Alfred owes his friend some money.
Who has the problem?	Alfred has a problem because he does not have the money to pay back his friend. The friend is angry. His friend also has a problem because he needs the borrowed money.
What are some other examples of this kind of problem?	When someone or a business goes bankrupt.
By when must it be solved?	It is not clear how long the friend will tolerate not being paid back, or how long Alfred can tolerate feeling guilty.
Why is it a problem?	Owing money may create a hardship for the lender and bad feelings in the lender and borrower.

---

some problem-defining strategy. Teachers need to strike a balance, teaching the skill in a sufficiently explicit manner but connecting it with subject matter and avoiding overstructuring instruction in ways that foreclose on the students' need to define and clarify problems on their own.

Setting Goals

Definition—In general terms, setting goals involves establishing direction and purpose. More specifically, setting goals is stating the outcomes one expects to attain.

Key Concepts and Issues—Problem defining and clarifying lead naturally to goal setting. In essence, the problem solver says, "Now that I know why this is a problem, what am I going to do about it?" However, goal setting may occur at any time or repeatedly in any given learning situation. We emphasize setting specific goals here because such goals limit the range of alternatives individuals must deal with, making action more purposeful.

A critical issue in American education today is the lack of opportunities for students to set their own goals. This is a problem from several perspectives. The authors of *Becoming a Nation of Readers*, for example, point to a sense of meaninglessness that arises when students engage in endless drill or other activities without having personal goals or even knowing the purpose of what they are doing (Anderson, Hiebert, Scott, & Wilkinson, 1986). Such practices deprive students of opportunities to understand the cause-and-effect relationship between a learning goal and the choice of an effective strategy (Borkowski & Buchel, 1983). Moreover, Brown, Campione, and Day (1981) discuss the merits of what they call informed learning as compared to uninformed or "blind" learning (cf. Anderson & Burlis, 1987). Finally, it is important for students to recognize that experts may experience frustration, clumsiness, and failure at setting appropriate goals and to learn to deal with the consequences of poor goal setting.

Strategies—While student goal setting is widely advocated, in practice it is often assumed that students will make poor choices. Clearly, though, students who are not given opportunities to set goals will remain unskilled in this area.

One strategy for teaching goal setting emerges from programs developed in the business community: (1) set short-term learning goals that encompass units of time as short as a single class period; (2) state the goals overtly in oral or written form; (3) make goals concrete and, if possible, measurable (Tice, 1976).

A second strategy, rooted in mathematics, involves assessing and monitoring the achievement of one's goals. Schoenfeld (1985) discusses the need for setting subgoals when it does not seem possible to achieve certain goals. Schoenfeld also stresses the importance of "debriefing" later on to establish precisely what goals were accomplished, how they were attained, what general principles were involved in the learning, and how the principles can be applied. This strategy can be used to address a broad range of problems in schools and in real life.

A third strategy for helping students set their own goals is K-W-L (Ogle, 1986). *K* stands for establishing what the students *k*now; *W* for what they *w*ant to know (their learning goals); and *L* for reflecting later on what they have *l*earned. In this strategy, goal setting occurs before and after an activity. For example, before reading an expository text on spiders, the students can brainstorm with each other categories of information commonly associated with spiders (e.g., habitat, appearance, and fears about spiders). Then they select which of these topics they would most like to learn something about. The chosen topics become goals for learning. After reading, the students refer back to the original list of topics to verify which learning goals were attained and raise questions for subsequent research.

Comments on Classroom Applications—Teaching students to set their own goals is an arduous task, and no doubt they will make some poor choices. Also, it is often a fine line between allowing students to set reasonable goals and allowing them to pursue their own interests in the extreme—a major problem of implementation of Dewey's philosophy, according to Cremin (1961). However, when practiced explicitly in the classroom with attention to cognitive development, goal setting provides direction, focus, and a means of evaluating individual and group performance. The skill may develop slowly in students, but it is worth nurturing both for its academic utility and its value throughout life.

Information-Gathering Skills

Information-gathering skills are the skills used to bring to consciousness the substance or content to be used for cognitive processing. The data may already be stored, or they may be newly collected. We will discuss two of these skills, observing and formulating questions, in this section and a related skill, recalling, in the following section.

Observing

Definition—Observing involves obtaining information through one or more senses. These senses are typically used to collect new information from the environment; they may or may not be focused on a particular aspect of it.

Key Concepts and Issues—In science, observation is considered the groundwork for presumably more complex operations such as classifying, hypothesizing, or inferring (Tweney, Doherty, & Mynatt, 1981). After determining a hypothesis to test or a problem to solve, an individual begins to take note of specific elements in the environment related to that problem or goal. Observation, then, is focusing perception on some phenomenon or object. As straightforward as this might seem, it has some hidden complexities.

First, we use "perception" here to mean highlighting only some of the information received through the five senses. This implies that an individual "dampens" some sensory information while focusing on other information. Additionally, perception involves making finer and finer distinctions within the type of sensory information that has been highlighted. For example, students make finer visual distinctions as they examine perspective and color in a painting or details of biological structures on a slide (Lindsay & Norman, 1977).

There is much research in science, psychology, and philosophy defining the nature of observation and perception, but very little revealing how students learn to perceive and observe. Therefore, the strategies below come not so much from specific research as from general principles of learning elaborated throughout this book.

Strategies—As with many thinking skills, a major portion of learning how to observe is domain-specific. An important part of learning what to observe about snails derives from various opportunities to observe many snails or specific instruction about what to observe. Accordingly, it is helpful to embed observation activities in content-area instruction. It is also useful to sequence observations from simple to complex or from familiar to unfamiliar, where possible. For example, the teacher might initially inform students about the type of information to be observed selectively. Later, students can determine the important aspects of phenomena to which they attend and describe differences they perceive in specific situations.

Although observation is clearly suited to science, it also applies in other content areas, including music, art, drama, and speech. For instance, students previewing any type of book can observe such things as title, underlining, italics, headings, charts, pictures, graphs, summaries, index, appendices, and table of contents.

Formulating Questions

Definition—Formulating questions involves clarifying issues and meaning through inquiry. Good questions focus attention on important information and are designed to generate new information. When students formulate questions, they are actively involved in learning.

Key Concepts and Issues—Very little research relates directly to teaching students to formulate their own questions. Much of the research on questioning centers on adjunct questions in textbooks, taxonomies of questions, the effects of teacher-generated questions, and efforts to train students to answer questions. While our focus is not directly on most of these areas, it may be helpful to refer the reader to two sets of studies that would influence how we teach students to formulate questions.

First, Andre (1987) discusses several taxonomies of questions that may be useful to consider in teaching students to ask questions about material they have read. Pearson and Johnson (1978), for example, argue that what is important in thinking about questions is understanding the question-and-answer relationship:

1. Some questions are textually explicit; they can be fully answered in the text.

2. Others are textually implicit; they ask about inferences from prior knowledge.

3. Still other questions cannot be answered from the text at all; they require answers based on prior knowledge.

Raphael (1984) and her colleagues improved both comprehension and retention of middle grade students by teaching them to distinguish these various types of questions and answers.

There are several subject-specific taxonomies. Armbruster and her colleagues developed a taxonomy of history questions (Armbruster, Anderson, Bruning, & Meyer, 1984). They also emphasize the importance of conceptualizing questions in relation to the nature of the answer. For example, many questions state an effect and ask about a cause. Sometimes the answer to such questions requires discussing the goals; for example, "Why did the Nez Perce leave Oregon?" Other causal questions require discussing the causes as conditions; for example, "Why did the stock market crash in 1929?"

One of Andre's major points is that question formats and their answers will vary markedly according to the subject matter. Another point he makes is that modeling questions and their answers is critical to teaching students to ask and answer questions effectively. Thus, teachers interested in teaching students to formulate questions may find subject specific taxonomies useful.

Strategies—Despite the dearth of research on student questioning, it is important for students to learn and to practice this skill. Four strategies relate directly to teaching students to formulate their own questions. First, study-skills strategies such as SQ3R (*Survey, Question, Read, Recite, Review*) ask the student to convert titles, headings, and subheadings into questions and then to read to answer the questions (Robinson, 1961; see also Tierney, Readence, & Dishner, 1985). Other study strategies focus on converting a main-idea sentence into a question. This procedure has support from research on particular study-skills strategies and from studies comparing reading without a specific purpose to reading for the purpose of answering a question. However, this literature does little to demonstrate that students internalize such strategies for long-term use.

Second, Ogle's (1986) *K-W-L Strategy*, described in the earlier discussion of goal setting, begins with teacher-generated questions but seeks to guide students in learning to ask questions themselves.

Third, the use of *frames* holds promise for helping students generate questions that integrate information and are fundamental to understanding. The key questions suggested for defining a problem are an example of a frame, in this case a *generic* frame because the questions can be applied to problems in many different subject areas. *Content-specific* frames are more difficult to generate and require considerable subject area expertise, so students are not usually asked to generate such frames, though they may learn to use frame questions generated by the teacher to guide their reflection and study. In research studies involving frames, the researcher typically provides frame questions and then teaches students to use generic questions to generate content-specific questions. Singer and Donlan (1982), for example, taught students to apply generic questions (e.g., "What is the character's goal?") to complex short stories. Their study is one of the few that have demonstrated spontaneous question formulation. (Other examples of generic frame questions may be found in Chapter 2.)

Fourth, Palincsar and Brown (1984) have incorporated student questioning in their research on *reciprocal teaching*. This strategy, explained in Chapter 4, makes self-questioning public. Students take turns being "the teacher," asking each other questions about matters that puzzle them or about points that seem important to them. Palincsar and her colleagues have demonstrated that even young children can be taught to generate critical questions spontaneously and with some degree of transfer to new materials.

Comments on Classroom Applications—Questioning seems to be difficult, especially for younger and lower achieving students. Teachers need to model self-questioning for students and guide them until they are comfortable asking themselves questions and able to ask useful and penetrating questions. A useful approach is to have students work in pairs or small groups, asking each other questions as an intermediate step to independent self-questioning.

Although the above strategies have been used mostly when students are reading various kinds of text materials, self-questioning should apply to many types of learning activities. For example, before beginning a writing assignment, students can ask themselves what they know about a topic and what they need to find out. Self-questions can also relate to audience; for example, "Will the people who read what I write understand what I'm saying, or do I need to give more background or more detail?" In mathematics, self-questioning seems especially important for problem solving. Questions might focus on plausible estimates of solutions, choice of solution routes, and evaluation of the answer obtained.

Formulating questions also applies, of course, to questioning others. This is particularly important in group discussions, where students ask each other to justify, clarify, and add information.

Remembering Skills

Remembering skills are activities or strategies that people consciously engage in to store information in long-term memory and to retrieve it. Many educators do not consider strategies such as mnemonics and rehearsal as thinking because they associate them with rote memory, but recent research defines remembering as a thinking activity. The greater the extent of thinking about something, the more likely it is that it will be remembered (Craik & Tulving, 1974; Jenkins, 1975). Indeed, most of the thinking skills in this chapter have been found to improve retention.

Encoding

Definition—Technically, encoding is the process of linking bits of information to each other for storage in long-term memory. In practice, however, similar strategies are also used to systematically retrieve the information, so the line between encoding and retrieval is fuzzy. Two encoding and retrieval strategies are rehearsal and mnemonics.

Strategies: Rehearsal—Rehearsal establishes simple associations or conceptual links among the items learned. That is, the learner links bits of information together by simply repeating the associations or conceptual linkages over and over again. Mnemonics link bits of information to each other and to prior knowledge through visual or semantic connections. Since these traditional encoding techniques are best defined by example, we present the strategies section before discussing the key concepts and issues.

Two rehearsal strategies are especially useful for remembering information in school. In *verbatim rehearsal*, the student repeats the information to be remembered, either overtly or covertly, using words or mental pictures. For example, various formulas for chemistry might be committed to memory in this way. Such rehearsal is most appropriate when students need to recall large bodies of information. In *generative rehearsal*, students use what they already know to select portions of information from a text—perhaps to copy, underline, or highlight—and then rehearse. For instance, they might highlight the attributes that distinguish the benefits from the side effects of various vitamin groups or medicines and repeat those attributes again and again, checking their recall against the list from time to time. (For a thorough treatment of rehearsal strategies, see Weinstein & Mayer, 1986.)

Strategies: Mnemonics—While numerous mnemonics have been documented in the literature, the *keyword method* seems particularly useful for school learning tasks. In this mnemonic strategy, the student finds a familiar "word" (the keyword) within an unfamiliar word or concept and relates it to the meaning of the new word or concept. Suppose the student had to learn the definition of *cataplexy*, which means a state of muscle rigidity. Rather than just rehearsing its definition, the student might identify the familiar word "cat" with the new word and visualize a cat in a rigid muscle state, thereby relating part of the word ("cat") to its meaning. Other mnemonics such as familiar location, the "one-is-a-bun" technique, and the keyword-pegword are essentially variations of this basic method, and all these mnemonics are usually used in conjunction with rehearsal.

Mnemonics are most useful for information that has little logical order, such as foreign words and their English equivalents. Successful application of the keyword method and its variations include learning new foreign words, vocabulary, inventors and their inventions, and state capitals—in short, whenever an association between two items must be learned. However, like rehearsal, mnemonics must be described as a memory aid that does not yield deep understanding. (For further discussion of mnemonics, see Klausmeier, 1985; Pressley & Levin, 1983.)

Key Concepts and Issues—An interesting feature of rehearsal and some mnemonics is that they permit self-testing. That is, students identify relatively easily what they do and do not recall. Low-achieving students and young children tend not to engage in rehearsal or to use mnemonics spontaneously. Even youngsters as old as 8 or 9 may not rehearse unless instructed to do so, but after age 10 or 11, rehearsal seems to be a part of their repertoire of remembering strategies. However, experience in using mnemonics successfully may provide dramatic evidence to both types of students that they can improve their learning capability (see Rohwer, 1971).

Recalling

Definition—The remembering strategies discussed so far are conscious, systematic efforts to store information for easy retrieval. These encoding strategies are initiated at the time of encoding and used again during retrieval. In contrast, recalling strategies are strategies generally unplanned and unsystematic and may be initiated, consciously or unconsciously, at any time during the learning process. Two recalling strategies will be discussed in this section: activating prior knowledge and retrieval strategies.

Strategies: Activating Prior Knowledge—Activating prior knowledge means thinking about something that has already been learned in school or from personal experience. It is clear that people raise prior knowledge for many different purposes, such as to make an inference or evaluate a statement according to a known standard.

For example, authors often do not directly state character traits. Students will need to activate prior knowledge, then, as they read the following:

Maria's thoughts were interrupted by the giggling of three girls as they bounded into the room. The word "hi" almost formed on her lips. But when the girls only nodded and then rushed over to Diane, her greeting remained unspoken (from "Maria's Big Experiment," by Shirlee P. Newman).

To understand this passage, students must use what they know about how people behave in this kind of social situation, using both recall and inference. One student might infer, based on past experience, that Maria is shy; another, that she is unfriendly. Both inferences are appropriate, given the limited information at this point in the story and each student's prior knowledge.

Obviously, differences in prior knowledge are among the most significant differences among human beings. Because of this, an abundance of teaching strategies exists for activating prior knowledge—for example, surveying or skimming the features of a problem, mentally reviewing what is known, or summarizing previous learnings. However, since most of these activities are embedded in complex study-skill strategies, there is little data on them as specific strategies.

Strategies: Retrieval—Retrieval strategies are techniques for recalling previously stored items of information when initial efforts to recall have failed. Retrieval strategies are based largely on the finding that people encode many attributes of the bits of information they process. These extra linkages can be used to "jog one's memory" and increase recall of specific information. Underwood (1969) calls these linkages "attributes of memory." For example:

- *Temporal*—Recalling the time something was learned (e.g., recall of a day, year, or occasion)
- *Spatial*—Recalling the place where something was learned (e.g., school, library)
- *Mode of presentation*—Recalling the modality in which information was given (e.g., visual, oral)

Some attributes are more helpful than others in recalling particular information. For example, going through the letters of the alphabet might help to recall a person's name but would be unlikely to help recall an event. Student-constructed graphics seem to focus attention on certain attributes, especially the visual, and can also aid recall.

Other retrieval strategies are aimed at making connections explicit *after* learning. Even college students may fail to use information they are given or knowledge they already have. Their knowledge is *inert*; that is, they do not associate or link that bit of information to the problem at hand (Bransford et al., 1986). Various strategies exist for dealing with this problem, such as asking students to discuss particular applications of concepts or principles.

Comments on Classroom Applications—Mnemonics can dramatically increase memory for specific information, but they must be taught explicitly, and they are highly domain-specific. We emphasize that mnemonics typically do not transfer to other types of information, at least not initially (Bransford et al., 1986). It may be necessary to apply a given mnemonic to many different learning contexts before students can incorporate the strategy into their repertoire and apply it spontaneously to new situations.

Rehearsal strategies may be more generally applicable because they encourage students to overlearn and self-test. Students might be encouraged to use particular retrieval strategies such as using attributes to jog their memory, especially in test situations. However, these recalling strategies add little to understanding, and they are difficult for children to learn. To improve understanding, we must turn to such skills as activating prior knowledge and to meaning-based retrieval strategies that have students devise applications or draw inferences. These more productive strategies are appropriate for all ages and ability groups.

Organizing Skills

Organizing skills are used to arrange information so it can be understood or presented more effectively. Through these skills, we impose structure on information and experience by matching similarities, noting differences, or indicating sequences. For example, students typically begin preparing a research paper by collecting relatively unorganized information from many sources. To complete the task successfully, they must organize the information. We will discuss four organizing skills: comparing, classifying, ordering, and representing.

Comparing

Definition—Comparing means identifying similarities and differences between or among entities. Finding similarities helps individuals organize both new and known information by establishing how things might be related (e.g., noting that computer A has a larger memory than computer B). Though finding differences is, more precisely, contrasting, we have chosen to consider both noting likenesses and noting differences as aspects of the skill of comparing.

Key Concepts and Issues—Comparing seems necessary for effective interaction with the environment. According to Feuerstein, this skill involves a number of cognitive operations: precision, discrimination, and judgment of similarities and differences (i.e., contrasting). Articulating the similarities and differences appears to be a natural final step in comparison (Feuerstein, Rand, Hoffman, & Miller, 1980).

Comparing may be simple or complex, depending on the particular task and the knowledge and skill of the individual making the comparison (Mandler, 1983). A young child might easily compare two dogs according to specified qualities of size and color and yet be unsuccessful in stating a comparison of a dog and a cow, because the latter requires verbalizing the superordinate (and relatively abstract) category animals.

Strategies—Stahl (1985) developed a comparing strategy involving four steps. The individual (1) identifies salient attributes to be compared, (2) rearranges them so that each attribute is adjacent, and (3) notes whether the attributes are the same or different. The results of these three steps are illustrated in a task involving comparison of two dinosaurs:

Dinosaur A	Dinosaur B	
60 feet long	50 feet long	*different*
30 tons	30 tons	*same*
6-toed feet	6-toed feet	*same*
round feet	almost-square feet	*different*

In the final step, (4) the learner states the similarities and differences as precisely as possible: "Both dinosaurs A and B weigh the same and have feet with six toes. But dinosaur A, which is 60 feet long, is 10 feet longer than dinosaur B. Their feet are also shaped differently. Dinosaur A has round feet; dinosaur B has almost-square feet."

Matrix outlining is a strategy that demonstrates the close connection between comparing and articulating comparisons (Jones, Amiran, & Katims, 1985). Students place information in two-dimensional matrices, such as the one for colonial governments in Figure 5.3. Students specify attribute categories (the column headings) and then use the matrix to create a summative statement involving attribute categories, details from the cells, and row generalizations. Further analytical statements can be made by answering questions that require applying and integrating information from the matrix, such as the puzzles in Figure 5.4. This method can increase students' long-term retention and improve their writing of comparison and contrast summaries where appropriate.

In Raphael and Kirschner's (1985) approach, students learn three organizational strategies for doing comparative summaries: whole/whole (describing all of one item first, then all of the second), part/part (comparing part of one item, then part of the other), and mixed. Both comprehension and comparative summary writing improve with this method, which makes use of "frame" questions and a matrix to integrate information from more than one text.

Comments on Classroom Applications—Making single comparisons is fairly easy. Making multiple comparisons involving many points of comparison is a difficult skill that involves precise attention to several points being compared, and to the alignment of information for each comparison. Thus, multiple comparisons may require sustained instruction with gradually decreasing teacher direction. Teachers should also stress the importance of articulating the comparisons, because formulating such statements in their own words helps students develop genuine understanding and consolidate the information.

All content areas invite comparisons. In literature, students can find similarities between or among stories, poems, novels, and their own experiences. In social studies, students can compare and contrast major movements. For example, migrations such as Europeans to America, the westward movement, and the black movement from the South to the North furnish rich comparisons that work well in both cooperative and individual learning situations. In science, students can construct matrices to compare and contrast any and all of the flora and fauna presented in zoological and biological phyla as well as the comparative information in earth science textbooks.

Classifying

Definition—Classifying (also called categorizing) is grouping items into categories (e.g., types of rocks) on the basis of their attributes (e.g., hardness).

Key Concepts and Issues—Classifying is an essential skill because the world consists of an infinite number of stimuli (Mervis, 1980). People make unfamiliar

Figure 5.3

Model Matrix and Summary of Levels of Colonial Government

Instructions

- READ the political essay, part 1.
- USE the information from the essay to FILL IN the government charts. The first column has been done for you.
- REMEMBER, if some of the information is only "partly there" or "not there," you should try to figure out or infer the answer.
- The information from this activity will be used in Lesson 3.

Colonial Government

Level 1

Who Governs?	What Powers Do They Have?	How Do They Get Their Powers?
governor	(can veto laws)	(from the colony's owner)
council	(pass laws for the entire colony)	(from the colony's owner)
assembly or legislature	(pass laws for the entire colony)	(elected by the colonists)

Level 2

Who Governs?	What Powers Do They Have?	How Do They Get Their Powers?
people at town meetings	(vote for government officials; make decisions on local problems)	Not there; figure out (infer) the answer if you can. (by being residents of the town)
justices of the peace	(make decisions that affect small areas of a colony)	(appointed by the governor)

Instructions

- USE the government charts on SN 72-73 to WRITE a two-paragraph summary of colonial government, one paragraph for each chart. The questions are included to help you organize your summary.
- USE cue words to help write your summary and be sure to USE complete sentences in your summary.

Title: Colonial Government in the English Colonies

Topic Sentence:

How many levels of colonial government were there in the English colonies?

Paragraph One

(There were two levels of colonial government in the English colonies.)

Level 1

Who Governs?

Who governed in the first level of colonial government?

(The governor, council, and assembly ruled in the first level.)

What Powers Do They Have?

What powers did the first level of colonial government have?

(In the first level of colonial government, the council and assembly passed laws for the entire colony, but the governor could veto these laws.)

How Do They Get Their Powers?

How did government officials in the first level of colonial government get their powers?

(The governor and council got their powers from the colony's owner, while the assembly or legislature was elected by the colonists.)

Figure 5.4

Application Activity for Classification Matrix

Homework — Colonial Government Puzzles

Instructions — USE the government chart and the Glossary Matrix page for <u>colonial government</u> to IDENTIFY which government office or power is being described in the following situations:

Situation One
You live in the colony of Massachusetts. You and your neighbor have a dispute about the boundary between your lands. Whom would you go to for help in settling this dispute and why? (You would go to town officials or to a town meeting, because in the New England colonies they made decisions about local problems.)

Situation Two
You live in the colony of Virginia and decide to run for elected office. You must get the votes of the majority of people to get elected. If elected to this position, you and other elected officials will have the power to pass laws for the entire colony of Virginia. What position are you running for and how do you know? (The Assembly; these officials are elected by the colonists and pass laws for the entire colony.)

Copyright © 1986b, Board of Education, City of Chicago, and Center for the Study of Reading, University of Illinois, Urbana-Champaign, p. 140. Reprinted with permission.

---

things familiar through classification because it links the new information to known categories. Also, generalizing about an object based on its category gives more information than just perceiving it. Classifying greatly facilitates comprehension and retention of information. In fact, Nickerson, Perkins, and Smith (1985) affirm that the ability to form conceptual categories is so basic to human cognition that it can be considered a necessary condition of thinking.

To classify, students must identify the features or attributes of entities, forming groups based on common features. Many instructional programs include classifying activities, ranging from relatively simple (such as classifying emotions into the categories "pleasant" and "unpleasant") to highly complicated such as the example in Figure 5.5 from Feuerstein's *Instrumental Enrichment*. In this exercise, the students must draw two pictures that differ from the model on the left in ways specified by the circled words. Thus, picture 1 must differ from the shaded triangle in size and form.

This classifying exercise is sophisticated in two ways. First, in these and similar exercises, students learn the range of attribute categories such as size and form along which items may vary. Second, the reasoning processes that students must go through to complete the exercise on the bottom row are highly complex, as indicated by the accompanying text (Feuerstein, Rand, Hoffman, & Miller, 1980).

Comments on Classroom Applications—Athough school-aged children typically can classify many items, they usually do not consciously use categories to remember information. There is some evidence that very young children and low-achieving students typically do not use categories unless instructed to do so or unless given category labels (e.g., Moeley, 1977). Furthermore, salient catego-

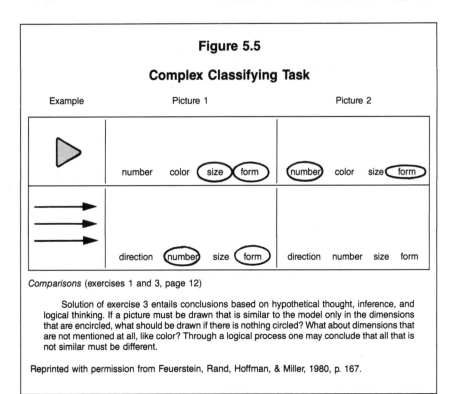

Figure 5.5

Complex Classifying Task

Comparisons (exercises 1 and 3, page 12)

Solution of exercise 3 entails conclusions based on hypothetical thought, inference, and logical thinking. If a picture must be drawn that is similar to the model only in the dimensions that are encircled, what should be drawn if there is nothing circled? What about dimensions that are not mentioned at all, like color? Through a logical process one may conclude that all that is not similar must be different.

Reprinted with permission from Feuerstein, Rand, Hoffman, & Miller, 1980, p. 167.

ries may differ according to culture. To encourage younger and low-achieving students to use classifying, it may be necessary to provide them with explicit instruction, extended practice, and feedback (see Jones, Amiran, & Katims, 1985).

In most situations, students should learn classifying not as an independent skill but as an aid to organizing content-related information. Examples of types of language arts content that can be classified in various ways are themes, plot structures, and characters. Teachers might begin by specifying a way to classify, but eventually students should form categories based on their own criteria. Even young children can do this, if encouraged.

For example, as part of a unit on plants, the teacher might put various plants in paper bags and ask students to describe their characteristics—first by touching and smelling them, then by looking at them, thereby establishing the salient attributes through various senses. Students in a health class might classify foods as healthy or unhealthy according to the amount of salt, sugar, and fat in the foods.

Ordering

Definition—Ordering is sequencing or ordering entities according to a given criterion. It is closely related to classifying and might even be considered a special case of that skill. Putting things into order provides logical organization that aids comprehension and recall. Examples include ordering a sequence of events in a historical narrative, such as constructing a biography or autobiography; generating a timeline (e.g., major events in the life of Lincoln, or events leading to the Civil War); and arranging three or more items in story problems or games according to height, weight, color and so on.

Key Concepts and Issues—Ordering is often surprisingly difficult for students, partly because textbooks and teachers are not always clear about the exact order in which things actually happened and about whether events and phenomena are causally related. Problems involving ordering may be especially difficult if they require integrating items of information from different sources.

Piaget's conservation studies indicate that young children sometimes do not order information in accord with adult logic. When asked to put a set of sticks that are all different lengths in order from the largest to the smallest, children may not be able to do the task at all, or they may group only three sticks from large to small, then another three from large to small, and so on, rather than putting the whole set in order. Piaget concluded that children do not usually master ordering until the concrete operational stage, usually about age 7 or 8, or even later (Piaget & Szeminska, 1941).

Strategies—There is little research on ordering strategies that can be used to help students learn, possibly because difficulties in ordering are usually defined as difficulties in representation, or because ordering is treated as comparing or classifying. We recommend teaching students to look for attributes and to compare attributes as a means to develop readiness for ordering.

Comments on Classroom Applications—Ordering can be a very useful content-related activity. For example, in studying African cultures, students might discuss cultural values and principles by ranking occupations according to how important they are in our society and then re-ranking them after reading about an African community. Class discussion could focus on analysis of students' reasons for their rankings before and after studying the other culture.

Teachers can help students understand the sequence of events by asking students to make time lines and flow charts. Ordering can be extended beyond simple ranking by using the concept of the continuum. Sometimes a classification scheme may involve changes in two or more dimensions at once, as when minerals are ordered according to both hardness and transparency.

Representing

Definition—When representing information, the learner changes its form to show how critical elements are related. Representations take many forms, the main ones being visual, verbal, and symbolic. They may be internal (as in a mental picture) or external (as in a drawing). Representing may be simple, as in using a symbol for a particular item or changing from decimals to fractions. However, representing can also be complex, such as constructing a matrix or other graphic display for prose information. A key characteristic of complex representation is that the learner makes the information more meaningful and cohesive by constructing linkages.

We identify representing as an analyzing skill because, although it may involve classifying or ordering, it goes beyond these skills. The organizing skills, as we have defined them, primarily involve perceptual discrimination. We suggest that representation is a special case of analyzing patterns and relationships. That is, to represent information, the learner identifies the parts and conceptualizes them in a new form, usually for a particular purpose, and is often led to new understandings and capabilities as a consequence of this reformulation. For example, when students correctly represent a mathematics problem, they can usually solve it correctly, whereas they would not have been able to do so without the representation. Presumably some insight was added that was not present without the representation—an insight that is probably analogous to the insight gained from discovering a pattern or a relationship. Similarly, when students represent things in graphic outlines, they are often led to insights about the information beyond the mere organization of its parts. In fact, in its extreme form, representing may even lead to restructuring.

Key Concepts and Issues—Research on representation focuses on both internal and external representation. One aspect of *internal representation* is the internal knowledge structures (called *schemata*) that humans acquire and store in memory. Because all humans have schemata and seem to acquire many of them without conscious effort, there is some debate whether this aspect of internal representation can be considered a skill at all. In Chapter 6 we discuss schemata at greater length. Here we will only note that internal representations can be activated for many purposes, among them the generation of external representations (e.g., students prepare a flow chart depicting steps in acquiring a driver's license). External representation, then, may be derived from internal representations or created from new information. Examples are models, drawings, blueprints, maps, hierarchical outlines, and concrete objects.

Strategies—Creation of external representations can be enhanced through instruction. For example, Bransford, Sherwood, and Hasselbring (in press) have taught low achievers how to represent math problems using the film *Raiders of the Lost Ark*. One problem was to estimate how far Indiana Jones had to swim to reach a boat in the middle of a river. Students learned to represent the problem in terms of the number of "lengths" of Indiana's body. Similarly, Feuerstein taught students to represent information in comparing and understanding directions on a map (Feuerstein et al., 1980). They represented objects on a map both in relation to each other and to the four compass directions.

Another strategy for the skill of representing is the use of graphic organizers and outlines. Graphics may lead students to generate new meaning in several important ways:

1. They permit, and often encourage, nonlinear thinking.
2. They can be used to synthesize complex information from diverse sources efficiently, helping students to identify patterns and relationships that are otherwise difficult to apprehend.
3. They help the user to generate information about the structure and

relationships among parts that may not have been clear in the original, non-graphic information.

How can students be taught to construct graphic representations? First, they can identify the critical aspects or components of something, using analytic and organizing skills. Then they ask themselves how the aspects are related and try to show these relationships in some visual array. Different graphic structures may be used to represent different types of information. This is an important principle in creating or selecting a graphic display. Figures 5.6, 5.7, and 5.8 illustrate three different graphic structures—hierarchies, chains, and webs or spiders—each representing different kinds of information. Notice that categorical information is best represented in the hierarchy, whereas a sequence of events is shown as links in a chain or a series of boxes. The web, or spider map, seems best for representing a major idea, theme, or concept. The central concept is in the main node, with minor or supporting ideas emanating from the node. Details can be added on lines connecting to the spokes (see Holley & Dansereau, 1984; Jones, Tinzmann, Friedman, & Walker, 1987; Van Patten, Chao, & Reigeluth, 1986).

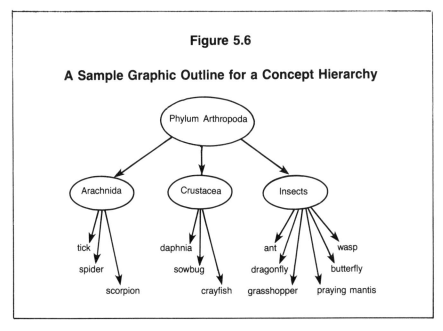

Figure 5.6

A Sample Graphic Outline for a Concept Hierarchy

Representation is also an important skill in mathematics. Primary teachers have long recognized the usefulness of having children represent mathematical concepts with Cuisenaire rods or other similar concrete materials to learn computation and regrouping. Moreover, changing the form but not the value of the mathematical expression is constantly used in mathematics. Numbers can be represented in limitless ways, some more useful than others (e.g., $4 = 2 + 2 = 11 - 7 = 8 \times \frac{1}{2}$).

Figure 5.7

Event Frame with an Example Chain of Events

(Frame)   **(Example)**

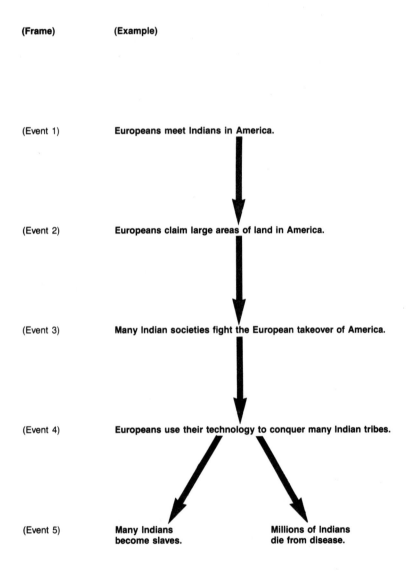

(Event 1)   Europeans meet Indians in America.

(Event 2)   Europeans claim large areas of land in America.

(Event 3)   Many Indian societies fight the European takeover of America.

(Event 4)   Europeans use their technology to conquer many Indian tribes.

(Event 5)   **Many Indians**   **Millions of Indians**
                   become slaves.   **die from disease.**

Figure 5.8

Spider Map

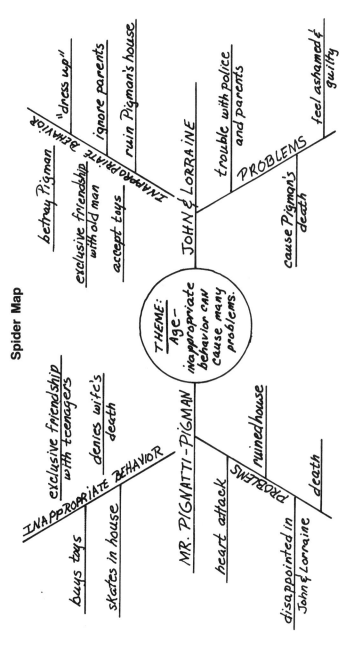

Reprinted with permission from Teaching Thinking Skills: English/Language Arts, p. 64, published by the National Education Association, 1987.

Representation can also be an important step in problem solving. Problem-solving research indicates that students often skip this step, focusing instead on so-called keywords and phrases (e.g., "how many more . . . " "how many all together . . ."), substituting the numbers in the problem statement and then computing. This strategy works at times with simple problems but not with problems that contain irrelevant information (as in Lester, 1985).

A better strategy is to represent the problem in real-world terms to understand its meaning before setting up a computation. For example, many adults set up an algebraic equation with the problem shown below:

Problem: Elsie brought home her paycheck. 1/3 of it went to rent. 1/4 of what remained went for food. 5/6 of the money that was then left went to pay the other bills, leaving her with $100. What was the amount of her paycheck?

Although an equation is not an incorrect strategy, a better one was devised by a remedial math student in the form of the representation shown in Figure 5.9.

Figure 5.9

Representation

RENT	RENT	FOOD	FOOD	$100	OTHER BILLS
RENT	RENT	OTHER BILLS	OTHER BILLS	OTHER BILLS	OTHER BILLS

(12 boxes: 4 for RENT, 2 for FOOD, 5 for OTHER BILLS, 1 for $100; 100 × 12 = $1,200 total)

Reprinted with permission from Simon, 1985, p. 108.

Comments on Classroom Applications—Representation works especially well when attention is given to meaning—that is, to understanding how the parts of something are related. Even young children seem capable of representing if their attention is directed to understanding of fundamental structures, such as story grammar elements (Stein & Glenn, 1979). Thus, teachers may need to focus on important elements of content early in instruction. Eventually, students may be guided to develop their own meaningful representations. Representation may be a crucial component of problem-solving instruction, a current concern of mathematics educators and researchers. Similarly, representation of text structures can positively affect understanding of concepts in the various content areas.

Analyzing Skills

Analyzing skills are used to clarify existing information by examining parts and relationships. Through analysis, we identify and distinguish components, attributes, claims, assumptions, or reasons. The function of analysis is to "look inside" ideas; it is at the core of critical thinking as defined by philosophers. Three analyzing skills will be described below—identifying attributes and components, identifying relationships and patterns, and identifying main ideas.

Identifying Attributes and Components

Definition—As an analyzing skill, identifying attributes and components requires an individual to recognize and then articulate the parts that together constitute a whole. Analyzing attributes and components should help students focus on the details and the structure of objects, ideas, designs, and so on.

Key Concepts and Issues—Philosophy focuses heavily on identifying the components of arguments as an initial step for evaluating them. (See section below on Evaluating.) The components of a simple argument can be expressed in terms of premises and a conclusion. Figure 5.10 shows the thinking process for analyzing arguments developed by Friedman (Jones, Tinzmann, Friedman, & Walker, 1987). This process can be used to analyze arguments in social studies, biology, health, or any content area involving opinions or a particular point of view such as an argument supporting vegetarianism. (The same process model can, of course, be used to generate the various parts of an argument.)

Identifying attributes and components is also central to concept formation (see Chapter 4). Attributes and components refer to types of information usually associated with certain concepts—for example, attributes of baroque music. Research on concept attainment suggests that directing students' attention to important attributes of examples and nonexamples promotes learning of well-structured concepts.

Comments on Classroom Applications—In social studies, students can identify the elements of arguments in persuasive essays or historical documents. In home economics or finance courses, they can develop a budget by writing down all the categories of essential information, such as rent or house payments and utilities.

Identifying Relationships and Patterns

Definition—As we have seen, when students identify attributes and components, they make distinctions among elements that constitute a whole; when identifying patterns and relationships, they articulate the interrelationships among these components. The relationships may be, for example, causal, hierarchical, temporal, spatial, correlational, or metaphorical.

Key Concepts and Issues—The ability to identify patterns and relationships depends heavily on knowledge of the content, according to Bransford, Sherwood, Rieser, and Vye (1986). In a famous study by de Groot (1965), chess experts were compared with ordinary players on ability to reproduce

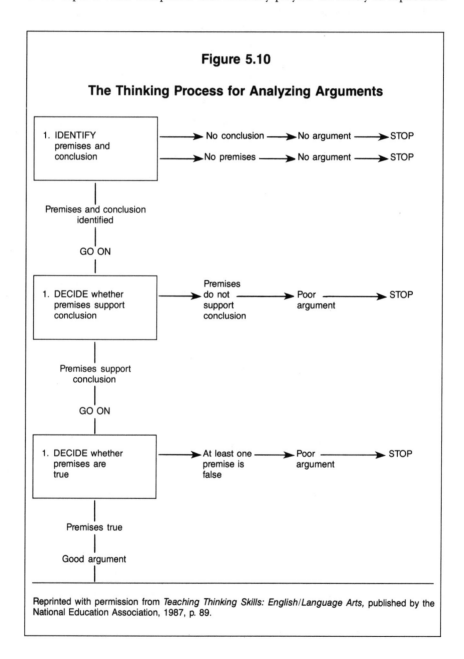

Figure 5.10

The Thinking Process for Analyzing Arguments

Reprinted with permission from *Teaching Thinking Skills: English/Language Arts*, published by the National Education Association, 1987, p. 89.

the positions of pieces on a chessboard after viewing them in midgame position for 5 to 10 seconds. The experts correctly reproduced the positions of 20 to 25 pieces almost without error, while ordinary players placed only about a half dozen pieces correctly. When the experiment was repeated with the pieces randomly arranged, however, only about 6 pieces were correctly placed by both groups. The experts had learned to recognize at a glance meaningful patterns or chunks of pieces on the board and to use such patterns to process information about the game.

Pattern recognition has also been linked to expertise in other games and in medical diagnosis. Good readers recognize letters and patterns that enable them to figure out words they have never seen before. Thus, the ability to recognize patterns and relationships seems to be related to expertise in a variety of domains.

There have been many attempts to identify important types of relationships between ideas (e.g., Kintsch & Van Dijk, 1978; Meyer, 1982). Marzano and Dole (1985) have classified many of the relationships in this literature into five basic categories useful for classroom instruction: time, causality, addition, contrast, and reference. These categories are presented in Figure 5.11 with their subtypes and linguistic cues. Teachers can use this list to help make students aware of the linguistic cues for the various types of relationships that are used in textbooks and in student writing to signal relationships. The ability to recognize and use signal words and phrases is important for understanding temporal sequences, cause-effect relations, and so on.

Strategies—Several relational strategies have been documented by researchers to help students analyze the relationships, among ideas in expository prose and student writing (see Holley & Dansereau, 1984). Essentially, students are asked to identify component parts of a message or text as reflecting specific types of relationships, such as equality, inequality, concept/example, cause/effect, and so on. However, these systems have been developed as a part of strategies for representing text, and the effects of this type of analysis by itself are not well documented (see section on Representing). Moreover, the relational strategies are often cumbersome to learn, and it is not clear that students would use them systematically without sustained instructional support.

Other strategies for learning and teaching patterns and relationships vary according to content areas. For instance, Strong (1986) is among the English educators who place signal words in the context of sentence-combining instruction—a useful alternative to teaching abstract definitions (as in parts of speech) that focus ineffectively on knowledge *about* rather than *use of* connectives.

Relationships and patterns are common in mathematics as well. For example, the teacher can guide students to discover the distributive principle in multiplication by working several problems that involve that principle, as noted in Figure 5.12.

Figure 5.11

Linguistic Signals of Relationship Between Ideas

Time

1. Subsequent Action:
afterwards, next, since, then, after that, later, in the end, shortly, subsequently, so far, as yet, before, until, finally

2. Prior Action:
after, earlier, initially, in the beginning, originally, at first, previously, beforehand, formerly, before that, before now, until then, up to now, by now, by then

3. Concurrent Action:
simultaneously, while, meanwhile, meantime, at this point, at the same time

4. Ordered Action:
first, second, secondly . . ., for a start, to begin with, next, then, finally

Cause

1. Direct cause:
by

2. Result:
consequently, hence, now, so, therefore, thus, as a consequence, for all that, as a result, whereupon, therefore, accordingly, hence, the result was, this is the reason why

3. Reason:
because, because of, in that, so that, since, so on account of, for the fact that

4. Inference:
else, otherwise, in that case, then

5. Condition:
now that, providing that, supposing that, considering that, granted that, admitting that, assuming that, presuming that, seeing that, unless . . . then, as long as, in so far as, if, where . . . there, when . . . then, no sooner . . .

Addition

1. Equality:
and, moreover, equally, too, besides, furthermore, what is more, likewise, similarly, as well, in addition, besides, at the same time

2. Restatement:
indeed, actually, in actual fact, in fact, namely, that is, that is to say, another way of saying this

3. Example: (Simple and Ordered)
for example, first, second, secondly, third . . . one, two, three . . . for a start, to begin with, next, then, finally, last, last but not least, for one thing, for another thing, another example would be

4. Summation:
altogether, over all, then, thus, in all, therefore, all in all, in conclusion, in sum, in a word, in brief, briefly, in short, to sum up, to summarize

Contrast

1. Antithesis:
but, yet, or rather, what is better, what is worse, contrariwise, conversely, oppositely, on the contrary, else, otherwise, on the other hand

2. Alternative:
alternatively, either . . . or, neither . . . nor, rather than, sooner than

3. Comparison:
in comparison, by comparison, in contrast, like

4. Concession:
however, anyhow, besides, else, nevertheless, nonetheless, only, still, though, in any case, in any event, for all that, in spite of that, all the same, anyway, though, at any rate, in any case, regardless of this

Reference

1. Personal
you, he, she, it, we, they, my, its, your, yours, her, hers, our, ours, their, theirs, mine, who, whom, which, that

2. Whole Idea Reference
this, that

3. Case Reference
where, when, why

Reprinted with permission from Marzano & Dole, 1985.

Figure 5.12

Problem: To discover the distributive principle for multiplication over addition, ask students to calculate the following without paper and pencil. Do not share the pattern until 90 percent of the students have discovered it.

$(23 \times 989) + (23 \times 11) = ?$ (The problem can be rewritten as $23 \times 1,000$)

$(41 \times 92) + (41 \times 8) = ?$ (The problem can be rewritten as 41×100)

$(35 \times 675) + (65 \times 675) = ?$ (The problem can be rewritten as 100×675)

$(4 \times 1,234) + (96 \times 1,234) = ?$ (The problem can be rewritten as $100 \times 1,234$)

Carpenter (1985) has classified the various types of mathematical relations in story problems. The three broad types are change, combine, and compare; each type has several subtypes. Such typologies can be useful for instruction.

Comments on Classroom Applications—Analyzing patterns and relationships is fundamental to success in school and in life. Certainly, its importance is reflected in the myriad of thinking skills programs that focus on analyzing patterns and relationships using geometric figures, numerical relationships, Venn diagrams, and logic. Nevertheless, there is little evidence that these programs transfer to learning situations in content courses, especially for low-achieving students. What is needed is more effort to develop content objectives that require students to analyze patterns and relationships.

Increasing experience with different kinds of relationships will help students to identify them. Equivalence, symmetry, and similarity are relationships found throughout the arts and sciences, along with difference, contradiction, and exclusion. Models, metaphors, analogies, and isomorphisms are relationships used in many fields to clarify and extend meaning. Recognizing them is a key skill in analysis.

The core thinking skill of identifying relationships is essential to the thinking process of principle formation discussed in the preceding chapter. Rules, principles, theories, and laws are based on relationships between and among concepts.

Identifying Main Ideas

Definition—Identifying main ideas is a special case of identifying patterns and relationships. In the past, this skill has been limited largely to finding the main idea or topic sentence in reading; however, it is a critical skill in processes such as oral discourse and scientific inquiry. The definition we prefer invjab01olves identifying the hierarchy of key ideas in a message or line of reasoning; that is, the set of superordinate ideas around which a message is organized plus any key details. As with establishing other patterns and relationships, sometimes main ideas may be stated explicitly; at other times, they must be inferred. Also, in many cases, the message unit may be a single paragraph, but more likely, it is a whole segment of text, passage, or chapter.

Key Concepts and Issues—Traditionally in schools, identifying the main idea has been defined in terms of finding the main idea sentence or topic sentence in a single paragraph. However, there is some question in the research literature on reading as to whether there is such a thing as a "free floating" main idea sentence in most paragraphs. Numerous researchers have identified various text structures for paragraphs and whole passages, such as problem and solution, compare and contrast, sequential or temporal, and so on (e.g., Anderson & Armbruster, 1985; Meyer, 1982). The main idea sentence for each type may vary greatly in terms of its structure and signal words. For example, the main idea sentence and signal words for a temporal paragraph discussing two concurrent events will be different from the main idea sentence and signal words for a paragraph stating a cause-and-effect relationship or even a sequence of events. Equally important, if students had to construct main idea sentences for such paragraphs, the search procedures and sentence structures they would use for each type would vary significantly.

Other problems compound these issues. First, textbook instruction in finding main idea sentences typically does not explicitly distinguish different types of text structures. Second, apart from the paragraphs that are specially constructed for these exercises, textbook paragraphs may not always have main idea sentences (Anderson & Armbruster, 1985). Third, even if they did, finding main idea sentences may not be particularly useful.

That is, finding the main idea as it is taught in basals usually focuses on paragraph-level information in specially constructed paragraphs designed specifically to teach main ideas. However, the skills required to do this may not apply to understanding either stories or expository prose, in part because the writing is different. Moreover, what is frequently more important in both instances is how the various elements of text are related. Thus, reading researchers nowadays emphasize the use of other skills and study strategies aimed at understanding whole passages and stories, particularly questioning, inferring, and mapping to establish key concepts, sequences of events, and elements in a description—regardless of where they are located in a text (e.g., Tierney, Readence, & Dishner, 1985). Thus, this research has essentially redefined the skill of identifying main ideas to focus on identifying the set of ideas that comprise the macro-structure of a message or message segment.

Strategies—Strategies for identifying the main idea are twofold. First, we would refer the reader to the variety of strategies emphasizing cognitive mapping (discussed under Representing), formulating questions, inferring (particularly the notion of retroduction), and summarizing. Second, if schools are determined to teach finding the main idea for individual paragraphs, it is vital to provide and identify different types of text structure and to teach students to find or construct main idea sentences for each type. Regardless of the particular strategy, what is critical is supporting one's analysis with supporting evidence and giving reasons for considering certain ideas as central.

Comments on Classroom Applications—Brown and Day's research on summarizing requires students to find or invent a topic sentence, but they found that younger children had difficulty doing this (Brown, Campione, & Day, 1981). However, Palincsar and Brown (1984) have documented that primary children can summarize key ideas of a text. We therefore assume that, with appropriate guidelines, it is possible to teach younger students to find main ideas.

Identifying Errors

Definition—This skill involves detecting mistakes in logic, calculations, procedures, and knowledge, and where possible, identifying their causes and making corrections or changes in thinking. Some elements may be biased, false, or ambiguous. Others may be inconsistent, irrelevant, or contradictory. Claims may be unwarranted. Omissions may limit comprehensiveness or break the chain of an argument.

Key Concepts and Issues—The literature from which we can learn about defining errors is extensive. There is, for example, an increasing body of research on comprehension monitoring that deals with faulty reasoning or poor understanding of content or procedures. We could also draw upon research on miscues and other reading problems such as the difficulty that some students have integrating contradictory or conflicting information. However, we will confine our discussion to understanding and correcting fallacies of logical reasoning in argumentation identified by philosophers.

Philosophers have identified an impressive array of *fallacies of argumentation* that to some extent overlaps with issues related to verification. In Figure 5.13 below, we present a few examples of the errors and fallacies

---

Figure 5.13

Examples of Fallacies from Unwarranted Assumptions

Asserting a False Cause: (a) Confusing temporal succession with causal sequence;   (b) Citing a mistaken cause

Evading the Issue: "Sidestepping" an issue by changing the topic

Appealing to Authority: Invoking an authority as the "last word" on an issue

Examples of Fallacies from Ambiguity

Equivocation: Using words or phrases in inconsistent ways

Accent: (a) Taking something out of context;   (b) Using italics, boldface, or other techniques to lend a false significance to a statement

Reprinted with permission from Toulmin, Rieke, & Janik, 1981, p. 158.

---

identified by Toulmin, Rieke, and Janik (1981). They posit two categories of fallacies. The first is fallacies of unwarranted assumptions, which result from information that cannot be supported. The second is fallacies that result from ambiguities; these fallacies are a product of imprecise or inaccurate use of language. Nickerson, Perkins, and Smith (1985) describe various categories of thinking skills programs that teach these fallacies. They also offer their own classification of errors and biases in reasoning.

Strategies—Strategies for making students aware of different types of errors and how to correct them differ markedly according to the subject matter. For errors and biases in reasoning, it is critical to have opportunities for recognizing the diversity of various types of fallacies in various learning contexts. While such opportunities may be structured by using well-developed programs, it is vital that students begin to internalize the various types of fallacies in everyday classroom situations.

Comments on Classroom Applications—Identifying errors is a skill that should be taught as soon as students begin to make errors. Moreover, the focus on understanding underlying principles, symbols, and lines of reasoning may be a significant deviation from classroom practices in many schools.

Generating Skills

Generating skills involve using prior knowledge to add information beyond what is given. Generating is essentially constructive, as connections among new ideas and prior knowledge are made by building a coherent organization of ideas (i.e., a schema) that holds the new and old information together. Organizing and analyzing involve showing how parts are related; in generating, new information and ideas come into play, often being recast into new structures. In this section, we will consider the generating skills of inferring, predicting, and elaborating.

Inferring

Definition—When we infer, we go beyond available information to identify what reasonably may be true. For example, when we smell smoke, we ask ourselves what could be the meaning of the smoke. Then we fill in the gap by reasoning that something is burning. Making inferences is pervasive to human activity and undoubtedly to survival.

Key Concepts and Issues—In traditional philosophical terms, making inferences refers largely to inductive and deductive reasoning (discussed under "Research" in Chapter 4). Deductive reasoning is the ability to extend an existing principle or idea in a logical manner; inductive reasoning refers to making generalizations and logical statements based on observation or analysis of various cases. Numerous typologies, treatises, and thinking skills programs define various inductive and deductive reasoning skills (Nickerson, Perkins, & Smith, 1985; Costa, 1985e).

Scholars in various fields have criticized traditional definitions on the grounds that reasoning is often more "messy" and nonlinear than earlier definitions suggest (Eco, 1976, 1979, 1984; Medawar, 1967; Percy, 1975; Deely, 1982). Many philosophers and educators have advanced the concept of *retroduction*, introduced by philosopher Charles Sanders Peirce, as a more fruitful approach to understanding the nature of inferential thinking. Retroduction, which can be likened to hypothesis making, is the act of generating and shaping an idea based on one or more cases. This is similar to the usual definition of induction, but Peirce held that retroduction is a construct that deeply enriches the understanding of inference. It has more utility, greater psychological reality, and wider applicability.

Strategies—Teachers in science and social studies classrooms can have students progressively generate and shape hypotheses as new information is provided through observations, discussion, research reviews, and systematic experimentation. When students observe the phenomenon of erosion, for example, they can (in line with Peirce's model) generate several "messy" guesses (retroduction) about the causes and consequences of this problem. They can then be asked to explore and refine these in oral and written form. Once this is done, students can describe and discuss the implications of the untested hypotheses (deduction). On the basis of this new information, students can select specific hypotheses for testing in a more systematic fashion (induction)—that is, through systematic observation and research or through actual experimentation, recognizing that the data collected will resolve some issues but raise many more.

Retroduction is at the heart of reading literary texts in which language is purposely ambiguous (Eco, 1979). The enjoyment of a Frost poem or a Steinbeck short story is largely derived from the fact that the multi-tiered meanings activate a variety of hypotheses within the reader. Moreover, different readers bring different backgrounds to the text, so oral discourse in the classroom is enhanced by the exchange of an immense variety of constructed meanings.

Many situations that call for inferring are well structured. That is, the information given is specific and limited, so there is little need to work through progressively refined hypotheses. In such instances, simple acts of inference suffice. Johnson and Johnson (1986, pp. 622-623) define 10 well-structured inferences that can be taught through explicit instruction. They refer, for example, to *problem-solution inferences* ("While I marched in the junior high band, my Dad cheered, and his eyes filled with tears. What feeling was he experiencing?"); *cause-effect inferences* ("The side of Ken's face was swollen, and his tooth throbbed. What should Ken do about this problem?"); *object inferences* ("The gleaming giant had 18 wheels, and it towered above lesser vehicles on the turnpike. What is the 'gleaming giant'?").

An effective strategy for teaching inferring is to have students (1) identify what is known, for sure, about the current situation; (2) identify similar situations from personal experience, generalizations, or reference to authorities; (3) identify what is known in the similar situations that may fill in a gap in information about the current situation; (4) determine whether the situations are similar enough to warrant an inference about the current situation; and (5) make an inference, citing as support the information from similar situations.

Comments on Classroom Applications—Acts of inference will take on somewhat different characteristics, depending on the subject area, the complexity of the material, and the age of the learner. For example, a beginning reader will form hypotheses about both the letters on the page and the meanings of the words and phrases (as well as the pictures) when reading a book such as *The Little Engine that Could*. A teacher would decode with automaticity and proceed quickly to hypothesize the upbeat outcome of the story, perhaps encouraging the child to predict by asking, "Do you think a little engine can do something big and important?" A literary scholar examining the same text might retroductively ascribe mythic qualities to the narrative, linking it with narrative patterns in which the weak overcome oppressive barriers.

Textbooks geared to establishing "the right answer" with little opportunity to consider ambiguity or levels of meaning may not foster this type of inferring. (For further discussion of classroom applications, see Carey, 1983; Cunningham & Luk, 1985; Harste & Stephens, 1984; Siegel, 1984.) Making retroductive inferences requires many pauses for reflection and a high level of interaction among the learner, the information, and the teacher. While model students may need little help in formulating hypotheses and supporting them with evidence, low-achieving students will need a lot of modeling and opportunities to practice this process.

Predicting

Definition—A prediction is a statement anticipating the outcomes of a situation. (We may think of these outcomes as "future" events even though in some cases, such as asking students to predict effects of the Louisiana Purchase on the course of U.S. history, some of them were actually in the past.) Predictions are usually made by assessing the likelihood of an outcome based on prior knowledge of how things usually turn out. The skill of predicting can probably be considered a special type of inference, much the same way that ordering is a special type of classification skill.

Key Concepts and Issues—To avoid confusion, it may be useful to point out that in everyday life, our predictions almost always deal with events that have not yet taken place. In school, however, students are more likely to be asked to anticipate outcomes of fictional or historical situations; then, strictly speaking, they are not predicting "future" events.

Students are unlikely to improve their skill in predicting unless they get feedback on the accuracy of their predictions. In fact, evidence from reading research shows that predicting by itself is not effective in improving comprehension, and indeed may hinder it. Anderson and Foertsch (in press) found that when students were asked to make a prediction for each paragraph (without relating the information in the paragraph back to the prediction), comprehension was markedly decreased for both high- and low-achieving students.

Strategies—Prediction is integral to such comprehension strategies as reciprocal teaching, content reading, and various directed reading strategies. In these strategies, the teacher generally has students predict in connection with skimming titles and subtitles, examining graphics and illustrations, or responding to introductory statements. These steps activate prior knowledge and help establish a purpose for reading. During reading, students are asked to pause (consciously or unconsciously) to check the validity of their predictions. They may ask themselves questions such as "Is my prediction confirmed or not?"; "What are the implications for what I already know?"; "Is it necessary to change what I formerly believed to be true?"; "What did I learn?" Such questions are essentially integrative because they relate parts of new information to each other and to students' previous understandings. (For further description of these strategies, see Herber, 1978; Palincsar & Brown, 1983; Tierney, Readence, & Dishner, 1985.)

This general procedure also applies to scientific experimentation in which students formulate and test a hypothesis and relate the results to their original hypothesis. Students also predict in mathematical problem solving when they hypothesize the nature of a problem, estimate its answer, predict the "best" solution strategy, solve it, and then compare the answer to their estimation (see Polya, 1945; Schoenfeld, 1985).

Comments on Classroom Applications—If used in the broad sense we advocate, making predictions can be effective in many learning situations. Teachers may need to ensure, through questioning and other activities, that students actually make predictions and then take time during the learning activity to check those predictions. It is important to note that students can change their predictions as they obtain more information about an experiment, story, or topic. Equally important, students should be informed that some predictions turn out to be "incorrect" but that such an outcome does not mean the student has failed. Teacher modeling can help make students more comfortable with predictions that might be disconfirmed. Also, examples of scientists' "failed" hypotheses and their attitudes toward such outcomes can be given. Scientists expect that many of their hypotheses will be discarded, but they usually view such "failures" as providing useful information—sometimes more useful than their "successes." Teachers can help students learn to analyze these "failures" for critical information.

Elaborating

Definition—Elaborating involves adding details, explanations, examples, or other relevant information from prior knowledge in order to improve

101

understanding. Consider the statement, "Many plants contain substances that are of pharmacological use." This statement could activate any number of mental elaborations:

1. Camomile is a plant that contains substances that are of pharmacological value.
2. My grandfather knew an herbal tea for every ache and pain.
3. Inhumane animal experiments are sometimes carried out by pharmacologists.
4. I'm imagining an old herb brewer in a hut, and a scientist studying botanical specimens in a lab.
5. *Pharmacological* is a term I don't know (Ballsteadt & Mandl, 1984, p. 331).

These elaborations are generative because they add meaning to the new information and link it to existing knowledge structures.

To elaborate as a skill, the learner actively generates statements or mental images that relate the information at hand to prior knowledge. Further, there are many different types of elaborations. The elaboration might be an example of a concept (elaboration 1 above). Alternatively, it might be an episode associated with some part of the statement (elaboration 2), an evaluation related to the statement or some part of it (elaboration 3), a visual image constructed to represent the statement (elaboration 4), or a metacognitive elaboration indicating a gap in vocabulary (elaboration 5).

Elaborations take several forms that can be complex, interrelated, and perhaps overlapping. More complex examples include constructing comparisons, metaphors, analogies, explanations, and mental models. Analogies in the research literature go beyond the traditional "A is to B as C is to . . ." format. Broadly conceived, analogies are comparisons of familiar and unfamiliar things—for example, using knowledge of typing and typewriters to understand key entry and computers. Explanations are statements telling why something works the way it does—for example, saying to oneself a statement such as "My word processing system says that the disk is full when I try to save a large file, even though more bytes are available than my file has. Why? I think this is because the system saves the new file before deleting the old file. So to save a new file, I probably need at least twice as many bytes as the new file." Each of these elaborations involves using one's knowledge about a familiar topic to understand something unfamiliar.

Key Concepts and Issues—Research indicates that all these types of elaborations aid comprehension, in some cases dramatically. Analogies and metaphors provide a model with which students can make predictions, assumptions, or generate questions about how the elements or components of something are related. They help students synthesize information into a familiar and usable format (see Klausmeier, 1985).

However, the research is less clear on the exact conditions that facilitate learning and thinking. For example, we know that when the learner is generating mental pictures for visual elaboration, if the items to be remembered together are not physically touching or interacting in the image, the strategy does not aid recall. Moreover, whether a given elaboration can be used or is appropriate depends on the information available and the prior knowledge of the individual.

Strategies—Explanations, analogies, and metaphors may be particularly powerful elements of teaching/learning strategies. They are especially useful in science and mathematics and in computer programming and use of complex computer equipment, probably because so much of that information is abstract and unfamiliar to students. Elaborations are also essential in developing ideas in oral discourse and in composing, and in any efforts to foster creative thinking (see Bransford, Sherwood, Rieser, & Vye, 1986; Mayer, 1984; Weinstein & Mayer, 1986 for examples).

Teachers and textbooks can elaborate information easily by using ideas and concepts that are likely to be within students' prior knowledge. For example, Vosniadou and Ortony (1983) found that *all* 1st- and 3rd-grade children were able to explain illnesses and diseases when given analogies comparing the spread of disease to the attack of an enemy. The children made comments such as, "Medicine is needed to stop infection because it is like water that pours on them (the germs) and they do not expect it" (p. 12). This analogy was so successful because all or almost all students already understood the concept of *enemy*.

Comments on Classroom Applications—The positive effects of explanations, analogies, metaphors, and other elaborations have been substantiated in many situations, especially when students have had sustained and explicit instruction in how to create and use them. In teaching composition, both conventional and process approaches dwell on eliciting elaborations like those cited in the pharmacology example above (e.g., exemplification and definition). Additionally, in recent years numerous strategies have been developed for eliciting strikingly original metaphoric language from students at all grade levels (e.g., Koch, 1970, 1974; Tsujimoto, in press).

Many elaborating strategies are especially effective with low-achieving students. For primary-grade students, teachers might generate analogies and discuss with students how they elaborate and explain new information. Although older students may need such instruction as well, it is important to encourage and guide them to generate their own elaborations. Teachers can also pose questions and develop activities that invite students to form their own extended analogies, as in Figure 5.14.

Integrating Skills

Whereas analyzing involves taking things apart, integrating skills involve putting together the relevant parts or aspects of a solution, understanding, principle, or composition. New information and prior knowledge are connected and combined as the learner searches for prior knowledge related to

---

Figure 5.14

Activity to Generate Analogies

Students select an abstract term such as honesty, courage, pride, or justice. Next, they select from a grab bag a concrete object such as a candle, tape dispenser, or Nike brand T-shirt. They then note the different parts of the objects and their various purposes. After listing the attributes of their objects, students elaborate those qualities in a metaphoric comparison to their abstract term.

Possible metaphoric elaboration for "Justice is a Nike T-shirt."

FRONT	LABEL
It must stretch to fit society.	It is "sewn" into the fabric of society.
People must be comfortable with it.	It provides guidance to society to take
It is attractive.	care of its members.
It makes a statement about a society.	It identifies what is harmful to a society.

SLEEVES	SEAMS
It allows for freedom of movement and	It creates and maintains order.
thought.	It gives confidence and security to people in
	a society.

From O'Keefe, 1986. Reprinted with permission.

---

incoming information, transfers that knowledge to working memory, builds meaningful connections between incoming information and prior knowledge, and incorporates this integrated information into a new understanding. The last of these distinguishes integration from generating and other skills.

Summarizing

Definition—Summarizing is combining information efficiently into a cohesive statement. It involves at least three cognitive activities—condensing information, selecting what is important (and discarding what is not), and combining original text propositions. A summary may be oral or written and is appropriate for many learning activities. Good summaries include important elements and their relationships, and sometimes supporting details.

Key Concepts and Issues—Summarizing can be powerful for comprehending, retaining, and studying information. For example, written summaries are effective if students are instructed in how to produce them and if instruction and assessment are aligned. For studying information, students receiving summarization instruction do better when tested on high-level information than when tested on recall of isolated facts. According to Hidi and Anderson (1986), other factors also seem to influence the quality of summaries:

1. Length—shorter summaries are easier to write than longer summaries.

2. Genre—children summarize narratives more easily than other genres.

3. Audience—summaries for oneself are easier than summaries for others, such as the teacher.

4. Presence of information—summaries are easier to write if a written text is available than if one is not (Hidi & Anderson, 1986).

Strategies—Three approaches to summarizing that are documented in research are the rule-based approach, graphic organizers, and informal oral summarizing.

1. The most well-known *rule-based approach*, which was developed by Brown and Day, has been tested with students of various ages (Brown, Campione, & Day, 1981). The rules are:

- Delete trivial material that is unnecessary to understanding.
- Delete redundant material.
- Substitute superordinate terms for lists (e.g., "flowers" for "daisies, tulips, and roses").
- Select a topic sentence, or invent one if it is missing.

As indicated earlier in the section on finding main ideas, results using these rules have been mixed. Research suggests that younger students (up to grade 8) and low-achieving students (including junior college students) may have difficulty using these rules, especially the last one. They may not know what a "good" summary is, and poor readers often select what interests them rather than what is important. The rules are also problematic because they do not guide students in the process of *how* to write a summary, they do not capture the central idea of relating parts to each other, and they are not sensitive to differences in text organizational patterns (e.g., comparison and contrast texts or texts organized sequentially). Thus, we caution readers to plan for extensive instructional support if they attempt to teach this summarizing strategy.

2. *Graphic organizers and outlines with frames*, discussed in connection with representing, can guide summarizing in ways that avoid most problems of rule-based approaches. Graphic organizers help students select important information, comprehend and use structural elements, and see relationships among parts. They also can provide students with organizational patterns that facilitate writing a summary (Van Patten, Chao, & Reigeluth, 1986).

Figure 5.15, for example, shows a brief summary generated from an interaction frame. The frame graphically depicts the interaction between two characters in a short story much more clearly than a traditional hierarchical outline could. The three main sections of the graphic (goals, interactions, results) serve as prompts for including information in the summary. In a longer summary, the questions and boxes would serve as appropriate paragraph topics or headings when the student writes a summary. Having the information for each group next to similar information about the other groups enables the student to make important comparisons.

Figure 5.15

Interaction Frame with Literature/Short Story

"The Dip" by Jan Andrews

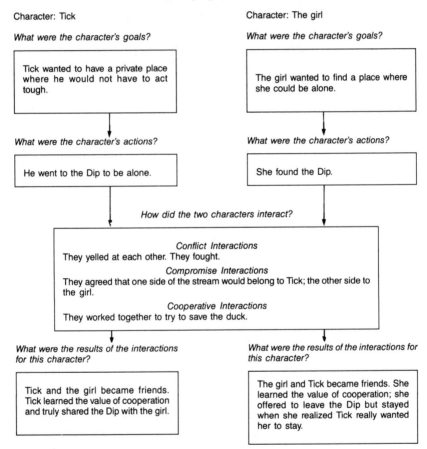

Character: Tick

What were the character's goals?

Tick wanted to have a private place where he would not have to act tough.

What were the character's actions?

He went to the Dip to be alone.

Character: The girl

What were the character's goals?

The girl wanted to find a place where she could be alone.

What were the character's actions?

She found the Dip.

How did the two characters interact?

Conflict Interactions
They yelled at each other. They fought.

Compromise Interactions
They agreed that one side of the stream would belong to Tick; the other side to the girl.

Cooperative Interactions
They worked together to try to save the duck.

What were the results of the interactions for this character?

Tick and the girl became friends. Tick learned the value of cooperation and truly shared the Dip with the girl.

What were the results of the interactions for this character?

The girl and Tick became friends. She learned the value of cooperation; she offered to leave the Dip but stayed when she realized Tick really wanted her to stay.

Summary of the Story

The Dip was a place in the woods that Tick Merrick had found where he could be alone and be himself and not act tough. One day a girl showed up who also wanted to be alone in the Dip. For a while Tick and the girl fought with each other over the Dip. Neither wanted to leave, so finally they agreed that each could stay but on separate sides of the stream. Their dislike for each other was forgotten when they found an injured duck and tried to nurse it back to health together. The duck did not survive, but Tick and the girl had learned the value of cooperation and found they had become real friends.

Reprinted with permission from *Teaching Thinking Skills: English/Language Arts*, published by the National Education Association, 1987, p. 36.

106

3. *Informal oral summarizing* can be elicited before, during, and after reading text segments in iterative fashion (Palinscar & Brown, 1984; Jones, et al., 1987). Before students read new content, a teacher or student may give a brief summary of previously learned content. During reading, the students and teacher pause to summarize and relate key points to prior knowledge. After reading, they summarize and identify relationships in what has been learned. This strategy differs from the first two because it does not have rules or graphics to structure the summary; moreover, informal oral summaries are done frequently, typically over small segments of text, and they have different purposes—to clarify and raise questions for events and ideas to come. Younger and lower achieving students seem to have fewer problems with this approach than with a rule-based method.

Comments on Classroom Applications—Because summarizing is a difficult skill, students of all ability levels will probably require considerable teacher guidance and modeling. In general, effective instruction includes:

- questions, rules, and graphic structures to organize written summaries;
- instruction in how to apply rules, questions, and graphics;
- models of the summary-making process and good examples of completed summaries of texts organized in various ways;
- coaching and practice, with feedback;
- emphasis on planning and revision;
- sequencing of summary assignments from simple, short, and familiar to complex, long and unfamiliar texts; and
- sequencing of summaries from writing for oneself to writing for others.

Restructuring

Definition—Restructuring is changing existing knowledge structures to incorporate new information. Because of new insights, the learner actively modifies, extends, reorganizes, or even discards past understandings because he or she recognizes that previously accepted concepts, facts, beliefs, or attitudes are no longer accurate or valid. This recasting of ideas is a major part of conceptual growth, and ultimately of cognitive development.

Key Concepts and Issues—Because of the predominance of Piaget's theories, the word *restructuring* often brings to mind the type of *global restructuring* that occurs as the individual moves from one stage to another. Such changes are marked by changes in the child's ability to represent thought (e.g., pre-operational), and it is assumed that such changes occur "naturally" through the maturation process. Vosniadou and Brewer (1987) argue that the notion of global restructuring has come under serious attack in recent years. Part of this concern centers on the importance of changes in domain-specific knowledge, especially the shift from novice to expert. In fact, there has been some movement to replace the notion of global restructuring with the notion of *domain-specific restructuring*, which occurs from the child's experience and instruction.

Domain-specific restructuring involves various kinds of changes, according to Vosniadou and Brewer. Sometimes, restructuring may occur from adding more or different relations among specific concepts. At other times, the restructuring may occur as the expert develops ways to organize thoughts more abstractly. Then, there are also more radical ways of restructuring, such as paradigm shifts as well as changes of theory and beliefs as the learner confronts misconceptions, conflicting or inconsistent ideas, and new theories. In fact, children's misconceptions are often efforts to integrate conflicting pieces of evidence.

Additionally, there is some debate about the role of prior knowledge. That is, if radical shifts are a desired objective, then the value of linking new information to prior knowledge is questionable. At the same time, dealing with prior knowledge seems essential for dealing with misconceptions and impoverished theories about the world. Our discussion below assumes that in most cases it is useful to relate the new information to prior knowledge.

Strategies—Research on expert learners suggests that perhaps the most important aspect of restructuring is to develop the disposition to be aware of contradictory and inconsistent information as well as an attitude of determination to persevere until some solution or resolution is found. Students should become aware of the types of situations that might require restructuring and build a repertoire of strategies that work, such as changing the problem.

Additionally, Posner, Strike, Hewson, and Gertzog (1982) have developed a teaching strategy for dealing with misconceptions that also applies to rigid, inflexible thinking and similar problems. They argue that for conceptual change to occur, it is necessary to help students identify precisely the ways in which past understandings conflict with new information, getting students to "buy into" the meaningfulness of the new information. Then, it is also important to articulate specifically what has to be learned by making specific comparisons between new and old information. It is also helpful for students to engage in concrete manipulations (including constructing diagrams) or experiments that demonstrate the correct conception. (Misconceptions are discussed further in Chapter 6.)

Yet other strategies for identifying misconceptions and inconsistencies are suggested by Vosniadou and Brewer (1987). They argue that Socratic dialog is necessary for the type of change which requires that old beliefs be abandoned and replaced with fundamentally different conceptual structures. Additionally, they show how analogies, metaphors, and physical models may help students construct new schemata as well as flesh out anomalies. Both strategies are primarily instructional strategies; however, students can be taught to use them spontaneously.

Comments on Classroom Applications—Many educators are concerned at the lack of flexible and inventive thinking in American schools. Part of the reason for these tendencies is that instructional objectives are often too shallow and narrowly focused. Some textbooks and teachers seek to avoid conflicts and dealing with contradictory information. Research in this area is relatively young and not widely disseminated.

Evaluating Skills

Evaluating skills involve assessing the reasonableness and quality of ideas. In this section, we will discuss two evaluating skills: establishing criteria and verifying. Most of this discussion is based on philosophical principles, although we refer also to psychological research.

Establishing Criteria: A Philosophical Perspective

Definition—From a philosophical perspective, establishing criteria refers to setting standards for judging the value or logic of ideas. These criteria are rational principles derived from culture, experience, and instruction. Suppose, for example, we make a judgment that *Illusions* by Richard Bach is an excellent book. This judgment is based on previously learned standards for evaluating books within prescribed categories. Regarding style (a typical category), we might say that it was creative or thought-provoking (the rational principle or criteria) and then go on to exemplify or support this judgment with illustrations (the supporting argument). Thus, the criteria have in fact functioned as the reason offered for making a favorable or nonfavorable judgment.

Key Concepts and Issues—In philosophy, much of the work on establishing criteria derives from defining pitfalls or problems in developing or applying criteria. Two problems are frequently evident when students (and many adults) deal with external criteria: choosing inappropriate categories of judgment and applying criteria ineptly. If someone claims that a book was good because the proceeds were going to charity and it was widely read, those categories would be irrelevant to the aesthetic worth of the book.

Sometimes appropriate categories of judgment are used, but they are applied in a faulty manner. One can know that good character development is an important criterion in judging a book yet be unable to distinguish excellent from poor character development—expecting, for example, broad and obvious depictions of character in every book.

Often, differences of opinion are based less on flaws in applying criteria than on the fact that discussants have selected different categories of judgment. Different principles of sorting are involved when one person says that *Illusions* was excellent because of the character development and theme, and another says it was poor because the script was flawed or the plot insufficiently developed (see Alston, 1964; Scriven, 1959; Slote, 1966).

Comments on Classroom Applications—In classroom teaching, it is important that evaluations and comparisons be accompanied by the identification of the criteria in terms of which the comparison was made. According to philosophers, students should be encouraged to provide such identifications as a matter of course. If someone asserts that John F. Kennedy was a better president than Lyndon Johnson, she should be challenged (preferably by other members of the class) to say whether she means in respect to foreign policy, domestic policy, or some other criterion. If someone says that tomatoes are fruits rather than vegetables, he should be challenged to provide the application that led him to make such a judgment. Specifying criteria is thus an invaluable resource for fostering classroom inquiry rather than invidious controversy.

Establishing Criteria: A Psychological Perspective

Definition—Psychological research has focused on how individuals establish criteria for judging the effectiveness of their own learning. These criteria are conceptualized in different ways from the philosophical notions above. The criteria here refer to the effectiveness of particular learning strategies, achievement of learning goals, and the like. Such criteria guide self-testing and are a major aspect of metacognitive activity.

Key Concepts and Issues—Most children younger than eight years are rather poor at judging whether they have learned information well enough to pass a test (Kail, 1984). Six-year-olds, when given a second opportunity to study, tend to waste time studying things they already know. Younger children and low-achieving students are also less proficient at monitoring their learning progress in other ways. For example, they are less likely to observe that they are holding contradictory points of view or to struggle to resolve them (e.g., Roth, 1985). It may be that self-directed learning does not fully develop until adolescence, about the time formal operations emerge. Thus, teachers will need to provide guidance if students (elementary students, at least) are to evaluate the quality of their own learning. Indeed, Vygotsky (1962, 1978) maintains that providing such guidance is a chief function of teachers and other adults in the child's environment.

Strategies—Metacognitive monitoring and evaluation seem to be vital to functioning during all cognitive operations (Brown, 1978; Sternberg, 1984a, 1984b). However, the specific strategies by which the student monitors and evaluates may vary greatly according to the cognitive process and task.

Many problem-solving researchers, for example, maintain that students of all ages should evaluate and monitor their processing at every stage in solving a problem. The teacher's role here would be (1) to help students establish criteria for effective problem solving and (2) to make them aware of their own metacognitive processing (or lack of it) so they will eventually internalize the process. The idea is to encourage "duality of self" where the students both do the work and judge the work according to the criteria. The doer (cognizer) does what the watcher (metacognizer) says. To promote this attitude, students can ask themselves the following metacognitive questions:

1. What is the situation? (How can I represent the problem?)
2. What exactly am I doing? (Can I describe it precisely?)
3. Why am I doing it? (How does it fit into the solution?)
4. How does it help me? (What will I do with the outcome when I obtain it?)

These four questions can be listed on a poster, or students can be asked to discuss them in small groups. Small groups may encourage more self-evaluation because students must defend their views when questions are raised by their peers.

Some of the above questions also apply to processes other than problem solving, but some processes may require different questions. For example, a major criterion for effective writing is whether or not the composition addresses the audience for which it is intended, a criterion that is not present in much problem solving; consequently, monitoring during composing might include self-questions focusing on how the writing relates to the audience. Additionally, teachers have specific criteria for judging the grammar, cohesiveness, organization, and style of student's written work, whether these standards are stated in the curriculum or not. To help students develop strategies for evaluating their own work, it is important to explain these criteria to them.

Verifying

Definition—Verification involves confirming or proving the truth of an idea, using specific standards or criteria of evaluation. Verification may be as formal as a scientific experiment or as casual as noticing that something does not make sense and checking the accuracy of facts.

Key Concepts and Issues—Verification of assertions and hypotheses is fundamental to scientific inquiry and philosophy, but because of its complexity and pervasiveness, we can only touch upon a few issues here. One outstanding issue is the relationship of verification to the notion of falsification. That is, when we seek to verify something, and it is true, we have an instance of verification. However, when we seek to verify something, and it turns out to be false, we have disconfirmed the idea or disproved it. Thus, verification and falsification are integrally related.

Verification takes on different meanings and procedures in different subject areas. In reading, for example, verification focuses on such procedures as checking the meaning or accuracy of the author's statement by looking back in the text, checking the accuracy of one's recall by self-testing, analyzing a line of reasoning for logic errors or fallacies, and verifying predictions of what is to come next in the text. Additionally, there is the entire area of research in the various social sciences whereby students use both quantitative methods such as surveys and qualitative methods such as case studies to verify or disconfirm hypotheses. In mathematics, verifying focuses heavily on evaluating the efficacy of decisions made and outcomes of executed plans (Lester, 1985). In such instances, the learner might pause to reflect, "I'd better check my steps again" or "This answer seems too big."

Strategies—There should be little difficulty devising classroom situations in which students confirm or disconfirm one another's observations. It is desirable, however, that they be conversant with the valid and invalid reasoning patterns that are presupposed in thinking about such observations. Figure 5.16 shows two valid forms of hypothetical deduction. Other patterns of reasoning may be found in the crop of research-based materials now available to schools.

Figure 5.16

Valid Forms of Hypothetical Deduction

Affirmation of the antecedent	If this is an acid, then the litmus will turn red. (hypothesis) <u>This is an acid.</u> (fact) The litmus will turn red. (judgment)
Denial of the consequent	If this is an acid, then the litmus will turn red. (hypothesis) <u>The litmus didn't turn red.</u> (fact) This is not an acid. (judgment)

Invalid Forms of Hypothetical Deduction

Denial of the antecedent	If this is an acid, then the litmus will turn red. (hypothesis) <u>This is not an acid.</u> (fact) (no conclusion follows logically)
Affirmation of the consequent	If this is an acid, then the litmus will turn red. (hypothesis) <u>The litmus will turn red.</u> (fact) (no conclusion follows logically)

Lipman, 1987, personal communication.

It is important to note that the nature of the relationship determines the nature of the method of verification. For example, verification that one thing causes another requires correlation, appropriate order of events, and the elimination of other possible causes. The verification of universality requires the absence of any counterexample. Correlation requires consistent covariation.

Comments on Classroom Applications—Students need to grow in their awareness of the richness of methods and procedures for confirming or disconfirming something; in understanding that the nature of the evidence must be related to the claim, and in their thoroughness in requiring firm evidence for truth claims.

Generalizations about Thinking Skills and Skills Instruction

In the beginning of this chapter, we referred to the repertoire of skills and strategies that characterize skilled thinkers. Now that we have described what we think those core skills are, we can consider some generalizations that apply to all of them. These themes are derived in part from what has already been said and in part from analyses of the nature of thinking.

- Thinking skills and strategies appear to develop *spontaneously*, in that more proficient students appear to acquire them without necessarily having received explicit instruction (Rohwer, 1971).

- Students' repertoires of skills and strategies *can be modified substantially*, however, by effective instructional conditions and methods. This is true not only for high-achieving and older students but also for low-achieving and younger students (Feuerstein, Rand, Hoffman, & Miller, 1980; Weinstein & Mayer, 1986).

- Much of skill learning is *content-specific* and *task-specific* (Bransford, Sherwood, Rieser, & Vye, 1986; Glaser, 1984, 1985).

- Model learners seem to be able to access skills and strategies *flexibly*; they know how to select a given skill or strategy appropriate to the task as well as how to monitor its progress, modify it in the face of obstacles or problems, and abandon it for a more effective strategy. Less proficient learners are more likely to select an inappropriate strategy and stick to it (Brown, 1980; Flavell, 1978; Nickerson, Perkins, & Smith, 1985).

- Similarly, high-performing students seem to have far greater *accessibility* to the knowledge they have; they can learn knowledge in one context and use it in another, whereas low-performing students are much less able to do so (Bransford, Sherwood, Rieser, & Vye, 1986).

- Model learners seem to have more skills functioning with some degree of *automaticity*; they execute them rapidly with little conscious thought, though the state of automaticity is achieved only after much practice and exposure to diverse learning contexts. Further, even expert learners may quickly revert to learning that is markedly slower and more conscious when confronted with unfamiliar content or tasks. Thus, expert learning is often characterized by cycles of more and less automaticity (Bransford, Sherwood, Rieser, & Vye, 1986; Meyer, 1985; Lesgold, 1986).

- Effective learning and thinking appears to be *nonlinear and recursive* in that (1) skilled learners frequently use the same skill repeatedly (iteratively) in solving a given problem, and (2) there is considerable effort to return to earlier thoughts for clarification and verification and for assimilating and restructuring information, and (3) there is often a tendency to see patterns and relationships that are nonlinear—to see nonlinear patterns and interacting factors (Nickerson, Perkins, & Smith, 1985; Resnick, in press).

• The repertoire of skills and strategies for model learners appears to be very *large*—both absolutely and relative to less proficient learners—and they appear to have a remarkable capacity for *selecting and combining sequences of skills and strategies* based on constant monitoring of the progress of learning.

There are also some themes regarding skills instruction. First, there is consistent and strong evidence that most students, but especially low-achieving and younger students, need sustained explicit skills instruction to become skilled thinkers and learners. Second, however, there is little evidence in the research literature for limiting instruction for less proficient or younger students to basic skills; nor is there much evidence that skills must be taught in a given order. Third, there is some quantitative evidence and much consensus among researchers that breaking down skills into hundreds of subskills fragments learning. Fourth, it is critical to provide skills instruction in various learning contexts that are legitimate and meaningful and to make specific provisions for transfer.

We have presented an array of skills that appear to be central in the cognitive growth of children, with special attention to teaching and learning these skills in school settings. Although classroom examples have been given throughout this chapter and previous ones, the question of how skills and processes relate to content area knowledge bears further discussion. That question is the focus of the next chapter.

6. The Relationship of Content-Area Knowledge to Thinking

SOME MAJOR QUESTIONS ABOUT TEACHING THINKING INVOLVE CONTENT-AREA knowledge: What are we teaching students to think about? Should thinking be taught in isolation or in relation to academic subject areas, or both? To what extent are thinking skills generic, and to what extent are they content-specific?

In fact, several cognitive theorists and researchers believe thinking skills cannot and should not be taught apart from content because content is inseparably linked with cognition. For example, Glaser (1985), after reviewing some major thinking-skills programs, suggests:

It thus seems best to teach thinking and learning skills in specific familiar knowledge domains. . . . Abilities to make inferences and to generate new information could be fostered by instructional methods that insure contact with prior knowledge, which is restructured and further developed as thinking and problem-solving occurs. Learning and thinking skills could be acquired as the content and concepts of a knowledge domain are taught (p. 616).

Certainly, efforts have been made in recent years to integrate thinking-skills instruction with content-area instruction. For example, writing-process instruction typically calls for brainstorming, dialoguing, informal outlining, and other activities that bring cognitive processes to the surface during prewriting and revision (Suhor, 1983).

The nature of content areas or "knowledge domains" implies another basis for teaching thinking. Each content area represents a particular way of mapping out the world, and each has specific approaches to investigation and analysis resulting in a body of ideas that are the discipline's conceptual core.

But this core is by no means fixed and absolutely stable. Content areas evolve as we gain new knowledge and as new techniques and technologies arise for more varied, more sophisticated analysis. Changes are constantly occurring in peripheral areas of our understanding of content areas, sometimes at the heart of a discipline. These changes have implications for teaching thinking in relation to the discipline.

In this chapter, then, we will consider four perspectives on content knowledge and discuss the implications of each:

- Content-area learning as schema-dependent
- Content areas as models and metaphors
- Content areas as changing bodies of knowledge
- Content areas as special approaches to investigation

Content-Area Learning as Schema-Dependent

Resnick (in press) clearly makes the case for teaching thinking in relation to particular disciplines. What we have called core thinking skills in the text—for example, defining problems or identifying patterns—may be simply impossible, Resnick says, if students do not have a store of knowledge about similar problems or if they do not know enough about the topic to recognize patterns. Even in the tasks used to assess general intelligence or scholastic aptitude, recent analyses have clearly shown that much depends on specific knowledge—of a particular vocabulary, of specific relationships, of possible transformations, and of different representations.

Theory and research on how we organize information in long-term memory underlines the importance of background knowledge. Different terms describe these types of organization. For example, in artificial intelligence, the terms *scripts, plans,* and *goals* are used (Schank & Abelson, 1977; Abelson, 1975). We will use the term *schema,* most commonly found in reading theory and research, to discuss background information.

Rumelhart (1975) believes that information is organized in memory in specific knowledge structures or "packages" called *schemata*. The schema example most often cited is going to a restaurant. Most people in our culture have an internalized restaurant schema that includes knowledge or expectations about reading a menu, ordering food, waiting for it to come, eating it with an array of utensils, and paying the bill. This schema may be related to many other schematic structures—for foods, for etiquette, or for dress. Although this example seems simple, a visitor from a nomadic tribe would utterly lack a restaurant schema and would be at a loss to function in an American restaurant—just as we, lacking a schema for desert survival, would be completely confused about nomadic dining.

Schema theory, then, furnishes powerful rationales for making links between students' individual backgrounds and specific subject area knowledge. Anderson (1984) summarized six ways in which schemata function in thinking and in remembering text information. We believe that his ideas apply equally well to information in nonprint forms.

First, most new knowledge is gained by assimilating new information into existing structures; therefore, subject matter learning should build on prior knowledge whenever possible. Second, the student's existing schemata help to allocate attention by focusing on what is pertinent and important in newly presented materials. Third, schemata allow and direct the inferential elaboration of incoming information and experience. Fourth, schemata allow orderly searches of memory by providing learners with a guide to the types of information that should be recalled. Fifth, schemata facilitate the thinking skills of summarizing and editing. Sixth, schemata permit inferential reconstruction when there are gaps in memory—that is, they help the learner generate hypotheses about missing information.

These functions have been well documented in a vast body of literature. Moreover, recent studies suggest that memory of particular cases plays a larger role in learning than was previously thought (Anderson & Pearson, 1985). As we shall see, though, accessing existing schemata and creating new schemata can be complex processes, especially when central understandings within subject areas shift over periods of time and when misconceptions must be "unlearned."

The educational implications of schema theory are straightforward: Student schemata should be developed for specific tasks and for specific content. For example, students who have no schemata about the traditions of knighthood would need some background information before reading Tennyson's *Idylls of the King* or seeing *Camelot*. Students in a social studies class who lack schemata for such ideas as "liberal," "moderate," and "conservative" would be unable to place political figures on a continuum ranging from radical left to radical right. These students lack a *content schema*—knowledge about objects, events, situations, and ideas.

In other cases, students may lack a *textual schema*—knowledge about how information is conventionally organized in texts. Poetic conventions such as meter and stanza are textual schemata needed for reading the Tennyson poem. Knowledge of the dramatic conventions of musical comedy texts and performances are background schemata needed for enjoying *Camelot*. In reading that play, students would need to know that "(*enter laughing*)" is a stage direction, not dialogue. In watching a performance, they should know that characters on stage do not hear "asides," even though they are spoken loudly. The social studies students would need to understand the convention that a single line can be used to represent a continuum.

In relation to schema theory, then, teachers should be aware of two potential problems: Students might fail to access the appropriate schema for understanding ideas in the text, or they might not even have the appropriate schemata for approaching a text. It is important to note that even simple schemata are rarely developed through "one shot" instruction. For example, it cannot be assumed that students know the conventions of dramatic texts simply because at the conclusion of a unit on theater they respond successfully to numerous test items about asides, stage directions, and the like. Nor does a student's successful interpretation of a continuum demonstrate enduring, in-depth learning about uses of continuum graphics. Repeated exposure to and application of textual and content schemata are required for students to develop important subject matter knowledge and learning strategies.

With that caveat, we suggest that specific networks of concepts should be identified in the various content areas, and that students should engage in activities intended to help develop domain-specific schemata. One of the most powerful of these techniques is semantic webbing, developed by Freedman and Reynolds (1980). Although designed to enhance primary-grade students' understanding of basal reading material, the technique applies to almost any grade level and any content area. Semantic webbing has four basic steps:

1. Formulate a core question and depict it as the center of the web.

2. Elicit from students possible answers to the core question and depict the answers as strands of the web.

3. Elicit support information for each of the web strands and relate the strand supports to the strands.

4. Guide students in relating the strands.

To illustrate, assume that a social studies teacher wanted to build students' schemata about the Bataan death march. She might formulate the question, "What were the events surrounding the Bataan death march?" She would then depict the question on the board or in a chart as the center of a web (see Figure 6.1). The teacher then would elicit answers to the core question (activating the students' skill at recalling) and depict these answers as web strands (see Figure 6.2). The teacher would then ask the students to fill in detail or add support to each of the strands. For example, the students might take the strand "forced march of prisoners" and add detail. This step would also take a graphic form (see Figure 6.3). Finally, the teacher would ask the students to identify relationships between the strands. For example, the students might hypothesize a cause-effect link between MacArthur leaving the islands and the Japanese takeover. Through systematic reinforcement provided by specific content-area schemata, students can understand the material central to a given content area.

Figure 6.1

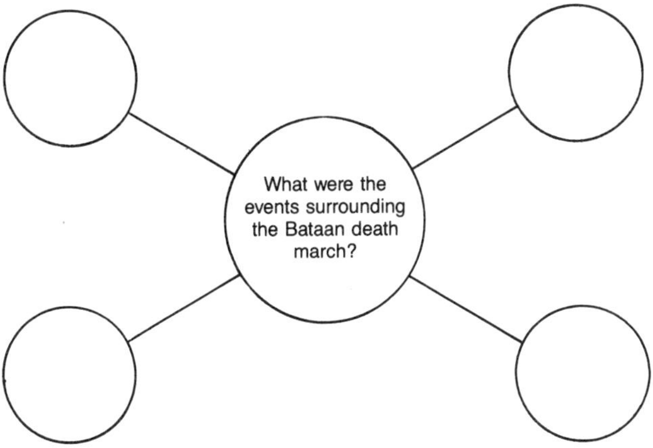

What were the events surrounding the Bataan death march?

Figure 6.2

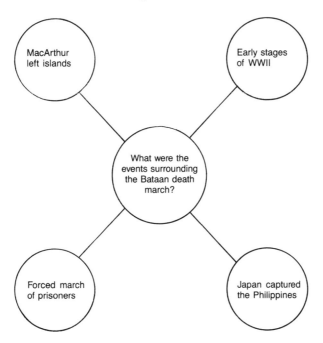

MacArthur left islands

Early stages of WWII

What were the events surrounding the Bataan death march?

Forced march of prisoners

Japan captured the Philippines

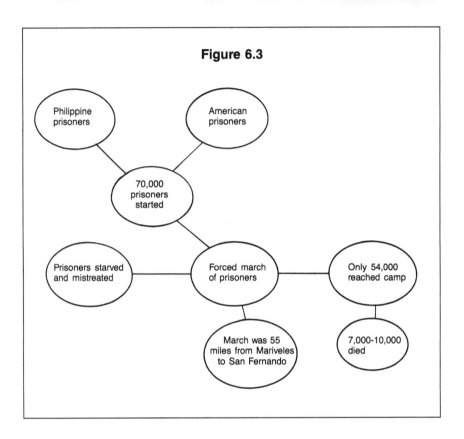

Figure 6.3

The meaning of a text is not contained wholly in the text. Rather, the *interaction* of the reader and the text yields meaning (Rosenblatt, 1978; Iser, 1978). Each student brings different schemata, drawn from his or her cultural background and individual experiences, to the learning task. He or she accesses these valuable schemata to generate some tentative ideas about the text's meaning, exercising skills in inferring and predicting. These ideas become a framework for further understanding of the text. As Probst (in press) notes, then, classroom discussion of a literary work

should not be . . . an effort to suppress the personal and idiosyncratic in the search for a purified reading. . . . Readers initially understand the work *only* on the basis of prior experience. They cannot make sense of a text except by seeing it in light of other experiences, other texts. The reader's background, the feelings, memories, and associations called forth by the reading are not only relevant—they are the foundation upon which understanding of a text is built.

Texts should be written in ways that help readers access textual schemata. Subheads, lists, graphs, charts, and italics and boldface text all signal the genre of the discourse and its organization. Recent research also suggests that school textbooks can be organized so that they more closely resemble plain-English, nontechnical texts (Graves, 1985). Unfortunately, educational and political pressures frequently prevent well-formed exposition in textbooks. Publishers resort to the superficial, destructive practice of "mentioning"—cramming concepts into the text artificially to include items that appear on scope and sequence charts mandated in various states and districts (Bernstein, 1985).

Students who lack appropriate textual schemata can be taught basic text structures so that they can recognize the purpose of an exposition and can move through it more easily (Barnett, 1984; Bartlett, 1978; Cook, 1983, as cited in Mayer, 1984). Teachers have long been accustomed to calling students' attention to structural elements of such literary genres as poetry, drama, and short stories, but other school subjects also have characteristic structures and conventions.

For example, when trained to identify a structural schema for scientific theories, students can better understand science material on plate tectonics. Brooks and Dansereau (1983) note description, inventor/history, consequences, evidence, and rival theories as pertinent structural elements. In other words, students are better able to read materials on scientific theories when they have specific schema for processing the information. Similarly, a schema-based strategy called OINC—identify *o*verall function, draw an *i*mage, focus on *n*ames, summarize *c*haracteristic functions (see Larson, et al., 1986)—enhances students' comprehension of technical material on oscilloscopes. We strongly urge a double-pronged approach. Students should learn more about textual schemata, and publishers of instructional materials should ensure that texts are written in ways that help the reader to access appropriate schemata.

Developing *frames* for content-specific texts or tasks is another way of helping students approach specific types of information (Jones, Tinzmann, Friedman, & Walker, 1987). As indicated earlier, frames are written or graphic devices that give us ways of perceiving how the ideas in a given text are related. For example, Figure 6.4 uses a series of key questions to help students analyze the meaning of a cartoon and its accompanying text from a social studies textbook. Within the larger context of the lesson, the teacher may guide the students to understand, for example, that the person in the back row represents the King of England (because he is wearing a crown and because he formed the "Dominion of England" lasso), that the lassos represent how England and the Albany Plan are a threat to the colonies' freedom, and that the overall meaning of the cartoon is that the colonists resisted attempts to unify them.

At their core, frames provide students with a loose structure that allows them to interact with a discipline. Frames shape information, making it compatible with students' background knowledge and their level of understanding of the content. Different theorists use different names for frames (Meyer, 1985; Brooks & Dansereau, 1983). For example, some researchers have shown that teaching students to use various frames for outlining will improve their ability to develop schemata (Armbruster, 1980; Brooks & Dansereau, 1983; Jones, Amiran, & Katims, 1985).

Figure 6.4a

Cartoon and Cartoon Analysis Frame

Another attempt to unite the colonies was called the Albany Plan of Union. In 1754, Benjamin Franklin proposed this plan to bring the 13 colonies under one central government. At that time, war seemed likely to erupt between England and France, and Franklin felt that the colonies could defend themselves better if they were united. Even though the French and their Indian allies surrounded the English settlements on all sides, the colonists disagreed with Benjamin Franklin. They refused to accept the Albany Plan of Union.

The Colonists Refused to Be Roped into Unification
The colonists opposed any attempts to bring them together as one body.

Figure 6.4b

Reference Box: Cartoon Analysis

The cartoons in a textbook, magazine, or newspaper serve two purposes:
- to help you understand important information
- to help you remember this important information

The cartoons help you understand and remember important information by summarizing or restating the information in a visual and memorable way.

Cartoon Analysis Questions

1. Who/what do the characters in the cartoon represent (stand for)?
2. What do the objects in the cartoon represent?
3. What is happening in the cartoon and what does this represent?
4. What does the cartoon mean?

Frames with particularly strong graphic aspects (see Figure 6.5) can be considered a type of representation, as described in Chapter 5. Using the skill of representing through the medium of a graphic device reinforces students' knowledge. To develop content-area schemata, students can use graphics or can learn how to create their own graphic representations for different types of content-area knowledge.

Content Areas as Models and Metaphors

Every course of study and textbook in a given discipline is an attempt to help students understand some aspects of that discipline's nature. How we conceptualize the core ideas in a subject area, and how we help students to do so, is important. Schwartz and Ogilvy (1979) suggests that we think about subject areas in terms of the creation of models and metaphors.

These models and metaphors form a kind of mental map of the actual world. The disciplines create models and metaphors for the way things are. These move out of the formal discipline to shape our common understandings and often back again to be applied in a new discipline. The physicist invents the hologram. . . . The brain theorist comes to understand the concept and sees in the hologram a metaphor for the complex system of brain functions leading to new avenues of research.

Together these models and metaphors form a kind of mental map of the actual world. They tell us what we know about the nature of things—what is real, what may be false, and what to pay attention to (p. 4).

Postman (1979) agrees that "every discipline . . . is based on powerful metaphors, which give direction and organization to the way we will do our thinking." The student who grasps the central metaphors in a subject area is "different from the student who can give you the facts" because the former "knows what is meant by a fact, and how that fact is different from an inference or theory." For example, the concept of language used imaginatively helps students organize the study of literature. Students who understand this idea have a useful perspective for grasping imaginative language of all kinds, from simple puns to lyric poems to *The Sound and the Fury*. For these students, facts about metrics, myths, or figures of speech are pertinent because they enhance the imaginative entry into a language-rich world.

Biology teachers have several alternatives for organizing and teaching their field. As Shulman (1986) notes, they can regard their discipline as a science of molecules, a science of ecological systems, or a science of biological organisms. "The well-prepared biology teacher will recognize these and other forms of organization and the pedagogical grounds for selecting one form under some circumstances and others under different circumstances" (p. 9).

The idea of content as metaphor is related to the instructional pedagogy of the 1960s. Bruner (1960) speaks of guiding students to discover the structure of a discipline, but "structure" implies more than information. For Bruner, the "process of education" involves actively grasping key principles and concepts.

Figure 6.5

A Detailed Representation of Meiosis

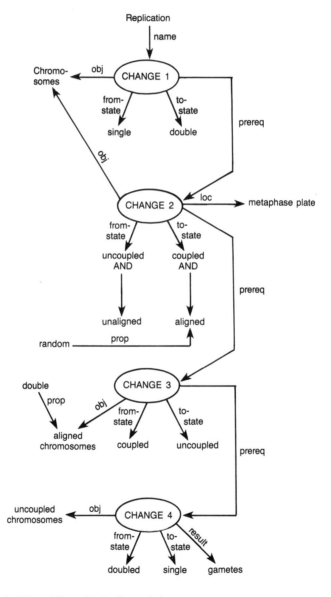

From Stewart, 1984, p. 240; reprinted with permission.

In combination with broader views of the fluid nature of disciplinary knowledge, the idea of content as metaphors, models, and mental maps takes on new power. Postman (1979) describes subject areas as "dialects of knowledge"— that is, the disciplines are different ways of articulating our understanding of ourselves and our universe.

Hawkins (1974) goes further, asserting that what is presented as subject-area content in a textbook or syllabus should be considered only the "surface curriculum." Underlying the academic disciplines are central concepts connecting other concepts in other content areas. He states that content-area tasks should be structured in an interdisciplinary fashion to uncover those connections and allow students to explore them.

Semiotic theorists, including Cunningham and Luk (1985), take a similar tack, viewing the various subject areas as alternative sign systems that constitute different but mutually enhancing "interpretants" of human experience. They point to semiotics-based approaches to curriculum that use many sign systems in the framework of existing subject-area study (Suhor, 1984). Dickson (1985) applies a semiotic view to interdisciplinary instruction with computers. He cites "thought-provoking" software that uses "the computer's capacity to provide rapid translation between symbol systems, e.g., oral, verbal, pictorial."

Even if teachers perceive their content areas as interconnected sets of mental maps or metaphors, other problems persist. Getting students to grasp these metaphors calls for skilled teaching—developing new, often complex and interrelated concepts and, in some instances, coping with misconceptions.

Another problem is that there is no agreement about a common vocabulary that teachers can use to communicate with one another about their fields. Bruner's (1960) notion of the structure of the discipline is perhaps most widely known, but we might seek broader languages for functional, cross-disciplinary communication. Among the various "candidate vocabularies," semiotics provides a powerful array of terms and concepts because it presents disciplines in terms of sign systems, each with its own semantic, syntactic (structural), and pragmatic elements. Perkins's (1984) idea of knowledge as design also provides a potentially useful language. He sees knowledge as "designs shaped by human invention," with the common elements of purpose, structure, model cases, and argument. His categories might serve as bridges for the everyday exchange of ideas among teachers of different subject areas.

Content Areas as Changing Bodies of Knowledge

The search for concepts central to each discipline does not imply that the disciplines are static. We agree with Haas (1986), who would encourage students to view content-area knowledge as "stories told by society to organize the world." Sometimes these stories change as we choose to organize the world differently. Sometimes we do not have a good story for certain phenomena or we are between stories.

Haas's (1986) approach is simply one way of saying that disciplinary knowledge constantly changes and reshapes itself. Knowledge is fluid not only in the minds of individuals but in an objective sense. This dynamic view of disciplinary knowledge differs from that of a century ago. Schwartz and Ogilvy (1979) speak of a "paradigm shift" that our understanding of disciplinary knowledge has undergone within the last century. They identify seven major areas of change in how we understand disciplines:

- *From simple to complex and diverse.* We once thought that the task of disciplinary knowledge was to reduce the information in a field to its simplest form. We no longer see the world as simple. Rather, we view disciplinary knowledge as comprising open systems, which interact with other open systems.

- *From hierarchical to heterarchical.* In the old understanding of content knowledge, the principles within it had a definite "pecking order"—a hierarchy of information. Now we tend to view information as organized heterarchically— as interlocking systems that create mutual constraints and influences. There are no immutable rules or principles "to discover" at the top of a discipline.

- *From mechanical to holographic.* In a mechanical view of content knowledge, one piece of information is linked in a simple way to another piece of information within the discipline, much as the parts of a machine are related to one another. In a holographic perspective, information is totally interconnected—each piece connected to every other piece, each containing the seeds of the others.

- *From determinate to indeterminate.* We once believed that if we knew all the information in a discipline, we could perfectly predict all events within the discipline. This situation would exist in a determinate system. In an indeterminate system, probabilities and possibilities can be known, but precise outcomes cannot be predicted.

- *From linear causality to mutual causality.* Linear causality assumes that simple actions always lead to the same results. A system operating on mutual causality assumes that effects feed information back to causes. When it mutually benefits both cause and effect, change occurs.

- *From assembly to morphogenesis.* In the old view of content knowledge, all components were created by assembling other parts or pieces of information. A morphogenic perspective includes the possibility that a new form, unpredicted by any of its parts, can arise in a system.

- *From objective to perspective.* Until this century, we were taught to believe that the way to know about the world was to stand outside of it and observe it objectively. We assumed that our mental processes and the techniques we used were somehow neutral. But we have discovered that it is virtually impossible to view the world neutrally. The assumptions we make, even the instruments we use, shape the information we perceive. This perspective view of content-area knowledge implies that the individual is inexorably linked to the content, which itself is fluid and changing. Curriculum and instruction, as functional context theorists note, must take into account not only the learners' prior knowledge, but also the academic and social contexts they are likely to experience in the future

(Sticht and Hickey, in press). Thus, students must be taught to think for themselves, lest they become entrapped in an information-bound view of content that virtually guarantees obsolescence.

Content Areas as Special Approaches to Investigation

Another important issue concerning content-area knowledge is how far students should be guided through the thinking processes and skills specialists use. As Presseisen (1985) notes, the nature of subject content is only part of the issue; the "ways the historian, mathematician, or author thinks in his or her subject matter is another dimension" (p. 51).

When we consider the relevance of specialists' thinking processes to classroom instruction in a discipline, some paradoxes and important differences come to light. In some subject areas, a wide chasm exists between the traditional presentation of content in schools and the specialist's methods of investigation.

For example, historians examine many primary sources to get a coherent interpretation of particular places, people, and periods. This specialized mode of inquiry involves, among other things, much deductive thinking, formulation of questions, and high inferential powers. Yet the results of historians' work are commonly written into narratives, which are summarized and then presented as mere declarative information in textbooks. The student reading history is hard pressed to infer the approaches the historian used.

By contrast, instruction in literature and the performing arts has traditionally relied on understanding and emulating the mental processes of expert critics and practitioners. Science educators, too, have long stressed the importance of processes and skills such as defining and analyzing problems; formulating principles; and observing, classifying, and verifying rather than memorizing facts (Bransford, Sherwood, Rieser, & Vye, 1986).

Referring to Whitehead's idea of inert knowledge, Bransford and his associates (1986) claim that mastering concepts in a discipline does not ensure transfer of learning or understanding of its real-world applications. Knowledge is inert when it is "accessed only in a restricted set of contexts," such as solving problems (and taking tests) in the classroom.

Experts acquire knowledge through particular mental process and approaches to investigation. But beyond that, they can apply disciplinary knowledge broadly and "debug" their thinking in pursuing further knowledge. Novices need to learn, through content-related instruction in thinking and through instruction in metacognitive strategies, how the classroom study of concepts—from logarithms to plot development to bicameral legislatures—relates to problems in the real world and to the expansion of their own powers of reflection and action.

Research on students' "misconceptions" reveals that the problem of teaching core ideas in relation to specialists' mental processes is much more complex than was previously believed. Studies of experts and novices in areas such as science and mathematics suggest that experts organize their knowledge around key concepts that result in a deep understanding of basic operating principles.

Novices do not have these key concepts—and research indicates that in many cases the concepts cannot be taught directly (Larkin, 1983; Greeno, 1983).

This startling research shows that students do not always simply add new knowledge to what they already know about a content area. As Anderson and Smith (in press) note, students must abandon ingrained habits of thought and adopt more complex and even counterintuitive ways of thinking—restructuring information, formulating new questions, and making bold inferences. Rather than viewing content knowledge in terms of a set of concepts, facts, and principles that students can add to incrementally, we need to see some content knowledge as information that gradually changes in structure, becoming much more sophisticated in the process.

Learning scientific information reveals characteristic student misconceptions. For example, even after students were specifically instructed in the New-tonian concept of gravity, they returned to naive preconceptions when describing forces that operate in flipping a coin. Similarly, a unit on photosynthesis did not result in the intended insights; students resorted to "commonsense" notions of fertilizer and soil as food for plants.

To learn subject-area content, then, students must replace misconceptions with newer, more accurate ideas. This process can involve a "radical restructur-ing" of knowledge in which prior knowledge is a barrier for students to over-come rather than schemata to build on. Imaginative teaching that relies heavily on oral discourse (especially Socratic dialogue) and analogies, metaphors, and physical models seems most useful in dealing with students' misconceptions (Vosniadou & Brewer, 1987).

Posner, Strike, Hewson, and Gertzog (1982) have suggested four conditions needed for students to change their central concepts:

• *There must be dissatisfaction with existing concepts.* Students must be aware of their own ideas and recognize the dissonance between their ideas and the scientific community's ideas.

• *A new concept must be intelligible.* Students must know what the idea means and be able to construct a representation of it. But students do not necessarily have to believe it to be true or related to the real world.

• *A new concept must be initially plausible.* Students must find the new concept to be potentially true and believable, consistent with their existing view of the world. They must be able to reconcile the new concept with their prior concepts.

• *A new concept must be fruitful.* If students are going to incorporate a new concept into an existing schema at the expense of a comfortable, long-held misconception, the reason must be convincing. Thus, the new idea must be more useful than the old idea. A new concept can be considered fruitful if it solves a previously unsolved problem, if it suggests new ideas, or if it gives better explanatory and predictive power (Roth, 1985, pp. 4-5).

Roth (1985) states that rather than present students with new information to be learned in an incremental fashion, teachers should present them with strat-

egies for forming new concepts and principles. Roth found that students have difficulty changing old ideas because of several information-processing errors:
- Overreliance on prior knowledge
- Overreliance on words in the text to complete a task
- Overreliance on unrelated facts in the text
- Separation of disciplinary knowledge and real-world knowledge

She states that students who more readily accomplish conceptual change are
- aware of key statements in the text that are incompatible with their prior knowledge;
- able to recognize the main goal concepts of the text;
- aware of the conflict between the text explanations and their own misconceptions and are willing to abandon misconceptions to resolve the conflict;
- aware that the text is leading to changes in their own thinking about real-world knowledge;
- aware of places where the text explanations are confusing because they conflict with the students' previous beliefs; and
- able to use text ideas to explain real-world phenomena.

Implications

Clearly, the role of knowledge is central to teaching thinking. We do not claim that thinking can be taught only in relation to the study of content areas. We suggest, though, that content instruction should be strongly linked with instruction in thinking. Consequently, content-area specialists should identify the important schemata, models and metaphors, and modes of investigation in their domains. These should be explicitly taught and reinforced in an integrated fashion with the skills, processes, and other dimensions described in this book. For example, teachers might stress a special approach to investigation as an adaptation of the process of research described in Chapter 5. Using the concept-formation or principle-formation processes described in Chapter 4, teachers might reinforce a specific schema.

Finally, content-area teachers should view their domain as fluid and ever-changing. Therefore, they should not be too rigid in demanding that students understand the content in one particular way. Instead, teachers should realize that the ultimate goal of content-area instruction is for students to integrate the knowledge into their existing store of ideas. This implies that students should process new knowledge in ways that are meaningful and useful to them as individuals.

7. Use of the Framework

Although we have discussed application of each of the dimensions in previous chapters, here we consider use of the framework as a whole for curriculum, instruction, and assessment.

Curriculum

What Is Taught

The dimensions are intended as aspects of students' cognitive growth that may be accounted for in any curriculum. Thus, a school that adopts our framework might include the following as general goals, implementing them appropriately at each grade level:

- Students should attain high levels of knowledge in the various subject areas.
- Students should have a repertoire of cognitive and metacognitive skills and strategies that they can call on as they engage in various cognitive processes.
- Students should be able to use these skills and strategies with increasing independence and responsibility for their own learning.
- Students should be aware of the nature of thinking and of their capability to control their attitudes, dispositions, and development.
- Students should have standards for evaluating what is "good" thinking and be able to think critically and creatively.

These goals should be integrated into the course of study for each content area. Cognitive and metacognitive skills should be taught when warranted by the content and the teaching process. Curriculum planners should identify the concepts, ideas, processes, and principles that are especially important for students to understand. Frames and graphic organizers, mental models and metaphors, and modes of investigation provide powerful tools for sequencing instruction in most subject areas, although much research is needed to go beyond our rudimentary knowledge of what the key questions and categories are in each area.

How the Curriculum Is Sequenced

As to sequencing, we strongly caution against rigid conceptions and lock-step applications of skill hierarchies and spiraled curriculum. Certainly, there are some valid skill hierarchies such as teaching addition before multiplication, short stories before the novel, or simple harmonies before dissonant chords. However, little evidence supports objectives that move in a lock-step fashion through skills hierarchies, reifying and overapplying concepts such as those in Bloom's taxonomy (Bloom, Engelhart, Furst, Hill, & Krathwohl, 1956). Research on memory, comprehension, and problem solving has questioned the idea that neatly ordered taxonomies are appropriate guides for educational objectives. Throughout this book, we have noted that high-level thinking skills such as verifying and summarizing are based on recalling and comparing information and are not somehow "above" these skills.

Many educators believe that instruction in thinking is not appropriate for younger students and low-achieving students. Clearly, younger or less proficient students may have difficulty learning complex skills such as restructuring and creating analogies. Yet these skills are fundamental not only to understanding but to conceptual change. Their difficulty should not preclude efforts to teach them.

From current research on cognitive development, we know that these and other skills can be taught successfully to these students—given instruction in cognitive and metacognitive strategies, appropriate sequencing, and adequate teacher support in modeling, coaching, and guided practice. In fact, recent data from Brown and Cane's (1987) research on primary-grade children suggest that with appropriate instruction, these children have a remarkable capability to transfer what they learn. Of course, teaching less capable students will not be easy. But substantial evidence indicates that these students do indeed benefit— sometimes dramatically—from cognitive instruction.

Finally, we caution against assumptions that young children cannot think abstractly, that objectives involving reflection and critical thinking must be reserved for upper elementary grades or high school. Although analyzing absolute phrases or discussing quantum theory with 5th-graders would be folly, children can have abstract ideas (e.g., about story structures) and can develop relatively sophisticated cognitive and metacognitive strategies.

One way of conceptualizing the sequencing of thinking-skills instruction is to use the "ski analogy," developed by Burton, Brown, and Fischer (1984; see also Lesgold, 1986). One ultimately wants to learn to ski with long skis, but learning to ski with long skis is cumbersome and inefficient. Teaching prerequisite skills (such as holding the poles, breathing, and turning) separately from the process of skiing in specific environments is not helpful. Learning to ski with short skis, using rudiments of the various skills needed for long skis, is more productive. Then, as the novice gains proficiency, the skis become longer, and the learning environments change to provide more challenging contexts.

This analogy applies to sequencing thinking skills both in adjunct courses and content courses. Instead of teaching dozens of discrete subskills in a progression from easy to difficult, schools might define a limited number of core skills for each content-area or skills course and focus on teaching these skills in ever more challenging learning contexts. What would be sequenced from easy to difficult would be not a broad array of discrete subskills, as is often the case in traditional skills instruction, but rather the content and tasks.

Collins, Brown, and Newman (in press) articulate three principles for sequencing curriculum consistent with the notion of holistic skills instruction: (1) increasing the complexity of the content and the task, (2) increasing the diversity of the applications, and (3) "scaffolding" (i.e., providing adequate supports for learning, with gradual transfer of responsibility for learning from teacher to student).

Consider summarizing, for example. Using traditional principles, we might sequence the summarizing rules so that the easiest rules are objectives for younger and less proficient students, and the more difficult rules are objectives for older and more proficient students (Brown, Campione, & Day, 1981). If, instead, we used the principles suggested by Collins, Brown, and Newman, we would teach summarizing holistically at all grade levels; we would sequence the content, tasks, and instruction to match the learners' capabilities. Thus, primary-grade students would first summarize concrete, familiar, simple, and short material (e.g., a short narrative passage), and the task would be relatively easy (e.g., constructing oral summaries).

Scaffolding—sequencing instruction so that students have a framework or "scaffold" on which they can construct new meaning—can be provided in a number of ways: modeling, coaching, asking the whole class to construct the summary, providing or eliciting a graphic representation of the text, or providing structural prompts such as partially completed summaries. The amount of scaffolding will, of course, depend on the students' capabilities.

As students gain proficiency in constructing oral summaries, teachers might make the task increasingly difficult by decreasing the various supports or by providing increasingly diverse applications. Teachers can introduce longer, more complex narratives. Subsequent objectives might focus on producing written summaries and increasing the diversity of the materials to be summarized.

Teachers can use similar principles to sequence instruction in metacognition. At the primary level, students can learn a simple metacognitive strategy such as asking the purpose of a particular task: "What am I trying to do right now?" Initially, teachers might activate this skill by posing the question and its answer aloud as well as discussing the usefulness of the skill. Teachers might then ask students to articulate their thinking about increasingly difficult tasks. At the secondary level, students can learn fairly complex metacognitive strategies such as those depicted in Figure 7.1, which include various aspects of self-knowledge as well as procedural and conditional knowledge.

Figure 7.1

1. *Refocusing*—students relax and end whatever previous activity they were engaged in.

2. *Awareness*—students notice:
   a. their level of distraction (e.g., how much they are attending to thoughts unrelated to the class),
   b. their attitude toward the class (e.g., if they believe the class is valuable or not valuable, interesting or boring),
   c. their attitude toward working (e.g., their commitment to the class),
   d. their attitude toward their ability (e.g., a sense of power about their ability to perform well in the class or a sense of sinking), and
   e. other attitudes.

3. *Commitment*—students:
   a. hold off or "bracket" any thoughts unrelated to the class,
   b. generate interest and value for the class,
   c. commit to being involved and exerting necessary effort,
   d. take a stand that they can do well, and
   e. make other commitments.

4. *Goal setting*—students:
   a. set some specific goals for the class, and
   b. integrate the teacher's goals with their own.

5. *Task engagement*—students:
   a. monitor whether they are getting closer to or further from their stated goals, and
   b. make any corrections necessary in their own behavior or seek help to further the attainment of their goals.

6. *Task completion*—students:
   a. determine if their goals were accomplished, and
   b. evaluate what worked and what did not work relative to their goals.

From Marzano and Arredondo, 1986.

Instruction

Our framework has far-reaching implications for teaching, affecting the role of the teacher, models of instruction, and lesson planning. Our analysis of the teacher draws upon the research on expert teaching, instruction, and learning because we believe that the teacher is also a learner; expert teachers are expert learners. This conception of the teacher and the process of instruction varies markedly from traditional views. To create a teaching force committed to and capable of carrying out cognitive instruction, we will need to change substantially preservice and inservice teacher education, teacher supervision, and ultimately teacher certification.

The Role of the Teacher

Throughout this framework, we have portrayed model students as strategic learners who have well-structured knowledge of content and a repertoire of cognitive and metacognitive strategies; who can access information and execute strategies flexibly; who strive to clearly conceptualize what they learn; who enjoy being productive, solving problems, and making decisions; and who can evaluate information critically and creatively.

Model teachers are also expert learners, based on recent research comparing the characteristics of expert teachers to experts in various content subjects (Berliner, 1986). Generally, both types of experts deeply understand the content as well as the processes of learning and teaching. Like model students, expert teachers spend a lot of time planning, recognize quickly many patterns related to the content subject and to classroom instruction, anticipate problems and solutions, monitor the process of learning and instruction, and change strategies when students are not meeting goals. Thus, model teachers function as strategic teachers in ways that are parallel to strategic learners, striving to attain cognitive and metacognitive goals in their professional lives and in the act of teaching.

What, specifically, are the roles of the expert teacher? Clearly, expert teaching has many facets. Based on data from effective-teaching research, Good and Brophy (1984) discuss the role of the teacher as manager. Among other things, the teacher keeps track of student achievements and problems and monitors the classroom for discipline, interpersonal relationships, and time on task. Berliner (1984a, 1984b) sees the expert teacher as an executive, deciding on the content and selecting cognitive processes to teach as well as deciding about levels of prior knowledge, grouping, and pacing. Certainly these roles are vital, but we need to go beyond them to explore what teachers do to help students learn.

The idea of the teacher as mediator in student cognitive processing (Winne & Marx, 1983; Wittrock, 1986) is highly consistent with our framework. *Mediate*, as used here, means to serve as a guide—to intercede between the learners, the substance of what is to be learned, and the context. A mediator, whether a parent or a friend or a teacher, works actively to help the learner interpret the environment. At times, mediating may involve helping students to formulate a question or construct a visual representation of a problem. At other times, mediating may involve guiding students to develop positive attitudes toward work. Mediating functions may also include focusing attention, linking new information to prior knowledge, and explaining how ideas are related (Duffy, Roehler, & Rackliffe, in press). Modeling the process of thinking by thinking aloud is another critical mediating strategy.

According to Feuerstein and Jensen (1980; Feuerstein, Jensen, Hoffman, & Rand, 1985), the mediating functions of teaching may make the difference between high and low achievement. Typically, low-achieving students have rela-

134

tively few contacts in which parents, teachers, or others actively mediate learning experiences. In contrast, high-achieving students often have access to a variety of mediating contacts from early childhood onward. Thus, Feuerstein's theory of mediated learning experiences is not only a concept about learning, it is a concept about interrelationships in society and differing access to educational experiences.

Models of Instruction

Teaching thinking requires specifying clearly and in detail the interaction between what is taught and the pedagogy used to teach it. The different types of knowledge identified within the dimensions often imply different pedagogies.

One way to view those types of knowledge is to consider some as more dynamic and others as more static. The term *dynamic* indicates that the knowledge is meant to be "executed" by students. Dynamic knowledge is meant to be used by students to perform some mental or physical operation. For example, knowledge of how to perform a specific type of experiment or how to compose a particular kind of essay is dynamic. Students must be able to execute a task mentally and physically. From this perspective, the following aspects of the dimensions are more dynamic:

- Metacognitive strategies
- Cognitive processes
- Core thinking skills and strategies
- Content-area procedural knowledge
- Special modes of investigating in content areas

All have a strong "performance" component. Students must be able to execute or perform metacognitive strategies, core thinking skills, and so on.

Static knowledge may be used in dynamic knowledge, but it cannot be "performed." For example, students' knowledge of concepts such as "equilibrium" and "propaganda" cannot be performed. That knowledge might be applied in a dynamic process such as solving a problem or making a decision, but the information itself involves no activity. From this perspective, the following dimensions can be considered more static:

- Concepts
- Principles
- Factual knowledge
- Content-area declarative and conditional knowledge

The pedagogy used to teach and reinforce dynamic knowledge normally differs from the pedogogy used for static knowledge. For example, pedagogy designed for dynamic knowledge must be sensitive to its developmental nature. Fitts (1964) explains that while acquiring dynamic knowledge, learners progress through three stages: the cognitive, the associative, and the autonomous.

First, during the cognitive stage, learners may be able to verbalize the strategy but be unable to execute it well. For example, when first learning a strategy for problem solving, such as brainstorming ideas for a solution, students may be poor at actually performing the process. Therefore, the teacher needs to help students understand the elements of that process—for example, generating ideas in abundance, stating hunches, and temporarily suspending judgment. The teacher might discuss those elements with students and list them on the board. She might then model the processes, pointing out various aspects or component parts. At this stage, the objective would be to deepen students' understanding of the process rather than to seek a high level of performance.

During the associative stage of acquiring dynamic knowledge, learners begin to smooth out the process, adding, changing, and deleting elements along the way. Here students take what the teacher has presented and *change* it, tailoring it to their own personal style. Thus, students might leave some elements out from those originally presented, add others, and modify still others. For example, a student composing a persuasive essay might choose to "free write" a first draft, intending to use the initial draft as raw material instead of jotting down key phrases and other notes in a quasi-outline form for a more orderly first draft. Such strategic differences and adaptations of the composing process are in fact common among skilled student and adult writers.

Any strategy may need to be adapted to fit the personality, needs, interests, and skills of the individual. We need to teach specific strategies to students, but the strategies should be considered a starting place. They provide a common vocabulary for teachers and students to use to discuss the dynamic knowledge being studied. Teaching of skills prescriptively can actually inhibit the learning process because it does not allow students to progress through the important "shaping" and "personalizing" stages of learning dynamic information (Combs, 1982; Lohman, 1986).

To guide students through the associative stage, the teacher provides guided practice, though not in a formulaic or prescriptive manner. Rather than monitoring students' performance to make sure they are "getting it right," teachers should ask probing questions to help guide students' decisions as they shape a particular process. The teacher does not automatically intervene when students are about to make an error. Instead, the teacher helps them to predict the possible consequences of their actions or to consider the implications of their line of thought—helping them, in effect, to learn to forecast possible errors in their own thinking.

Finally, to help students reach the level of autonomy (the automatic stage) (Kamii, 1984), to help them perform the strategy with little conscious effort, the teacher provides for independent practice. Here we disagree with Hunter's (1984) statement that "independent practice is assigned only after the teacher is reasonably sure that students will not make serious errors" (p. 176). Although not intended by Hunter, this position can foster a lack of trust in students' abilities to shape effective strategies independently. If guided practice makes students aware that they might have "bugs" in their strategies, then the teacher gives the students opportunities to continue to develop individual strategies, even without strong direction. Groen and Resnick dramatically illustrate this idea in their 1977 study: Preschoolers were taught an addition algorithm that was clumsy to use; with practice but without further instruction, the children transformed the routine into a more efficient one.

Static knowledge, like dynamic knowledge, implies specific pedagogies. When knowledge is static, the instructional goal is for students to assimilate the information into their existing knowledge base. Therefore, the pedagogy should emphasize various representational techniques and schema-development techniques like those described in Chapters 4 and 5. The teacher works to eliminate misconceptions and to develop textual schemata. The instructional principles of guided practice and independent practice have little application, since there is relatively little "performance" per se. Rather, the teacher provides many opportunities for students to see, hear, and manipulate static information, including wide reading and rich language experiences, as well as opportunities for application and discussion of future applications.

The broad dynamic-static knowledge distinction, if misunderstood, can be applied inappropriately. For example, students "perform" in a real sense when they read to acquire static knowledge, since reading is an interaction between reader and text. But the distinction between dynamic and static knowledge illustrates that no single pedagogical model fits all types of knowledge equally well.

Assessment

Doyle's (1983) study of academic work in American schools reveals that what we assess and how we assess it drive both the curriculum and the tasks we present to students in the classroom. As a result, students tend to take seriously only tasks that we hold them accountable for by testing. If we want students to take instruction in thinking seriously, then we must somehow hold them accountable for their performance on the processes, skills, and other aspects of the dimensions. But many dimensions cannot be accurately assessed with paper-and-pencil tests. Furthermore, successfully teaching critical and creative thinking does not often lead students to a single "right answer."

Nevertheless, if it is correct that students concentrate on what is to be tested, two things are immediately obvious: Teachers need to create better classroom tests as magnets for student attention, and we need to expand the concept of test to include the richer, more dynamic aspects of thinking described here.

Applying Criteria for Effective Assessments

There are no de facto heroes or villains inherent in the distinctions often made among assessment types: qualitative versus quantitative, paper-and-pencil tests versus performance tests, observation scales versus interviews. Each type of assessment can be effectively used or badly abused. The most important applied criterion in designing an assessment is its content validity, its degree of overlap with the skills and dispositions being fostered in the classroom. The assessment must be sensitive to capturing and reflecting any improvements that might have occurred in the students' thinking skills and dispositions. Here most assessments go astray. The assessment must be reliable; different evaluators should reach the same conclusion about the quality of students' thinking. To make these conclusions possible, it is important to state explicitly the behavioral criteria that all raters will use. Also, assessments must be diagnostic, with the potential to provide feedback to students that will enable them to improve their thinking. The behavioral criteria for successful thinking should be so clearly specified from the beginning that students can use these before the assessment to monitor their own thinking.

Creating Better Classroom Tests

Several new sources enable teachers to create better paper-and-pencil tests that require students to use their knowledge rather than merely recall it. They include Carlson's (1985) compendium of ten designs for assessment and instruction, with applications for English, social studies, and science, and Stiggins, Rubel, and Quellmalz's (1986) guidelines for teachers to use in incorporating recall, analysis, comparison, inference, and evaluation in oral questions and performance and paper-and-pencil tests.

Recently developed statewide assessments also have the potential to influence classroom tests. New reading assessments in Michigan and Illinois take into account schema theory and contextual concerns such as the use of entire selections instead of snippets (Peters, 1987; Valencia, 1987). Massachusetts has recently integrated critical reading and critical thinking skills into its latest statewide assessment (Massachusetts Department of Education, 1987). California has recently tried to merge critical thinking skills with the assessment of social studies (Kneedler, 1984).

Using Performance Tasks on Large-Scale Assessments

Recent assessments have tried to evaluate more complex student performance in large-scale assessment settings. Burstall (1986) describes some techniques used in Britain's national assessments in English oracy, foreign languages, scientific inquiry, and mathematical problem solving. Since 1980, the Connecticut Assessment of Educational Progress program has used performance tasks on statewide student samples in art and music, business and office education, English language arts, science, foreign language, and industrial arts (see Figure 7.2). Baron (1985) provides evidence from Connecticut's performance tests in language arts and science that demonstrates how teachers reach different conclusions when, instead of analyzing multiple-choice data, they observe student behavior and talk with students engaged in sustained tasks. Baron (1987) reviews Pittsburgh's approaches to evaluate classroom discussions; Bristol's (Connecticut) approach, supported by a Carnegie Foundation grant, to integrate reading, writing, and thinking in a high school; and researchers' approaches to studying

138

Figure 7.2

Performance Testing in the Connecticut Assessment of Educational Progress Program, 1980-87

Subject	Year	Grades Tested	Performance Task	Whole Sample or Subsample	Administration Time	When scored? (After self-administered testing or during other-administered testing)
Art	1980-81	4, 8, 11	Draw a room wall and draw a table with people around it	Subsample	1 class period	After
Music	1980-81	4, 8, 11	Sing "America" and complete a musical phrase	Subsample	A few minutes	During
Business and Office Education	1983-84					
Accounting		12	Make journal entries and complete a payroll record	Whole	1 class period	After
General Office		12	Timed typing	Whole	1 class period	After
Secretary		12	Type and compose part of a letter	Whole	1 class period	After
			Take shorthand	Whole	Part of a class period	After
English Language Arts	1983-84	4, 8, 11	Write 2 essays	Subsample	1 class period	After
			Take a dictated spelling and word usage exercise	Subsample	Part of a class period	
			Revise errors in focus, organization, support and mechanics	Subsample	1 class period	After
			Take notes from a taped lecture	Subsample	Part of a class period	After

continued

Figure 7.2
continued

Subject	Year	Grades Tested	Performance Task	Whole Sample or Subsample	Administration Time	When scored? (After self-administered testing or during other-administered testing)
Science	1984-85	4, 8, 11	Use scientific apparatus: weigh, meas-ure, focus microscope, etc.	Subsample	1 class period	During
		8, 11	Design and conduct an experiment	Subsample	1 class period	During
Foreign Language French German Italian Spanish	1986-87	9-12	Write a letter Speak to an interviewer	Whole Subsample	1 class period 1 class period	After During
Industrial Arts and Technology Education	1986-87					
Drafting		12	Produce a series of drawings	Subsample	3¼ hours	During
Graphic Arts		12	Produce a brochure	Subsample	5½ hours	During
Small Engines		12	Service and repair small engines	Subsample	3¼ hours	During

For information, contact Joan Boykoff Baron, Connecticut State Department of Education, P.O. Box 2219, Room 342, Hartford, CT 06145.

how thinking-skills programs affect attitudes and dispositions. Stiggins, Conklin, and Bridgeford (1986) provide some criteria for designing effective performance tasks for use in classrooms, including "clearly articulating and communicating scoring criteria, defining acceptable levels of performance, repeating observa-tions, keeping written records, and checking judgments against other data (e.g., test scores)" (p. 9).

Using Classroom-Based Qualitative Evaluation

Classroom-based qualitative evaluation has been developed in various con-tent areas. For example, in assessing reading competency, Goodman (1978) recommends "kid watching," which involves observing, interacting, document-ing, and interpreting. The teacher observes students as they use reading materials, interacting with them and gathering clues about their thinking processes. Anec-dotal records of these interactions become a resource for interpreting student strengths and weaknesses. Assessment, then, does not occur only at testing time. Rather, it is an ongoing part of the teaching and learning process as students get feedback on their progress on daily tasks.

A recent article by Gable and Rogers (1987) describes some additional interactive approaches (i.e., small-group interviews, situational pictures, card sorting, learning logs, and an open-ended version of the conventional teacher-made test) that one teacher used to assess the depth of his 5th-grade students' understanding of the Bill of Rights and the Constitution. Baron and Kallick (1985) have also suggested informal evaluations.

Distinguishing Good Assessments from Good Instructional Tasks

Good assessments are more similar to than different from good instruc-tional tasks. Both use rich, sustained, and complex tasks to provide opportunities for the desired thinking skills and dispositions to surface. Both articulate the criteria for effective performance and give students meaningful feedback. Yet assessments differ from instructional situations in at least two important ways: the teacher's role and the importance of assessing transfer.

The teacher's role in the instructional setting is often catalytic or structuring, providing the scaffolding needed to help students make the necessary connec-tions or fill in the gaps in their thinking. But in evaluation, the teacher generally plays a more passive role, except with Campione and Brown's (undated) "dy-namic assessment" technique. Campione and Brown developed the technique for use with any set of cognitive operations. Building on Vygotsky's concept of a "zone of proximal development," they recommend presenting students with increasingly explicit cues for performing a task:

If they [students] are unable to solve a particular problem, they are given a series of hints to help them. The initial hints are very general ones, and succeeding ones become progressively more specific and more concrete with the last "hint" actually providing a detailed blueprint for generating the correct answer. This . . . allows us to estimate the *minimum* amount of help needed by a given child to solve each problem. The metric of learning efficiency is the number of hints required for the attainment of the learning criterion (pp. 12-13).

A second difference between assessment and instruction emerges when the teacher structures the assessment both to foster and to measure the transfer of learning. Although the tasks will be similar to those used to learn the skills, they will not be identical. Just how they differ and how much they differ are important considerations in developing an effective assessment. The assessment task should be similar enough to the instructional task so that its contextual cues elicit the transfer of appropriate skills and dispositions from the instructional situation to the new one. If the assessment is too different, students may not perceive it as an appropriate opportunity to use the skills and strategies they have learned. Teachers will need to experiment with different degrees of difference to strike the best balance.

Using Standardized, Norm-Referenced Basic Skills

Because of their entrenched presence in American schools, we must consider the appropriate role of nationally normed, standardized, basic-skills tests in assessing thinking. We suggest that the teachers and administrators responsible for designing the assessment of thinking skills in their schools closely scrutinize these national tests to answer one central question: If students have improved their thinking, will the scores on this test improve? If the answer is yes, the tests are a valid indicator of improvement; if the answer is no, then the district should look for different assessment strategies to monitor growth in thinking skills.

"Teaching to" or "Studying for" the Test

As the ultimate criterion in designing effective assessments, teachers and administrators should ask whether a test or performance task is worth "teaching to" or "studying for"? That is, if students structure their study and practice time to learn the skills and strategies required to do well on the assessment, would the time be well spent? Indeed, assessments should be put in place as magnets for study only if they have intrinsic merit and only if they provide an opportunity for students to display a broad array of the skills, processes, and dispositions called for in this book. Otherwise, we will be perpetuating an all-too-common practice that Kerr (1975) describes in "On the Folly of Rewarding A, while Hoping for B."

Constructing the Future of Thinking in Schools

Dimensions of Thinking has been written as a framework for curriculum and instruction. The framework of a house provides a structure for the dwelling, but both labor and materials are added to the framework before construction is complete and someone can live in the home. Likewise, the authors of *Dimensions of Thinking* invite educators to build the curriculum, the instructional strategies, the staff development programs, and the assessment designs that will enable our students to live in schools where thinking is modeled, taught, monitored, and honored.

Appendix A.
Glossary of Terms

Activating prior knowledge: recalling something learned previously relative to the topic or task.

Analyzing skills: core thinking skills that involve clarifying information by examining parts and relationships.

Attention: conscious control of mental focus on particular information.

Attitudes: personally held principles or beliefs that govern much of one's behavior.

Classifying: grouping entities on the basis of their common attributes.

Commitment: an aspect of knowledge and control of self that involves a decision to employ personal energy and resources to attain a goal.

Comparing: noting similarities and differences between or among entities.

Composing: the process of developing a composition, which may be written, musical, mechanical, or artistic.

Comprehending: generating meaning or understanding.

Concept formation: organizing information about an entity and associating that information with a label (word).

Conditional information: information about the appropriate use of an action or process important to a task.

Core thinking skills: cognitive operations used in thinking processes.

Creative thinking: original and appropriate thinking.

Critical thinking: using specific dispositions and skills such as analyzing arguments carefully, seeing other points of view, and reaching sound conclusions.

Curriculum: what is taught in the classroom.

Decision making: selecting from among alternatives.

Declarative information: factual information.

Defining problems: a focusing skill used in clarifying puzzling situations.

Dimensions of thinking: major themes commonly found in discussions of human cognition that can be used in planning for curriculum and instruction.

Dispositions: inclinations to engage in some types of behavior and not to engage in others. Certain dispositions are associated with critical and creative thinking.

Elaborating: adding details, explanations, examples, or other relevant information from prior knowledge.

Encoding skills: remembering skills that involve storing information in long-term memory.

Establishing criteria: setting standards for making judgments.

Evaluating (as applied to metacognition): assessing one's current knowledge state.

Evaluating skills: core thinking skills that involve assessing the reasonableness and quality of ideas.

Executive control: evaluating, planning, and regulating the declarative, procedural, and conditional information involved in a task.

Focusing skills: core thinking skills that involve attending to selected pieces of information and ignoring others.

Formulating questions: an information-gathering skill that involves seeking new information through inquiry.

Generating skills: core thinking skills that involve producing new information, meaning, or ideas.

Identifying attributes and components: determining characteristics or parts of something.

Identifying errors: disconfirming or proving the falsehood of statements.

Identifying relationships and patterns: recognizing ways elements are related.

Inferring: going beyond available information to identify what reasonably may be true.

Information-gathering skills: core thinking skills that involve bringing to consciousness the relevant data needed for cognitive processing.

Integrating skills: core thinking skills that involve connecting or combining information.

Knowledge and control of process: a component of metacognition that involves executive control of declarative, procedural, and conditional information relative to a task.

Knowledge domain: a body of information commonly associated with a particular content area or field of study.

Metacognition: a dimension of thinking that involves knowledge and control of self and knowledge and control of process.

Mnemonics: a set of encoding strategies that involve linking bits of information together through visual or semantic connections.

Observing: an information-gathering skill that involves obtaining information through one or more senses.

Oral discourse: talking with other people.

Ordering: sequencing entities according to a given criterion.

Organizing skills: core thinking skills that involve arranging information so that it can be used more efficiently.

Philosophic tradition: an approach to studying thinking that focuses on broad issues about the nature and quality of thinking and its role in human behavior.

Planning: selecting strategies to fulfill a specific goal or subgoal relative to a task.

Predicting: anticipating the outcome of a situation.

Principle formation: recognizing a relationship between or among concepts.

Problem solving: analyzing and resolving a perplexing or difficult situation.

Procedural information: information about the various actions or processes important to a task.

Psychological tradition: an approach to studying thinking that focuses on the nature of specific cognitive operations.

Recalling skills: remembering skills that involve retrieving information from long-term memory.

Regulating: checking one's progress toward a goal.

Rehearsal: an encoding strategy that involves processing information over and over.

Remembering skills: core thinking skills that involve conscious efforts to store and retrieve information.

Representing: changing existing knowledge structures to incorporate new information.

Research: the process of conducting scientific inquiry.

Restructuring: changing existing knowledge structures to incorporate new information.

Retrieval: accessing previously encoded information.

Schemata: knowledge structures associated with a specific state, event, or concept.

Self-knowledge and self-control: a component of metacognition that involves commitment, attitudes, and attention.

Setting goals: a focusing skill that involves establishing direction and purpose.

Summarizing: combining information efficiently into a cohesive statement.

Thinking processes: relatively complex and time-consuming cognitive operations—such as concept formation, problem solving, and composing—that commonly employ one or more core thinking skills.

Verifying: confirming the accuracy, truth, or quality of an observation, hypothesis, claim, or product.

Appendix B.
Summary Outline of
Dimensions of Thinking:
A Framework for Curriculum
and Instruction

A. Introduction
This book provides a framework intended to help educational leaders (principals, supervisors, curriculum directors, and teachers) plan programs for incorporating the teaching of thinking throughout the regular curriculum.

B. Metacognition
Metacognition refers to awareness and control of one's thinking, including commitment, attitudes, and attention.

C. Critical and Creative Thinking
The terms "critical" and "creative" are ways of describing the way we go about thinking. The two are not opposite ends of a single continuum but are complementary.

1. *Critical thinking* is "reasonable, reflective thinking that is focused on deciding what to believe or do" (Ennis). Critical thinkers try to be aware of their own biases, to be objective and logical.

2. *Creative thinking* is "the ability to form new combinations of ideas to fulfill a need" (Halpern) or to get "original and otherwise appropriate results by the criteria of the domain in question" (Perkins).

D. Thinking Processes
A thinking process is a relatively complex sequence of thinking skills.

1. Concept formation: organizing information about an entity and associating that information with a label (word).

2. Principle formation: recognizing a relationship between or among concepts.

3. Comprehending: generating meaning or understanding by relating new information to prior knowledge.

4. Problem solving: analyzing and resolving a perplexing or difficult situation.

5. Decision making: selecting from among alternatives.

6. Research: conducting scientific inquiry.

7. Composing: developing a product, which may be written, musical, mechanical, or artistic.

8. Oral discourse: talking with other people.

E. Core Thinking Skills

Thinking skills are relatively specific cognitive operations that can be considered the "building blocks" of thinking. The following (1) have a sound basis in the research and theoretical literature, (2) are important for students to be able to do, and (3) can be taught and reinforced in school.

FOCUSING SKILLS—attending to selected pieces of information and ignoring others.

1. Defining problems: clarifying needs, discrepancies, or puzzling situations.

2. Setting goals: establishing direction and purpose.

INFORMATION-GATHERING SKILLS—bringing to consciousness the relevant data needed for cognitive processing.

3. Observing: obtaining information through one or more senses.

4. Formulating questions: seeking new information through inquiry.

REMEMBERING SKILLS—storing and retrieving information.

5. Encoding: storing information in long-term memory.

6. Recalling: retrieving information from long-term memory.

ORGANIZING SKILLS—arranging information so it can be used more effectively.

7. Comparing: noting similarities and differences between or among entities.

8. Classifying: grouping and labeling entities on the basis of their attributes.

9. Ordering: sequencing entities according to a given criterion.

10. Representing: changing the form but not the substance of information.

ANALYZING SKILLS—clarifying existing information by examining parts and relationships.

11. Identifying attributes and components: determining characteristics or parts of something.

12. Identifying relationships and patterns: recognizing ways elements are related.

13. Identifying main ideas: identifying the central element; for example, the hierarchy of key ideas in a message or line of reasoning.

14. Identifying errors: recognizing logical fallacies and other mistakes and, where possible, correcting them.

GENERATING SKILLS—producing new information, meaning, or ideas.

15. Inferring: going beyond available information to identify what reasonably may be true.

16. Predicting: anticipating next events, or the outcome of a situation.

17. Elaborating: explaining by adding details, examples, or other relevant information.

INTEGRATING SKILLS—connecting and combining information.

18. Summarizing: combining information efficiently into a cohesive statement.

19. Restructuring: changing existing knowledge structures to incorporate new information.

EVALUATING SKILLS—assessing the reasonableness and quality of ideas.

20. Establishing criteria: setting standards for making judgments.

21. Verifying: confirming the accuracy of claims.

F. The Relationship of Knowledge to Thinking

Some aspects of thinking are inseparably linked to content-area knowledge. We can define problems or identify patterns only if we know enough about the topic in question. Knowlege is stored in memory in structures called "schemata," and can sometimes best be represented by models and metaphors.

G. Using the Framework

Schools should teach thinking to all students in the context of academic courses. To that end, teachers should be thinkers themselves, modeling metacognition, goal setting, and problem solving.

References

Abelson, R. (1975). Concepts for representing mundane reality in plans. In D. Bobrow & A. Collins (Eds.), *Representation and understanding: Studies in cognitive science*. New York: Academic Press.

Alston, William. (1964). *Philosophy of language*. Englewood Cliffs, NJ: Prentice-Hall.

Amabile, T.M. (1983). *The social psychology of creativity*. New York: Springer-Verlag.

Anderson, C.W., & Smith, E.L. (1984). Children's preconceptions and content-area textbooks. In G. Duffy, L. Roehler, & J. Mason (Eds.), *Comprehension instruction: Perspectives and suggestions*. New York: Longman.

Anderson, C.W., & Smith, E.L. (in press). Teaching science. In V. Koehler (Ed.), *The educator's handbook: A research perspective*. New York: Longman.

Anderson, J. (1983). *The architecture of cognition*. Cambridge, MA: Harvard University Press.

Anderson, R.C. (1977). The notion of schemata and the educational enterprise. In R.C. Anderson, R.J. Spiro, & W.E. Montague (Eds.), *Schooling and the acquisition of knowledge*. Hillsdale, NJ: Erlbaum.

Anderson, R.C. (1984). Role of reader's schema in comprehension, learning, and memory. In R.C. Anderson, J. Osborn, & R.J. Tierney (Eds.), *Learning to read in American schools: Basal readers and content texts*. Hillsdale, NJ: Erlbaum.

Anderson, R.C., & Freebody, P. (1981). Vocabulary knowledge. In J.T. Gurthrie (Ed.), *Comprehension and teaching*. Newark, DE: International Reading Association.

Anderson, R.C., & Pearson, P.D. (1985). A schema-theoretic view of basic processes in reading comprehension. In P.D. Pearson (Ed.), *Handbook of reading research*. New York: Longman.

Anderson, R.C., Hiebert, E.H., Scott, J.A., & Wilkinson, I.A. (1986). *Becoming a nation of readers*. Washington, DC: National Institute of Education.

Anderson, T.H., & Armbruster, B.B. (1985). Studying. In P.D. Pearson (Ed.), *Handbook of reading research*. New York: Longman.

Anderson, T.H., & Foertsch, D.J. (in press). *On making frequent predictions while reading expository text*. Urbana, IL: University of Illinois, Center for the Study of Reading.

Anderson, V., & Burlis, P.J. (1987, June). *Improving teachers' abilities to foster intentional learning and remedial reading lessons*. Paper presented at the Third National Thinking Skills Conference, Cincinnati, Ohio.

Andre, T. (1987). Questions and learning from reading. *Questioning Exchange, 1*, 47-86.

Applebee, A.N. (1984). Writing and reasoning. *Review of Educational Research, 54*, 577-596.

Armbruster, B.B. (1980, April). *Mapping: An innovative reading comprehension/study strategy*. Paper presented at the annual meeting of the American Educational Research Association, Boston.

Armbruster, B.B., Anderson, T.H., Bruning, R.H., & Meyer, L.A. (1984). *What did you mean by that question?: A taxonomy of American history questions* (Technical Report No. 308). Urbana, IL: University of Illinois, Center for the Study of Reading.

Ballsteadt, S.P., & Mandl, H. (1984). *Diagnosis of knowledge structures in text learning* (Technical Report No. 37). Tubingen, West Germany: Deutsches Institute fur Fernstudien an der Universitat Tubingen.

Baron, J. (1985). Assessing higher order thinking skills in Connecticut. In C.P. Kearney (Ed.), *Assessing higher order thinking skills* (ERIC/TME Report 90). Princeton, NJ: Educational Testing Service.

Baron, J. (1987). Evaluating thinking skills in the classroom. In J.B. Baron & R.J. Sternberg (Eds.), *Teaching thinking skills: Theory and practice*. New York: Freeman.

Baron, J.B., & Kallick, B. (1985). Assessing thinking: What are we looking for? And how can we find it? In A. Costa (Ed.), *Developing minds: A resource book for teaching thinking*. Alexandria, VA: Association for Supervision and Curriculum Development.

Barron, F. (1969). *The creative person and creative process*. New York: Holt, Rinehart & Winston.

Berliner, D.C. (1984a, October). *Contemporary teacher education: Timidity, lack of vision, and ignorance*. Paper presented to the National Academy of Education, Berkeley, CA.

Berliner, D.C. (1984b). The half full glass: A review of research in teaching. In P.L. Hosford (Ed.), *Using what we know about teaching*. Alexandria, VA: Association for Supervision and Curriculum Development.

Berliner, D.C. (1986). In pursuit of the expert pedagogue. *Educational Researcher, 15,* 5-14.

Bernstein, H. (1985). When more is less: The mentioning problem in textbooks. *American Educator, 9,* 26-29, 44-55.

Black, M. (1962). *Models and metaphors: Studies in language and philosophy*. Ithaca, NY: Cornell University Press.

Blasi, A., & Oresick, R. (1986). Emotion and cognition in self-inconsistency. In D.G. Bearison & J. Zimiles (Eds.), *Thought and emotion*. Hillsdale, NJ: Erlbaum.

Bloom, B.S., Engelhart, M.D., Furst, E.J., Hill, W.H., & Krathwohl, D.R. (Eds.). (1956). *Taxonomy of educational objectives: The classification of educational goals. Handbook I: Cognitive domain*. New York: David McKay.

Board of Education, City of Chicago, and the Center for the Study of Reading, University of Illinois. (1986a). *Investigating United States History: CIRCA Summary Text, Grade 7, Units 1 and 2* (pp. 44 and 69). Chicago: Board of Education, City of Chicago.

Board of Education, City of Chicago, and the Center for the Study of Reading, University of Illinois. (1986b). *Investigating United States history: CIRCA teacher manual, units 1 and 2* (pp. 135, 139, 140, 260). Chicago: Board of Education, City of Chicago.

Borkowski, J.G., & Buchel, F. (1983). Learning and memory strategies in the mentally retarded. In M. Pressley & J.R. Levin (Eds.), *Cognitive strategy research*. New York: Springer-Verlag.

Brandt, R. (1986). On creativity and thinking skills: A conversation with David Perkins. *Educational Leadership, 43,* 12-18.

Bransford, J., Sherwood, R., & Hasselbring, T. (in press). Effects of the video revolution on development: Some initial thoughts. In G. Forman and P. Pufall (Eds.), *Constructivism in the classroom*. Hillsdale, NJ: Erlbaum.

Bransford, J., Sherwood, R., Rieser, J., & Vye, N. (1986). Teaching thinking and problem solving: Research foundations. *American Psychologist, 41*, 1078-1089.

Bransford, J.D., & Stein, B.S. (1984). *The IDEAL problem solver.* New York: Freeman.

Bransford, J.D., Stein, B.S., Delclos, V., & Littlefield, J. (1986). Computers and problem solving. In C.K. Kinzer, R.D. Sherwood, & J.D. Bransford (Eds.), *Computer strategies for education.* Columbus, OH: Merrill.

Britton, J., Burgess, T., Martin, N., McLeod, A., & Rosen, H. (1975). *The development of writing.* London: Macmillan.

Brooks, L.W., & Dansereau, D.F. (1983). Effects of structured schema training and text organization in expository prose processing. *Journal of Educational Psychology, 75*, 811-820.

Brown, A.L. (1978). Knowing when, where, and how to remember: A problem of metacognition. In R. Glaser (Ed.), *Advances in instructional psychology.* Hillsdale, NJ: Erlbaum.

Brown, A.L. (1980). Metacognitive development and reading. In R.J. Spiro, B.C. Bruce, & W.F. Brewer (Eds.), *Theoretical issues in reading comprehension.* Hillsdale, NJ: Erlbaum.

Brown, A.L., Campione, J.C., & Day, J. (1981, April). Learning to learn: On training students to learn from texts. *Educational Researcher, 10*, 14-24.

Brown, A.L., & Cane, M.J. (1987, April). *Factors that promote flexible access to knowledge in young children.* Paper presented at the annual meeting of the American Educational Research Association, Washington, DC.

Bruner, J.S. (1960). *The process of education.* Cambridge, MA: Harvard University Press.

Bruner, J.S. (1978). The role of dialogue in language acquisition. In A. Sinclair, R.J. Jarvelle, & W.J.M. Levelt (Eds.), *The child's conception of language.* New York: Springer-Verlag.

Bruner, J.S., Goodnow, J.J., & Austin, G.A. (1977). *A study of thinking.* New York: Wiley.

Burns, M. (1986). Teaching "what to do" in arithmetic vs. teaching "what to do and why." *Educational Leadership, 43*, 34-38.

Burstall, C. (1986). Innovation forms of assessment: A United Kingdom perspective. *Educational Measurement: Issues and Practice, 5*, 17-22.

Burton, R., Brown, J.S., & Fischer, G. (1984). Skiing as a model of instruction. In B. Rogoff & J. Lave (Eds.), *Everyday cognition: Its development in social context.* Cambridge, MA: Harvard University Press.

Campione, J.C., & Brown, A.L. (undated). *Dynamic assessment: One approach and some initial data.* Champaign, IL: University of Illinois.

Carey, R. (1983, June). *Some implications of semiotics for theory, research, and practice in education.* Paper presented at the Fourth International Summer Institute for Semiotics and Structural Studies, Boomington, IN.

Carlson, S.B. (1985). *Creative classroom testing.* Princeton, NJ: Educational Testing Service.

Carpenter, T.P. (1985). Learning to add and subtract: An exercise in problem solving. In E.A. Silver (Ed.), *Teaching and learning mathematical problem solving.* Hillsdale, NJ: Erlbaum.

Carroll, J.B. (1964). Words, meanings, and concepts. *Harvard Educational Review, 34*, 178-202.

Carroll, J.B. (1974). Potentialities and limitations of print as a medium of instruction. In D.R. Olson (Ed.), *Media and symbols: The forms of expression, communication, and education.* Chicago: University of Chicago Press.

Chance, P. (1986). *Thinking in the classroom.* New York: Teachers College Press.

Chance, P. (1987). The one I didn't know. *Psychology Today, 21*(1), 20-21.

Chew, C.R., & Schlawin, S.A. (Eds.). (1983). *Written composition: Process, product, program.* New York: New York State English Council.

Clement, J. (1983, April). *Analogical problem solving in science and mathematics.*

Paper presented at the annual meeting of the American Educational Research Association, Montreal, Canada.

The College Board. (1983). *Academic preparation for college: What students need to know and be able to do.* New York: The College Board.

Collins, A. (1986). *A sample dialogue based on theory of inquiry reading* (Technical Report No. 367). Urbana, IL: University of Illinois, Center for the Study of Reading.

Collins, A., & Brown, J.S. (in press). Cognitive apprenticeship: Teaching students the craft of reading, writing, and mathematics. In L.B. Resnick (Ed.), *Cognition and instruction: Issues and agendas.* Hillsdale, NJ: Erlbaum.

Collins, A., Brown, J.S., & Newman, S. (1986). Cognitive apprenticeship: Teaching the craft of reading, writing, and mathematics. In L.B. Resnick (Ed.), *Cognition and instruction: The nature of expertise.* Hillsdale, NJ: Erlbaum.

Combs, A.W. (1982). *A personal approach to teaching: Beliefs that make a difference.* Boston: Allyn & Bacon.

Commission on Media of the National Council of Teachers of English. (1984). *Rationale for integrating media into English and the language arts.* Urbana, IL: National Council of Teachers of English.

Commission on Reading of the National Academy of Education. (1985). *Becoming a nation of readers.* Springfield, IL: Phillips Brothers.

Condon, J.C. (1968). *Semantics and communication.* New York: Macmillan.

Conot, R. (1979). *A streak of luck.* New York: Seaview.

Cooper, M., & Holzman, M. (1983). Talking about protocols. *College Composition and Communication, 34*, 284-293.

Costa, A. (1984). Mediating the metacognitive. *Educational Leadership, 42*, 57-62.

Costa, A. (1985a). *Developing minds: A resource book for teaching thinking.* Alexandria, VA: Association for Supervision and Curriculum Development.

Costa, A.L. (1985e). Toward a model of human intellectual functioning. In A.L. Costa (Ed.), *Developing minds: A resource book for teaching thinking.* Alexandria, VA: Association for Supervision and Curriculum Development.

Covington, M. (1983). Motivation cognitions. In S.G. Paris, G.M. Olson, & H.W. Stevenson (Eds.), *Learning and motivation in the classroom.* Hillsdale, NJ: Erlbaum.

Craik, F., & Tulving, E. (1974). Depth of processing and retention of words in episodic memory. *Journal of Experimental Psychology: General, 104*, 288-294.

Cremin, L.A. (1961). *Transformation of the school: Progressivism in American Education—1876-1957.* New York: Random House.

Cunningham, D., & Luk, H. (1985, March). *Student as semiotician.* Paper presented at the annual meeting of the American Educational Research Association, Chicago.

Cyert, R.M. (1980). Problem solving and educational policy. In D.T. Tuma & F. Reif (Eds.), *Problem solving and education: Issues in teaching and research.* Hillsdale, NJ: Erlbaum.

de Bono, E. (1970). *Lateral thinking.* New York: Harper & Row.

de Bono, E. (1983). The cognitive research trust (CORT) thinking program. In W. Maxwell (Ed.), *Thinking: An expanding frontier.* Philadelphia: Franklin Institute Press.

Deely, J. (1982). *Semiotics: Its history and doctrine.* Bloomington, IN: Indiana University Press.

de Groot, A.D. (1965). *Thought and choice in chess.* The Hague: Mouton.

Dewey, J. (1916). *Democracy and education.* New York: Macmillan.

Dickson, W.P. (1985). Thought-provoking software: Juxtaposing symbol systems. *Educational Researcher, 14*, 30-38.

Doyle, W. (1983). Academic work. *Review of Educational Research, 53*, 159-199.

Duffy, G.G., Roehler, L.R., & Rackliffe, G. (in press). Constraints on teacher change. *Journal of Teacher Education.*

Eco, U. (1976). *A theory of semiotics.* Bloomington, IN: Indiana University Press.

Eco, U. (1979). *The role of the reader.* Bloomington, IN: Indiana University Press.

Eco, U. (1984). *Semiotics and the philosophy of language.* Bloomington, IN: Indiana University Press.

Education Commission of the States. (1982). *The information society: Are high school graduates ready?* Denver, CO: Education Commission of the States.

Educational Policies Commission. (1961). *The central purpose of American education.* Washington, DC: National Education Association.

Ehrenberg, S.D., Ehrenberg, L.M., & Durfee, D. (1979). *BASICS: Teaching/learning strategies.* Miami Beach, FL: Institute for Curriculum and Instruction.

Ennis, R.H. (1985). Goals for a critical thinking curriculum. In A. Costa (Ed.), *Developing minds: A resource book for teaching thinking.* Alexandria, VA: Association for Supervision and Curriculum Development.

Ennis, R.H. (1987). A taxonomy of critical thinking dispositions and abilities. In J. Baron & R. Sternberg (Eds.), *Teaching thinking skills: Theory and practice.* New York: Freeman.

Feuerstein, R., Jensen, M., Hoffman, M.B., & Rand, Y. (1985). Instrumental enrichment, an intervention program for structural cognitive modifiability: Theory and practice. In J.W. Segal, S.F. Chipman, & R. Glaser (Eds.), *Thinking and learning skills* (Vol. 1). Hillsdale, NJ: Erlbaum.

Feuerstein, R., & Jensen, M.R. (1980). Instrumental enrichment: Theoretical basis, goals, and instruments. *Educational Forum, 46,* 401-423.

Feuerstein, R., Rand, Y., Hoffman, M.B., & Miller, R. (1980). *Instrumental enrichment.* Baltimore, MD: University Park Press.

Fitts, P.M. (1964). Perceptual-motor skill learning. In A.W. Melton (Ed.), *Categories of human learning.* New York: Wiley.

Flavell, J.H. (1976). Metacognitive aspects of problem solving. In L.B. Resnick (Ed.), *The nature of intelligence.* Hillsdale, NJ: Erlbaum.

Flavell, J.H. (1977). *Cognitive development.* Englewood Cliffs, NJ: Prentice-Hall.

Flavell, J.H. (1978). Metacognitive development. In J.M. Scandura & C.J. Brainerd (Eds.), *Structural/process theories of complex human behavior.* Netherlands: Sijthoff and Noordoff.

Flower, L.A., & Hayes, J.R. (1980a). The cognition of discovery: Defining a rhetorical problem. *College Composition and Communication, 13,* 21-32.

Flower, L.A., & Hayes, J.R. (1980b). The dynamics of composing: Making plans and juggling constraints. In L.W. Gregg & E.R. Steinberg (Eds.), *Cognitive processing in writing.* Hillsdale, NJ: Erlbaum.

Flower, L.A., & Hayes, J.R. (1981). A cognitive process theory of writing. *College Composition and Communication, 32,* 365-387.

Frederiksen, N. (1984). Implications of cognitive theory for instruction in problem solving. *Review of Educational Research, 54,* 363-407.

Freedman, G., & Reynolds, E.G. (1980). Enriched basic reader lessons with semantic webbing. *Reading Teacher, 33,* 677-683.

Gable, R., & Rogers, V. (1987, May). Taking the terror out of research. *Phi Delta Kappan,* 690-695.

Gagne, R.M., & Briggs, L.J. (1979). *Principles of instructional design.* New York: Holt, Rinehart & Winston.

Gardner, H. (1983). *Frames of mind: The theory of multiple intelligence.* New York: Basic Books.

Glaser, R. (1984). Education and thinking: The role of knowledge. *American Psychologist, 39,* 93-104.

Glaser, R. (1985). Learning and instructions: A letter for a time capsule. In S.F. Chipman, J.W. Segal, & R. Glaser (Eds.), *Thinking and learning skills* (Vol. 2). Hillsdale, NJ: Erlbaum.

Goldman, L. (1984). Warning: The Socratic method can be dangerous. *Educational Leadership, 42*, 57-62.

Good, T.L., & Brophy, J.E. (1984). *Looking in classrooms*. Cambridge, MA: Harper & Row.

Goodlad, J.I. (1984). *A place called school*. New York: McGraw-Hill.

Goodman, K. (1978). Kid watching: An alternative to testing. *National Elementary School Principal, 57*, 41-45.

Graves, M. (1985, June). *Could textbooks be better written, and would it make a difference?* Paper presented at the Convention on Textbook Reform: The Cooperative Agenda, Washington, DC.

Greene, M. (1984). Philosophy, reason, and literacy. *Review of Educational Research, 54*, 547-559.

Greeno, J.G. (1983). Forms of understanding in mathematical problem solving. In S.G. Paris, G.M. Olson, & H.W. Stevenson (Eds.), *Learning and motivation in the classroom*. Hillsdale, NJ: Erlbaum.

Groen, G., & Resnick, L.B. (1977). Can preschool children invent addition algorithms? *Journal of Educational Psychology, 69*, 645-657.

Guilford, J.P. (1956). Traits of creativity. In H. Anderson (Ed.), *Creativity and its cultivation*. New York: Harper & Row.

Haas, T. (1986). *The shifting paradigm*. Paper presented at the National Parent/Professionals Task Force on Collaboration, Washington, DC.

Halliday, M.A.K. (1975). *Learning how to mean—Explorations in the development of language*. London: Edward Arnold.

Halpern, D.F. (1984). *Thought and knowledge: An introduction to critical thinking*. Hillsdale, NJ: Erlbaum.

Harman, W., & Rheingold, H. (1984). *Higher creativity: Liberating the unconscious for breakthrough insights*. Los Angeles: Jeremy P. Tarcher.

Harste, J., & Stephens, D. (1984). *Toward a practical theory of literacy and learning*. Bloomington, IN: Indiana University Press.

Harter, S. (1980). The perceived competence scale for children. *Child Development, 51*, 218-235.

Hawkins, D. (1974). *The informed vision: Essays in learning and human nature*. New York: Agathon Press.

Herber, H.L. (1978). *Reading in the content areas (Text for teachers)*. Englewood Cliffs, NJ: Prentice-Hall.

Hidi, S., & Anderson, V. (1986). Producing written summaries: Task demands, cognitive operations, and implications for instruction. *Review of Educational Research, 56*, 473-494.

Hillocks, G. (1986). *Research on written composition*. Urbana, IL: ERIC Clearinghouse on Reading and Communication Skills and National Conference on Research in English.

Holley, C.D., & Dansereau, D.F. (1984). *Spatial learning strategies: Techniques, applications, and related issues*. New York: Academic Press.

Hughes, C.S. (1986). Teaching strategies for developing student thinking. *School Library Media Quarterly, 15*, 33-36.

Hunter, M. (1984). Knowing teaching and supervising. In P. Hosford (Ed.), *Using what we know about teaching*. Alexandria, VA: Association for Supervision and Curriculum Development.

Iser, W. (1978). *The act of reading: A theory of aesthetic response*. Baltimore: Johns Hopkins University Press.

Jenkins, J. (1975). Remember that old theory of memory? Well, forget it! *American Psychologist, 29*, 785-795.

Johnson D., & Johnson R. (in press). Structured controversy. *Educational Leadership*.

Johnson, D., & Johnson, R. 1986. Ten inference types and a three-step teaching procedure for inferential comprehension. *Journal of reading, 29*, 622-625.

Johnson, D.W., Johnson, R.T., Roy, P., & Holubec, E.J. (1984). *Circles of learning: Cooperation in the classroom.* Alexandria, VA: Association for Supervision and Curriculum Development.

Johnson-Laird, P.N. (1983). *Mental models.* Cambridge, MA: Harvard University Press.

Jones, B.F., Palincsar, A.S., Ogle, D.S., & Carr, E.G. (1987). *Strategic teaching: Cognitive instruction in the content areas.* Alexandria, VA: Association for Supervision and Curriculum Development.

Jones, B.F. (1985, April). *Guidelines for constructing graphic representations of texts.* Paper presented at the annual meeting of the American Educational Research Association, Chicago.

Jones, B.F., Amiran, M.R., & Katims, M. (1985). Teaching cognitive strategies and text structures within language arts programs. In J.W. Segal, S.F. Chipman, & R. Glaser (Eds.), *Thinking and learning skills. Volume 1: Relating instruction to research.* Hillsdale, NJ: Erlbaum.

Jones, B.F., Friedman, L.B., Tinzmann, M., & Cox, B.E. (1984). *Content-driven comprehension instruction: A model for army training literature* (Technical Report). Alexandria, VA: Army Research Institute for the Behavioral Sciences.

Jones, B.F., Tinzmann, M., Friedman, L.B., & Walker, B.J. (1987). *Teaching thinking skills: English/language arts.* Washington, DC: National Education Association.

Kail, R. (1984). Use of strategies and industrial difference in children's memory. *Developmental Psychology, 15*, 251-255.

Kamii, C. (1984, February). Autonomy: The aim of education envisioned by Piaget. *Phi Delta Kappan, 65* (6), 410-415.

Katz, S.E. (1976). *The effect of each of four instructional treatments on the learning of principles by children.* Madison, WI: University of Wisconsin, Wisconsin Research and Development Center for Cognition Learning.

Kerr, S. (1975). On the folly of rewarding A, while hoping for B. *Academy of Management Journal, 14*, 769-783.

Kintsch, W. (1974). *The representation of meaning in memory.* Hillsdale, NJ: Erlbaum.

Kintsch, W. (1979). On modeling comprehension. *Educational Psychologist, 14*, 3-l4.

Kintsch, W., & Van Dijk, T.A. (1978). Toward a model of text comprehension and production. *Psychological Review, 85*, 363-394.

Kirkpatrick, W.U. (1936). *Remaking the curriculum.* New York: Newson.

Klausmeier, H.J. (1985). *Educational psychology* (5th ed.). New York: Harper & Row.

Klausmeier, H.J., & Sipple, T. (1980). *Learning and teaching concepts.* New York: Academic Press.

Kneedler, P.E. (1984). *Assessment of critical thinking skills in history-social science.* Sacramento: California State Department of Education.

Koch, C., & Brazil, J. (1978). *Strategies for teaching the writing process.* Urbana, IL: National Council of Teachers of English.

Koch, K. (1970). *Wishes, lies, and dreams.* New York: Chelsea.

Koch, K. (1974). *Rose, where did you get that red?* New York: Random House.

Larkin, J.A. (1980). Teaching problem solving in physics: The psychological laboratory and the practical classroom. In D.T. Tuma & F. Reif (Eds.), *Problem solving and education: Issues in teaching and research.* Hillsdale, NJ: Erlbaum.

Larkin, J.A. (1983). Research on science education. In A.M. Lesgold & F. Reif (Chairs), *Computers in education: Realizing the potential* (Report of a Research Conference). Washington, DC: Office of the Assistant Secretary for Educational Research and Improvement.

Larson, C., et al. (1986). Technical training: An application of a strategy for learning structural and functional information. *Contemporary Educational Psychology, 11*, 217-228.

Lesgold, A.M. (1986, April). *Producing automatic performance*. Paper presented at the annual meeting of the American Educational Research Association, San Francisco.

Lester, F.K. (1985). Methodological considerations in research on mathematical problem-solving instruction. In E.A. Silver (Ed.), *Teaching and learning mathematical problem solving*. Hillsdale, NJ: Erlbaum.

Lindsay, P.H., & Norman, D.A. (1977). *Human information processing*. New York: Academic Press.

Lipman, M., Sharp, A.M., & Oscanyan, F.S. (1980). *Philosophy in the classroom*. Philadelphia: Temple University Press.

Lohman, D.F. (1986). *Predicting mathemathanic effects in the teaching of higher order thinking skills*. Iowa City, IA: University of Iowa.

Luria, A. (1973). *The working brain*. New York: Basic Books.

Mandler, G. (1983). The nature of emotions. In J. Miller (Ed.), *States of mind*. New York: Pantheon Books.

Marzano, R.J., & Dole, J. (1985). *Teaching basic patterns and relationships among ideas*. Aurora, CO: Mid-continent Regional Educational Laboratory.

Massachusetts Department of Education. (1987). *Reading and thinking: A new conceptual framework*. Quincy: Massachusetts Educational Assessment Program, Bureau of Research and Assessment.

Mayer, R.E. (1984). Aids to text comprehension. *Educational Psychologist, 19*, 30-42.

Medawar, P.B. (1967). Two conceptions of science. In J.P. Medawar (Ed.), *The art of the soluble*. London: Methuen.

Mellon, J.C. (1969). *Transformational sentence-combining* (NCTE Research Report No. 10). Urbana, IL: National Council of Teachers of English.

Mervis, C.B. (1980). Category structure and the development of categorization. In R.J. Spiro, B.C. Bruce, & W.F. Brewer (Eds.), *Theoretical issues in reading comprehension*. Hillsdale, NJ: Erlbaum.

Meyer, B.J.F. (1982). Reading research and the composition teacher: The importance of plans. *College Composition and Communication, 33*, 37-49.

Meyer, B.J.F. (1985). The structure of text. In P.D. Pearson (Ed.), *Handbook of reading research*. New York: Longman.

Meyer, R.E. (1985). Implications of cognitive psychology for instruction in mathematical problem solving. In R.A. Silver (Ed.), *Teaching and learning mathematical problem solving*. Hillsdale, NJ: Erlbaum.

Miller, G.A. (1973). Some preliminaries to psycholinguistics. In F. Smith (Ed.), *Psycholinguistics and reading*. New York: Holt, Rinehart & Winston.

Moely, B.E. (1977). Organization in memory. In R.V. Kail & J.W. Hagen (Eds.), *Perspectives on the development of memory and cognition*. Hillsdale, NJ: Erlbaum.

Moffett, J. (1968). *Teaching the universe of discourse*. Boston: Houghton Mifflin.

Nagy, W.E. (1985). *Vocabulary instruction: Implications of the new research*. Paper presented at the National Council of Teachers of English Conference, Philadelphia.

Nagy, W.E., & Herman, P.A. (1984). *Limitations of vocabulary instruction* (Technical Report No. 326). Champaign, IL: University of Illinois, Center for the Study of Reading.

Nagy, W.E., Herman, P.A., & Anderson, R.C. (1985, April). *The inference of word and text properties in learning from context*. Paper presented at the annual meeting of the American Educational Research Association, Chicago.

National Commission on Excellence in Education. (1983). *A nation at risk: The imperative for educational reform*. Washington, DC: Government Printing Office.

Newell, A., & Simon, H.A. (1972). *Human problem solving*. Englewood Cliffs, NJ: Prentice-Hall.

Nickerson, R.S. (1984). Kinds of thinking taught in current programs. *Educational Leadership, 42*, 26-37.

Nickerson, R.S., Perkins, D.N., & Smith, E.E. (1985). *The teaching of thinking*. Hillsdale, NJ: Erlbaum.

Norman, G.R. (1969). *Memory and attention*. New York: Wiley.

O'Keefe, V.P. (1986). *Affecting critical thinking through speech*. Urbana, IL: ERIC Clearinghouse on Reading and Communication Skills; and Annandale, VA: Speech Communication Association.

Ogle, D. (1986). K-W-L: A teaching model that develops active reading of expository text. *The Reading Teacher, 39*, 564-576.

Palincsar, A.S., & Brown, A.L. (1984). Reciprocal teaching of comprehension-fostering and comprehension-monitoring activities. *Cognition and Instruction, 1*, 117-175.

Palincsar, A.S., & Brown, A.L. (1985). Reciprocal teaching: Activities to promote reading with your mind. In T.L. Harris & E.J. Cogen (Eds.), *Reading, thinking, and concept development: Strategies for the classroom*. New York: The College Board.

Palincsar, A.S., Ogle, D.C., Jones, B.F., & Carr, E.D. (1986). *Teaching reading as thinking (facilitators' manual)*. Alexandria, VA: Association for Supervision and Curriculum Development.

Paris, S.G., & Cross, D.R. (1983). Ordinal learning: Pragmatic connections among children's beliefs, motives, and actions. In J. Bisanz, G. Bisanz, & R. Kail (Eds.), *Learning in children*. New York: Springer-Verlag.

Paris, S.G., & Lindauer, B.K. (1982). The development of cognitive skills during childhood. In B.W. Wolman (Ed.), *Handbook of developmental psychology*. Englewood Cliffs, NJ: Prentice-Hall.

Paris, S.G., Lipson, M.Y., & Wixson, K.K. (1983). Becoming a strategic reader. *Contemporary Educational Psychology, 8*, 293-316.

Paris, S.G., & Winograd, P. (in press). Metacognition in academic learning and instruction. In B.F. Jones (Ed.), *Dimensions of thinking: A review of research*. Hillsdale, NJ: Erlbaum.

Paul, R.W. (1984). Critical thinking: Fundamental to education for a free society. *Educational Leadership, 42*, 4-14.

Paul, R.W. (1986a, December). *Critical thinking, moral integrity, and citizenship: Teaching for the intellectual virtues*. Paper distributed at ASCD Wingspread Conference on Teaching Skills, Racine, WI.

Paul, R.W. (1986b). Program for the Fourth International Conference on Critical Thinking and Educational Reform. Rohnert Park, CA: Sonoma State University, Center for Critical Thinking and Moral Critique.

Paul, R.W. (1987). Critical thinking and the critical person. In *Thinking: Report on research*. Hillsdale, NJ: Erlbaum.

Paul, R.W. (undated). Some conference vocabulary and distinctions. *Fourth international conference on critical thinking and educational reform*. Rohnert Park, CA: Sonoma State University, Center for Critical Thinking and Moral Critique.

Paul, R.W., & Bailin, S. (undated). *The creatively critical and critically creative thinker*. Unpublished manuscript.

Paul, R., Binker, A.S.A., & Charbonneau, M. (1986). *Critical thinking handbooks: K-3. A guide for remodeling lesson plans in language arts, social studies, and science*. Rohnert Park, CA: Sonoma State University, Center for Critical Thinking and Moral Critique.

Pearson, P.D., & Johnson, D.D. (1978). *Teaching reading comprehension*. New York: Holt, Rinehart & Winston.

Percy, W. (1975). *The message in the bottle*. New York: Farrar, Strauss & Giroux.

Perkins, D.N. (1981). *The mind's best work*. Cambridge, MA: Harvard University Press.

Perkins, D.N. (1984). Creativity by design. *Educational Leadership, 42*, 18-25.

Perkins, D.N. (1985). *Where is creativity?* Paper presented at the University of Iowa Second Annual Humanities Symposium, Iowa City, IA.

Perkins, D.N. (1986). *Knowledge as design*. Hillsdale, NJ: Erlbaum.

Peters, Charles W. (1975-76). The effects of systematic restructuring upon the comprehension process. *Reading Research Quarterly, 1,* 87.

Peters, C. (1987, March). *Innovative tests in reading: The Michigan effort.* Paper presented at the Spring Conference of the National Council of Teachers of English, Louisville, KY.

Piaget, J. (1963). *The psychology of intelligence.* Paterson, NJ: Littlefield, Adams, & Co.

Piaget, J. (1967). *The language and thought of the child* (M. Gabain, Trans.). Cleveland, OH: World Publishing.

Piaget, J. (1971). *Genetic epistemology* (E. Duckworth, Trans.). New York: Norton.

Piaget, J. (1972). Intellectual evolution from adolescence to adulthood. *Human Development, 15,* 1-12.

Piaget, J. (1976). *The grasp of consciousness.* Cambridge, MA: Harvard University Press.

Piaget, J., & Szeminska, A. (1941). *The child's conception of number.* Atlantic Highlands, NJ: Humanities Press.

Polya, G. (1945). *How to solve it.* Princeton, NJ: University Press.

Popper, K. (1962, 1978). *Conjectures and refutations.* London: Routledge & Kegan Paul.

Posner, G.J., Strike, K.A., Hewson, P.W., & Gertzog, W.A. (1982). Accommodation of scientific conception: Toward a theory of conceptual change. *Science Education, 66,* 211-227.

Postman, N. (1979, November). *Teaching into the future.* Address at the 69th annual convention of the National Council of Teachers of English, San Francisco, CA.

Presseisen, B.Z. (1985). *Thinking skills throughout the K-12 curriculum: A conceptual design.* Philadelphia: Research for Better Schools.

Pressley, M., & Levin, J.R. (Eds.). (1983). *Cognitive strategy research: Educational applications.* New York: Springer-Verlag.

Probst, R. (in press). Transactional theory in the teaching of literature. *ERIC Digest.*

Proett, J., & Gill, K. (1986). *The writing process in action.* Urbana, IL: National Council of Teachers of English.

Rankin, S.C. (1964). *A theory of an isomorphism-model-hypothesis method of thought.* Unpublished doctoral dissertation, Wayne State University, Detroit, MI.

Rankin, S.C., & Hughes, C.S. (1986). The Rankin-Hughes framework. *Focus, 2* (Fall), 10-20.

Rankin, S.C., & Hughes, C.S. (1987a). Framework highlights thinking skills. *Oklahoma Educator, 16,* 1-2.

Rankin, S.C., & Hughes, C.S. (1987b). The Rankin-Hughes framework. In C. Canning and K. Bunting (Eds.), *Developing thinking skills across the curriculum.* Westland, MI: Michigan Association for Computer Users in Learning.

Raphael, T.E. (1984). Teaching learners about sources of information for answering comprehension questions. *Journal of Reading, 27,* 303-311.

Raphael, T.E., & Kirschner, B.M. (1985, August). *The effects of instruction in compare/contrast text structure on sixth-grade students' reading comprehension and writing products* (Research Series 161). East Lansing, MI: Michigan State University, Institute for Research on Teaching.

Raudsepp, E. (1983). Profile of the creative individual: Part I. *Creative Computing, 9,* 170-179.

Remy, Richard C. (1980). *Handbook of basic citizenship competencies: Guidelines for comparing materials, assessing instruction, and setting goals.* Alexandria, VA: Association for Supervision and Curriculum Development.

Resnick, L.B. (in press). *Education and learning.* Pittsburgh, PA: University of Pittsburgh, Learning Research and Development Center.

Robinson, F.P. (1961). *Effective Study* (rev. ed.). New York: Harper & Row.

Rogers, C. (1961). *On becoming a person.* Boston: Houghton Mifflin.

Rohwer, W.D., Jr. (1971). Prime time for education: Early childhood or adolescence? *Harvard Educational Review, 41*, 316-341.

Rosenblatt, L. (1978). *The reader, the text, the poem: The transactional theory of the literary work*. Carbondale, IL: Southern Illinois University Press.

Roth, K.J. (1985, April). *Conceptual change, learning, and student processing of science texts*. Paper presented at the annual meeting of the American Psychological Association, Chicago.

Rowe, H. (1985). *Problem solving and intelligence*. Hillsdale, NJ: Erlbaum.

Rumelhart, D. (1975). Notes on a schema for stories. In D. Bobrow & A. Collins (Eds.), *Representation and understanding: Studies in cognitive science*. New York: Academic Press.

Rumelhart, D. (1980). Schemata: The building blocks of cognition. In R.J. Spiro, B.C. Bruce, & W.F. Brewer (Eds.), *Theoretical issues in reading comprehension*. Hillsdale, NJ: Erlbaum.

Rumelhart, D., & Ortony, A. (1977). The representation of knowledge in memory. In R. Anderson, R. Spiro, & W. Montague (Eds.), *Schooling and the acquisition of knowledge*. Hillsdale, NJ: Erlbaum.

Russell, B. (1971). *The conquest of happiness*. New York: Liveright.

Samples, R. (1976). *The metaphorical mind*. Reading, MA: Addison-Wesley.

Scardamalia, M., Bereiter, C., & Steinbach, R. (1984). Teachability of reflective processes in written composition. *Cognitive Science, 8*, 173-190.

Schank, R., & Abelson, R. (1977). *Scripts, plans, goals, and understanding*. Hillsdale, NJ: Erlbaum.

Schlesinger, M. (1971). Production of utterances and language acquisition. In D.I. Slobin (Ed.), *The ontogenesis of grammar*. New York: Academic Press.

Schoenfeld, A.H. (1985). *Mathematical problem solving*. New York: Academic Press.

Schwartz, P., & Ogilvy, J. (1979). *The emergent paradigm: Changing patterns of thought and belief*. Menlo Park, CA: Values and Lifestyles Program.

Scriven, M. (1959). The logic of criteria. *Journal of Philosophy, LXVI*, 357-368.

Seiger-Ehrenberg, S. (1985). Educational outcomes for a K-12 curriculum. In A. Costa (Ed.), *Developing minds: A resource book for teaching thinking*. Alexandria, VA: Association for Supervision and Curriculum Development.

Sherwin, S. (1969). *Four problems in teaching English: A critique of research*. Scranton, PA: International Textbook.

Shulman, L.S. (1986). Those who understand knowledge growth in teaching. *Educational Researcher, 15*, 4-14.

Siegel, M.G. (1984). *Reading as signification*. Unpublished doctoral dissertation, Indiana University.

Silver, E. (1986, July). *Research in mathematical problem solving in the United States of America*. Paper presented at the United States-Japan Seminar in Mathematics Problem Solving, Honolulu, HI.

Simon, H.A. (1973). The structure of ill-structured problems. *Artificial Intelligence, 4*, 181-201.

Simon, M.A. (1986). D Diagram drawing in the math classroom: Eddie's story. In M. Driscoll, J. Confrey (Eds.), *Teaching mathematics: Strategies that work*. Portsmouth, NH: Northeast Regional Exchange and Heineman Educational Books.

Singer, H., & Donlan, D. (1982). Active comprehension: Problem-solving schema with question generation for comprehension of complex short stories. *Reading Research Quarterly, 17*, 166-186.

Slote, M.A. (1966). The theory of important criteria. *Journal of Philosophy, LXIII*, 221-224.

Smith, F. (1982). *Understanding reading*. New York: Holt, Rinehart & Winston.

Sorensen, T.C. (1965). *Kennedy*. New York: Harper & Row.

Stahl, R.J. (1985). *Cognitive information processes and processing within a uniprocess superstructure/ microstructure framework: A practical information-based model.* Unpublished manuscript, University of Arizona, Tucson.

Stahl, S.A., & Fairbanks, M.M. (1986). The effect of vocabulary instruction: A model-based meta-analysis. *Review of Educational Research, 56,* 72-110.

Stanton, J. (1984). Thinking together: Interaction in children's reasoning. In C. Thaiss & C. Suhor (Eds.), *Speaking and writing K-12.* Urbana, IL: National Council of Teachers of English.

Stein, M.I. (1974). *Stimulating creativity. Volume 1: Individual procedures.* New York: Academic Press.

Stein, N.L., & Glenn, C.G. (1979). An analysis of story comprehension in elementary school children. In R. Freedle (Ed.), *New directions in discourse processing.* Norwood, NJ: Ablex.

Sternberg, R.J. (1977). *Intelligence, information processing, and analogical reasoning: The componential analysis of human abilities.* Hillsdale, NJ: Erlbaum.

Sternberg, R.J. (1980). A componential approach to intellectual development. In R.J. Sternberg (Ed.), *Advances in the psychology of human intelligence.* Hillsdale, NJ: Erlbaum.

Sternberg, R.J. (1981a). Intelligence as thinking and learning skills. *Educational Leadership, 39,* 18-20.

Sternberg, R.J. (1981b). Nothing fails like success: The search for an intelligent paradigm for studying intelligence. *Journal of Educational Psychology, 73,* 142-155.

Sternberg, R.J. (1984a). *Beyond IQ: A triarchic theory of human intelligence.* New York: Cambridge University Press.

Sternberg, R.J. (1984b). What should intelligence tests test? *Educational Researcher, 13,* 5-17.

Sternberg, R.J. (1985b). *Understanding and increasing intelligence.* New York: Harcourt Brace Jovanovich.

Sternberg, R.J., & Davidson. (1986). What is insight? *Educational Horizons, 64*(4), 177-179.

Stewart, J.H. (1984). The representation of knowledge: Curricular and instructional implications for science teaching. In C.D. Holley & D.F. Dansereau (Eds.), *Spatial learning strategies: Techniques, applications, and related issues,* (pp. 235-253). New York: Academic Press.

Sticht, T.G., & Hickey, D.T. (in press). Functional context theory, literacy, and electronics training. In R. Dillon & J. Pellegrino (Eds.), *Instruction: Theoretical and applied perspectives.* New York: Praeger.

Stiggins, R., Conklin, N.F., & Bridgeford, N.J. (Summer 1986). Classroom assessment: A key to effective education. *Educational Measurement: Issues and Practice.*

Stiggins, R., Rubel E., & Quellmalz, E. (1986). *Measuring teaching skills in the classroom.* Washington, DC: National Education Association.

Strong, W. (1986). *Creative approaches to sentence combining.* Urbana, IL: ERIC Clearinghouse on Reading and Communication Skills and the National Council of Teachers of English.

Suhor, C. (1983). Thinking skills in the English language arts. *Problem Solving, 5* (June 1983), 1-4.

Suhor, C. (1984). Toward a semiotics-based curriculum. *Journal of Curriculum Studies, 16,* 247-257.

Suhor, C. (1986). Jazz improvisation and language performance: Parallel competencies. *Et Cetera, 43,* 133-139.

Taba, H. (1967). *Teacher's handbook for elementary social studies.* Reading, MA: Addison-Wesley.

Tennyson, R.D., & Cocchiarella, M.J. (1986). An empirically based instructional design theory for teaching concepts. *Review of Educational Research, 56,* 40-71.

Thaiss, C. (1986). *Language across the curriculum in the elementary grades*. Urbana, IL: ERIC Clearinghouse on Reading and Communication Skills and National Council of Teachers of English.

Tice, L. (1976). *Achieving your potential*. Seattle, WA: Pacific Institute.

Tierney, R.J., Readence, J.E., & Dishner, E.K. (1985). *Reading strategies and practices—A compendium* (2nd ed.). Boston: Allyn Bacon.

Tough, J. (1974). *Talking, thinking, and growing*. New York: Schocken Books.

Tough, J. (1976). *Listening to children*. London: Schools Council Publications.

Toulmin, S., Rieke, R., & Janik, A. (1981). *An introduction to reasoning*. New York: Macmillan.

Tsujimoto, J. (in press). *Teaching poetry writing to adolescents*. Urbana, IL: ERIC Clearinghouse on Reading and Communication Skills and the National Council of Teaachers of English.

Tweney, R.D. (1986). *Scientific thinking: New possibilities for enhancing education*. Paper presented at the Wingspread Conference on Thinking, Racine, WI.

Tweney, R.D. (1987, April). *What is scientific thinking?* Paper presented at the annual meeting of the American Educational Research Association, Washington, DC.

Tweney, R.D., Doherty, M.E., & Mynatt, C.R. (1981). *On scientific thinking*. New York: Columbia University Press.

Underwood, B.J. (1969). Attributes of memory. *Psychological Review, 76*, 559-573.

Valencia, S. (1987, April). *Novel formats for assessing prior knowledge and measures of reading comprehension*. Paper presented at the annual meeting of the American Educational Research Association, Washington, D.C.

van Dijk, T.A. (1980). *Macrostructures*. Hillsdale, NJ: Erlbaum.

van Dijk, T.A., & Kintsch, W. (1983). *Strategies of discourse comprehension*. Hillsdale, NJ: Erlbaum.

Van Patten, J.R., Chao, C.I., & Reigeluth, C.M. (1986). A review of strategies for sequencing and synthesizing information. *Review of Educational Research, 56*, 437-472.

Vosniadou, S., & Brewer, W.F. (1987). Theories of knowledge restructuring in development. *Review of Educational Research, 57*, 51-67.

Vosniadou, S., & Ortony, A. (1983). *The influence of analogy in children's acquisition of new information from text: An exploratory study* (Technical Report No. 281). Urbana, IL: University of Illinois, Center for the Study of Reading.

Vygotsky, L.S. (1962). *Thought and language*. Cambridge, MA: MIT Press.

Vygotsky, L.S. (1978). *Mind in society: The development of higher psychological processes*. Cambridge, MA: Harvard University Press.

Wales, C.E., Nardi, A.H., & Stager, R.A. (1986). Decision making: New paradigm for education. *Educational Leadership, 43*, 37-41.

Wales, C.E., Nardi, A.H., & Stager, R.A. (1987). *Thinking skills: Making a choice*. Morgantown, W. Va.: Center for Guided Design.

Walsh, D., & Paul, R.W. (undated). *The goal of critical thinking: From educational ideal to educational reality*. Washington, DC: American Federation of Teachers.

Weiner, B. (1972). Attribution theory, achievement motivation and the educational process. *Review of Educational Research, 42*, 203-215.

Weiner, B. (1983). Speculations regarding the role of affect in achievement-change programs guided by attributional principles. In J.M. Levine & M.C. Wang (Eds.), *Teaching and student perceptions: Implications for learning*. Hillsdale, NJ: Erlbaum.

Weinstein, C.E., & Mayer, R.E. (1986). The teaching of learning strategies. In M.C. Wittrock (Ed.), *Handbook of research on teaching*. New York: Macmillan.

Weinstein, R. (1982). *Student perceptions of schooling*. Paper presented at the Conference on Research on Teaching: Implications for Practice, Warrenton, VA.

Whimbey, A., & Lochhead, J. (1985). *Problem solving and comprehension*. Hillsdale, NJ: Erlbaum.

Whorf, L. (1956). *Language, thought, and reality*. New York: Wiley; and Cambridge, MA: MIT Press.

Wickelgren, W.A. (1974). *How to solve problems*. San Francisco: Walt Freeman.

Winne, P., & Marx, R.W. (1983). *Student cognitive processes while learning from teaching* (Vols. 1 & 2). Instructional Psychology Research Group (NIE Final Report, Grant No. NIE-G-79-0098). Burnaby, British Columbia: Simon Frasier University.

Winograd, P.N., & Hare V.C. (in press). Direct instruction of reading comprehension strategies: The nature of teacher explanation. In E. Goetz, P. Alexander, & L.C. Weinstein (Eds.), *Learning and study strategy research: Issues in assessment, instruction, and evaluation*. New York: Academic Press.

Wittrock, M.C. (1986). Students' thought processes. In M. Wittrock (Ed.), *Handbook of research on teaching* (3rd ed.). New York: Macmillan.